KU-714-386

All in One
Cook Book

Published by
The Hamlyn Publishing Group Limited
for the makers of
Stork and Oxo

Acknowledgements
Dishes and accessories used in the photographs
in this book kindly loaned by:
Heal's, Habitat, Casa Pupo, Elizabeth David, John Barker,
Selfridges, Conran, Josiah Wedgwood and Sons Limited.
Photographs on pages 34, 38 and 41 taken on Nauticalia,
the floating shop on the Thames at Shepperton

Photography by Iain Reid
Photograph on page 91 by John Lee

Jacket and colour illustrations by Robin Laurie
Black and white illustrations by Ann Rees

Published by
The Hamlyn Publishing Group Limited
London · New York · Sydney · Toronto
Astronaut House, Feltham, Middlesex, England
for
Van den Berghs and Jurgens/Brooke Bond Oxo
© Copyright Van den Berghs and Jurgens/Brooke Bond Oxo 1976

ISBN 0 600 39147 7

Printed in England by Jarrold and Sons Limited, Norwich

Contents

Introduction

This cookery book is designed for YOU – whether you are a beginner or an accomplished cook. Two of Britain's most popular household names have jointly sponsored this detailed guide to cooking and kitchen know-how.

For over 50 years we at Stork and Oxo have provided housewives with cookery advice and recipes. This experience has taught us just the sort of hints, information and recipes you want.

We hope this book provides a new and complete approach to your cooking and that you will gain pleasure and enjoyment from it for many years.

If you do have any queries or problems with your cooking, you can always write to us!

Stork Cookery Service
Department H.E.
Van den Berghs
Sussex House
Burgess Hill
West Sussex
RH15 9JN

Oxo Meal Planning Service
Brooke Bond Oxo
Leon House
Croydon
Surrey
CR9 1JQ

Useful facts and figures

Throughout the book you will find that quantities have been given in metric as well as Imperial measures. The metric conversions have been calculated and carefully tested to give results as close as possible to the Imperial ones, so that there is no difference whether you are using quantities according to the metric or the Imperial list. For simplicity we have rounded off metric quantities to the nearest 25 grams, which means that conversions are not exact but recipes are easier to work with.

In nearly all cases people using this book will wish to work entirely with either Imperial measures or metric ones. However, there might be times when you want to convert from one to the other and the table below will help you do this.

For quantities over 20 oz. divide the amount into suitable quantities so as to add the appropriate figures in the centre column, and then round off to the nearer multiple of 25. For example, 38 oz. is 18 plus 20 oz. which in metric is 1081 g. rounding off to 1075 g.

As a rough guide, a kilogram (kg.) is therefore a little less than $2\frac{1}{4}$ lb.; a litre is a little more than $1\frac{3}{4}$ pints.

This conversion from Imperial to metric works well in nearly all recipes, but the conversion from 4 oz. does present some problems. From the centre column in the table you can see that it could be rounded off equally well to 125 g. or to 100 g.

Generally speaking we have used the 100 g. conversion but, in baking recipes, we have used 125 g. as this gives a better end result which is in fact nearer to the Imperial one. A good example of this would be the recipe for a Victoria sandwich. If 100 g. was taken the end result would be a rather smaller cake than you are used to.

Another reason for taking 125 g. as the better conversion is that Stork margarine and other cooking fats will in fact be sold in packs of 250 g. so that a quantity of 125 g. means you only have to slice it in half as before.

Canned and packaged food At the present time most cans and packets are marked in both Imperial and metric quantities and usually a straight conversion to metric from Imperial is given. We have followed this custom when mentioning can or packet sizes. Thus the label on a

14-oz. can of tomatoes would read 14 oz. (397 g.) and this is how we use it in the recipes.

Spoons as a measure You will see that many smaller measures are given in spoons. All spoon measures in this book are based on the new British Standard measuring spoons so that to give correct results these are the spoons you should use too. The 15 ml. spoon corresponds to the old tablespoon and the 5 ml. spoon to our teaspoon. *All spoon measures are level.*

Linear measures The metric unit of length is the metre which is roughly 3 feet 3 inches. There are 100 centimetres (cm.) to the metre and 1 inch is 2.54 cm. In this book we have usually rounded up or down to the nearest whole centimetre, so a 7-inch cake tin has been converted to an 18-cm. tin (exactly 17.76 cm.).

Lemon juice note Half a lemon yields $1\frac{1}{2}$–2 tablespoons juice. One lemon yields 3–4 tablespoons juice. The grated lemon rind gives 2–3 teaspoons.

Oven temperatures

Oven temperatures on modern electric cookers are marked in degrees Celsius (°C are the same as Centigrade) and the chart below shows the recommended equivalent heats.

Ounces/fluid ounces	Approx. g. and ml. to nearest whole figure	Recommended g. and ml. conversion to nearest unit of 25
1	28	25
2	57	50
3	85	75
4	113	100
5 ($\frac{1}{4}$ pint)	142	150
6	170	175
7	198	200
8 ($\frac{1}{2}$ lb.)	226	225
9	255	250
10 ($\frac{1}{2}$ pint)	283	275
11	311	300
12	340	350
13	368	375
14	396	400
15 ($\frac{3}{4}$ pint)	425	425
16 (1 lb.)	452	450
17	484	475
18	512	500
19	541	550
20 (1 pint)	569	575

Description	°F.	°C.	Gas Mark
Cool	225	110	$\frac{1}{4}$
Extremely slow	250	120	$\frac{1}{2}$
Very slow	275	140	1
Slow	300	150	2
Very moderate	325	160	3
Moderate	350	180	4
Moderately hot	375	190	5
Fairly hot	400	200	6
Hot	425	220	7
Very hot	450	230	8
Very hot	475	240	9

Recipes with this symbol are suitable for freezing

Cookery know-how

It is always irritating to come across an unfamiliar term when you are using a cookery book. Here is a list of quite commonly used cookery terms.

Al dente A term usually used to describe the length of time to cook pasta or rice; cooked – but firm to the bite.

Bain marie A bath of water which is used for cooking food slowly in the oven or on top of the cooker. You can make one by half-filling a roasting tin with water and placing in it the dish holding the food to be baked, e.g. an egg custard.

Bake blind A method of baking pastry until set before the filling is added. The most usual method is to place the flan ring or pie dish lined with pastry on a baking sheet, cut out a circle of greaseproof paper or foil slightly larger than the flan, put this on top of the pastry. Cover with baking beans, rice or breadcrusts and bake in the oven for 15 minutes. Remove the baking beans and greaseproof paper or foil and allow to cook for a further 10 minutes, or put in the filling as directed in the recipe.

Baste A process usually carried out during roasting or baking when hot fat is spooned over food while it is in the roasting tin, to keep the food moist and improve the appearance.

Beat A method of introducing air into a mixture; usually done with a wooden spoon or an electric beater.

Bind Adding liquid, egg or melted fat to a dry mixture in order to hold it together.

Bisque A rich fish or shellfish soup.

Blanch Placing food in boiling water in order to whiten or to remove the skin, salt or a strong flavour from food. It is also used prior to freezing vegetables (see page 189).

Blend Used to describe the process of adding the thickening agent, such as flour or cornflour mixed to a smooth paste with water, to a liquid mixture. It is also used to describe the process of liquidising fruit, vegetables, soups, etc., in an electric blender.

Bouchée A small puff pastry case. A *vol au vent* is a puff pastry case which can be any size.

Bouillon A strong clear stock made from fish, game, poultry, meat or vegetables.

Bouquet garni A bunch of fresh mixed herbs tied together with string, normally comprising parsley, thyme, peppercorns and bay leaf; or ready-made sachets. Gives aromatic flavour to stews, casseroles and soups. Remove before serving.

Boil There are few occasions in the kitchen when food is actually boiled except for vegetables and this often refers to the simmering process, when liquid is brought to the boil and then kept piping hot on a low heat.

Brown Placing a cooked dish under a grill or in the oven for a short time to produce an appetising golden brown colour.

Canapé A small slice of bread which can be cut with a fancy cutter, spread with a fat, fried or toasted and used as a base for savouries.

Caramelise To melt and cook sugar with water until it turns a dark brown colour.

Casserole An ovenproof dish with a lid, usually used for savoury dishes which can be served straight from the oven to the table.

Chine A method of preparing neck or loin joints for easier carving – the bone at the wide end of the chops is cut away from the meat so that portions can be carved easily.

Clarify To clear stock with crushed eggshells, lightly beaten egg whites and raw minced meat. To clarify fat is to boil it up with water, allow it to cool and strain to leave pure fat.

Croûtons Small cubes of bread fried in oil and used as a garnish for soups and other savoury dishes.

Darioles Small individual moulds which can be used for sponge puddings or custards.

Emulsify To mix ingredients together, usually oil and another liquid, so that they blend and thicken, e.g. mayonnaise.

Escalopes Very thin slices, usually of veal or pork.

Farce Forcemeats and stuffings.

Flake Separating cooked fish into small pieces.
Grating chocolate or cheese into small slivers.
Knocking up the pastry edges of a pie using the blade of the knife.

Flambé To sprinkle a dish with brandy or liqueur and ignite it.

Flute To decorate the edge of a pie with a knife or the handle of a fork.

Fold To blend a light mixture into a heavier one, usually with a sharp-edged metal spoon, e.g. folding flour into a creamed mixture for a sandwich cake, or folding beaten egg white into a soufflé.

Forcemeat Finely chopped meat or fish which has been seasoned to use as a stuffing or garnish.

Galantine Boned meat or poultry stuffed and cooked in stock, glazed with aspic and served cold.

Glaze To brush meat with stock to give a shiny appearance.
To brush bread, buns or pastry with beaten egg or milk before baking.
To brush hot baked items with a sugar syrup or to brush the fruit for fruit flans.

Gratin A dish browned under the grill or quickly in the oven; dishes cooked in this way are usually sprinkled with breadcrumbs, fat and possibly grated cheese.

Hors-d'œuvre The first course of a meal made up of cold savoury items; also single hors-d'œuvre such as smoked salmon, avocado.

Infuse To steep herbs, tea leaves or other flavourings in boiling liquid, e.g. milk, water or stock, to extract the flavour.

Julienne strips Matchstick strips of vegetables or pared citrus fruit rind.

Knead Working dough lightly, using the fingertips for pastry-making and the knuckles for bread-making. Bread-making can also be done with the dough hook attachment of an electric mixer.

Knock back To punch or knock down once-risen yeast dough.

Macédoine A variety of fruits or vegetables cut into small cubes and used for salad.

Macerate To steep prepared fruits in a syrup, perhaps with an alcoholic liquor added, to allow the flavours to blend and develop.

Marinade A liquid usually prepared with wine or oil and herbs to steep pieces of meat or fish to tenderise and give extra flavour.

Mask To cover with a sauce.

Mirepoix A basic mixture usually composed of roughly chopped onions, carrots, celery and ham – used for braising, soups and sauces.

Mousse A mixture normally made of eggs, cream and gelatine which is light and which can be savoury or sweet.

Panada A binding agent, usually a thick mixture of flour and fat with a little liquid, used as a foundation in soufflés. (See Sauces section page 130.)

Parboil Boiling food for a short time to cook partially.

Pâté Strictly speaking a meat or fish dish enclosed in pastry but now usually used for a mixture of meat or fish which has been baked in a mould and is served as a first course, often called a terrine, if home-made.

Poach A method of cooking food gently in liquid which has been brought to the boil and is simmered just below boiling point.

Pot au feu A traditional French beef broth.

Purée Solid foods rubbed through a sieve or put in a liquidiser or electric blender.

Quenelles Forcemeat rolled in different shapes and either cooked in boiling water or steamed.

Raspings Breadcrumbs which have been prepared from crusts of bread dried in the oven.

Reduce Boiling a liquid uncovered in order to evaporate some of the water content and make the liquid more concentrated.

Refresh To place fruit, meat or vegetables which have previously been blanched, under cold running water.

Roux A thickening agent for soups and sauces normally made with equal quantities of fat and flour.

Rubbing-in A method of incorporating fat into flour, e.g. for short-crust pastry, when the fat is rubbed in with the tips of the fingers.

Sauté Shallow frying to obtain a pale golden brown colour. Shake the pan frequently during cooking.

Sear To seal the outside of meat or poultry in hot fat to form a coating which seals in the juices during the next stage of cooking.

Stiffen To cook meat or poultry in fat for a short time without colouring or cooking through.

Sweat To cook vegetables in a little fat and then cover with a lid to cook in their own juice for a few minutes without browning.

Truss Usually used in connection with poultry, where the legs are tied together.

Velouté A foundation white sauce made from fish, poultry or meat stock.

Whip or whisk Adding air quickly to a mixture by beating with a hand whisk, rotary beater or electric mixer.

Zest Outer skin of citrus fruits which is grated or thinly pared off for flavouring and garnishing.

Eating for health

Most people enjoy eating, indeed many of us tend to enjoy it too much and become overweight! However, we all need food and it is a help to know a little about the foods the body really needs to keep it in good working order. There are three main reasons for eating sensibly and this knowledge can help you plan meals which taste good and *are* good for the family.

1 To supply the body with energy and warmth.

2 To provide the raw materials which are needed for the growth of new tissues or the renewal of established tissues.

3 To supply the substances which the body needs in order to function properly. This helps maintain good health.

No single food contains all the substances, usually referred to as nutrients, that the body needs. It is by eating a combination of many different foods that we obtain all we need in the right amounts and as often as we need them.

Planning a menu for the family

It is helpful to plan menus well ahead to ensure catering for the family runs smoothly. If you plan menus for a week at a time, it will be easier to keep within your housekeeping budget and also help you to make efficient use of your time so that quick, easy meals are planned for rushed days. Meals requiring more attention can be cooked on days when you have more time available.

A most important point to keep in mind when planning meals for your family is their individual likes and dislikes. Good nutrition only begins when food is *eaten* so try to tempt the family each meal-time with attractively served food of varied colours, textures and flavours.

If the foods below are eaten daily, you can be sure your family is getting a satisfying, well balanced diet.

Milk and cheese These provide significant amounts of protein and calcium needed especially by bones and teeth. Whilst $\frac{1}{2}$ pint (275 ml.) milk a day is sufficient for an adult, ideally allow 1 pint (575 ml.) daily for growing children. If your family includes grandparents or other more elderly people, do make sure that they have at least $\frac{1}{2}$ pint (275 ml.) milk each day to help protect their bones.

Since cheese is made from milk, it also contains protein and calcium. Enjoy cheese in sandwiches, sauces, salads, grated on hot soup, etc. The hard English cheeses such as Cheddar are particularly rich sources of calcium.

Meat and fish Include a serving of meat or fish in main meals as often as possible. An average serving of meat is 4 oz. (100–125 g.) raw weight off the bone, a serving of fish is normally a little heavier. Although these foods tend to be expensive, they are a valuable source of protein. Textured vegetable protein (see opposite), often known as TVP, is now available and can be added to meat dishes such as minced meat and stews to make meat go further and so reduce costs. If you are going to use this 'new' food, do read the instructions on each packet as they vary according to the brand. Some convenience foods already contain a proportion of this kind of protein food.

When choosing meat and fish for the week's meals, it is wise to include liver, kidney or heart once a week since these meats are particularly rich sources of iron, the mineral needed to prevent anaemia. Do encourage adolescents to eat these foods. They are growing rapidly at this stage and have an extra requirement for iron.

Another item to include once a week at least is oily fish such as herrings, mackerel or one of the canned fish such as sardines, pilchards or tuna. These fish supply vitamin D.

Also include pig meats such as bacon, ham, pork, pork luncheon meat and sausages in the family meals. These meats are valuable sources of thiamine, part of the vitamin B complex.

Eggs Eggs make a useful basis for a simple meal and have many cookery uses, so do keep a stock of these available. They contain protein, the yolks contain iron and small amounts of some vitamins. Egg yolks are also a rich source of another fatty substance, cholesterol. People who have high blood cholesterol levels may be advised to limit the number of eggs they eat.

Fruit and vegetables Try and give everyone as many servings as the family budget will allow since they supply vitamin C and also roughage.

In the summer there are plenty of fresh vegetables and soft fruits available making a wide variety of vitamin C-rich foods to choose from. During the winter months, potatoes will continue to supply a little vitamin C but add to this by encouraging your family to eat citrus fruits. Vitamin C is now added to some fruit drinks and instant mashed potatoes. Do remember, however, that vitamin C is destroyed by prolonged cooking.

Cereals Flour, bread and other flour-based products. Some sources of carbohydrate in the diet are essential but the secret here is for each individual to eat just what he or she needs for energy purposes. If you eat more carbohydrate than you need, you will store the excess as fat and become overweight. If you are overweight, keep these kinds of foods to a minimum but do include some as the cereals are sources of vitamin B.

Fats Many of the foods already mentioned contain fat, but extra fat used when preparing meals makes food more attractive and satisfying to eat. Like carbohydrate, fats such as in fried food, cream, nuts, etc., which are another principal source of energy, should be restricted so that you do not become overweight. However, everyone should eat ½–1 oz. (15–25 g.) margarine or butter daily to supply the vitamins A and D that these fats contain.

Textured vegetable protein
Textured vegetable protein (TVP) is something we will all be hearing a great deal more about in the future. With the rising cost of animal protein foods like meat, vegetable proteins, e.g. soy, cotton seed and groundnut, are being used more by the food industry, often in the form of TVP which is made to resemble meat in texture. The major source for TVP is the soya bean. It is already available in a variety of shapes and sizes in health food stores – there are granules, flakes and fibres. TVP supplies nutritious yet inexpensive food extenders which partially replace the more expensive foods such as meat, fish and poultry without sacrificing taste, quality or texture. In addition to good quality protein, the mixture even contains vitamins and minerals to aid dietary needs.

TVP is already used by the catering trade and now some varieties are sold for use at home. Always read the instructions carefully before using to obtain the best results. Do look out for these useful food extenders as they come on to the market.

Body needs

Nutrient	What it does	Where it comes from
Protein	Of prime importance as a raw material in the growth of new body tissues. Also provides some energy.	Animal sources – meat, fish, eggs, milk, cheese. Vegetable sources – cereals including flour-based products, peas, beans, lentils, nuts and textured vegetable protein (TVP).
Fat	Provides energy in a concentrated form, essential fatty acids and helps to make other foods attractive to eat.	White cooking fat and cooking oils, margarine, butter, cream, full fat cheese, nuts.
Carbohydrate	Provides energy.	Sugar, syrup, honey, potatoes, rice and other cereals, flour and flour-based products such as bread, pasta.

Vitamins and minerals

Smaller amounts of vitamins and minerals are required by the body but nevertheless they are still very important for the maintenance of good health.

Vitamin	What it does	Where it comes from
Vitamin A	Aids normal growth of soft tissues such as the eye and vision in dim light.	Margarine, butter and dairy produce, liver, oily fish, carrots, and dark green leaf vegetables.
B Vitamins – a complex of a number of vitamins	Controls the release of energy from food. Helps to maintain a healthy nervous system.	Cereals, meat especially pig meats and offal, yeast and fish roes.
Vitamin C	Essential for healthy tissues, e.g. clear skin. Also helps the body absorb iron.	Fresh fruit and vegetables including citrus fruit, green vegetables and potatoes.
Vitamin D	Promotes strong bones and teeth because it helps the body to absorb calcium.	Margarine, butter, oily fish. Also produced by the action of sunlight on the skin.

Mineral	What it does	Where it comes from
Calcium	Needed for structure of bones and teeth. Controls muscle function.	Milk, cheese, bread, canned fish, e.g. sardines.
Iron	Needed for formation of red blood cells.	Liver, kidney, heart, corned beef and other red meats, egg yolks, bread, flour, cocoa.
Sodium	Controls water balance in the body.	Common salt, seafood and vegetables.
Potassium	Controls water balance in the body.	Meat, fish, fruit and vegetables.

Pastry-making

Pastry is such a marvellous way to produce interesting and exciting dishes that a whole chapter has been devoted to the different methods of producing really mouth-watering light pastries. There are simple step-by-step photographs to guide beginners and those of you who are more experienced but may have difficulty with one type or another.

Anyone can make delicious light pastry, especially now that softer blend margarines are available for simply made all-in-one shortcrust. After mixing lightly with a fork, all-in-one pastry requires slightly more kneading than the traditional rubbed-in type and can in fact take quite a lot of handling without toughening the end result. Here are a few simple rules to help you make perfect pastry:

1 Plan to do your pastry-making before the kitchen becomes warm and humid with other cooking – a damp atmosphere does not help to produce good pastry. A cool temperature is ideal as it will prevent the fat from oiling.

2 Use *sieved* plain flour if possible, to incorporate air, as it produces better pastry textures – that is, crisp and short as opposed to the spongy texture produced by self-raising flour.

3 Handle flour lightly when rubbing in the fat, lift and crumble the mixture between the tips of the fingers as this helps to add air to the pastry and give it a light texture. Shake the bowl after a few seconds to bring lumps to the surface and rub in as before.

4 Add ice cold water for mixing. The amount of water may vary very slightly as flour can become very dry depending on where it is stored. A mixture which is too dry will make the dough difficult to handle; after baking it will be crumbly and when eaten it will taste dry. A wet pastry dough will shrink and lose shape while baking and will make a tough hard pastry to eat.

5 Try to allow the pastry to rest in a refrigerator or cool place wrapped in a polythene bag or in foil for at least 30 minutes. This allows it to relax and removes the elasticity which causes shrinkage round the edge of the dish when cooked.

6 Roll out pastry on a cool surface. A marble slab is ideal but formica kitchen tops are also suitable. A plain wooden rolling pin is best and the worktop should only be lightly floured or the balance of the recipe will be altered if too much flour is used.

Note If a recipe requires 8 oz. (225 g.) pastry, the 8 oz. (225 g.) refers to the quantity of flour used *not* the made-up weight of the dough.

Top shelf: bacon plait (page 81), steak and kidney pudding (page 54) and raspberry flan (page 149). Bottom shelf: devilled ham bouchées (page 80), savoury fish pie (page 36) and choux fruit puffs (page 17)

11

All-in-one shortcrust pastry ❄

This method for making pastry is completely different from the traditional method. Stork, water and some of the flour are creamed together with a fork to form an emulsion of water-in-fat, which is stabilised by the flour. The rest of the flour is added and the flour particles are surrounded by the emulsion, which prevents the joining together of the gluten. The pastry dough can be kneaded without developing the gluten (which toughens pastry).

IMPERIAL/METRIC
5 oz./150 g. Stork margarine, at room temperature
2 tablespoons water
8 oz./225 g. plain flour, sieved

Place the margarine, water and one-third of the flour in a mixing bowl and cream with a fork for about ½ minute until well mixed (see steps 1–2). Add the remaining flour and work into a firm dough (steps 3–4). Turn out on to a lightly floured worktop and knead thoroughly until smooth and silky. Chill, then roll out and use as required.
Makes 8 oz. (225 g.) pastry

Freezing note The uncooked dough can be frozen, well wrapped in cling wrap and then foil.

Variations
Rich flan pastry Add an extra 1 oz. (25 g.) Stork margarine and mix with 1 tablespoon castor sugar dissolved in 1 egg yolk and 2 teaspoons water.
Cheese pastry Add 2–3 oz. (50–75 g.) grated cheese and a pinch of mustard and cayenne with the flour.

Quantities of shortcrust pastry required
For an 8- to 9-inch (20- to 23-cm.) covered plate pie, you will need 10 oz. (275 g.) pastry made with 10 oz. (275 g.) flour.
For a 6-inch (15-cm.) flan ring, you will need 4 oz. (125 g.) pastry made with 4 oz. (125 g.) flour.
For a covered pie in a 6- to 7-inch (15- to 18-cm.) pie dish you will need 6 oz. (175 g.) pastry made with 6 oz. (175 g.) flour.

1. *In a mixing bowl, adding the cold water to a third of the flour and the 5 oz. (150 g.) Stork margarine, brought to room temperature.*

2. *Creaming the ingredients with a fork until the mixture forms a sticky consistency.*

3. *Sieving the remaining two-thirds of the flour into the creamed mixture.*

4. *Mixing the flour in with a palette knife until a firm dough is formed.*

Lining a flan tin with shortcrust pastry

5. *Rolling out the pastry gently on a lightly floured board into a circle 2 inches (5 cm.) larger than the flan tin.*

6. *Lifting the pastry very carefully over a rolling pin to position the pastry in the flan tin.*

Traditional shortcrust pastry ❄

This is the simplest and most popular of all the pastries; it is called short because 'short' fibres are developed during the preparation. If a rich shortcrust pastry is required include egg. For sweet pastry use castor sugar dissolved in the water.

IMPERIAL/METRIC
4 oz./125 g. Stork margarine, straight from the refrigerator
8 oz./225 g. plain flour, sieved
2–3 tablespoons water

In a mixing bowl, rub the margarine into the flour until the mixture resembles fine breadcrumbs (see step 1). Add the water and stir into a dough (steps 2–3). Knead together on a floured worktop with the fingertips until smooth (step 4). Chill, then roll out and use as required.
Makes 8 oz. (225 g.) pastry

Freezing note Either freeze the prepared dough shaped into an oblong and wrapped in cling wrap and foil, or roll it out and use it to line foil dishes, then wrap.

Variations
Savoury pastry Use 2 Red, Chicken or Curry Oxo cubes and crumble into the rubbed-in ingredients.
Rich flan pastry Use 6 oz. (175 g.) Stork margarine and 8 oz. (225 g.) flour. Add 1–2 oz. (25–50 g.) castor sugar to the rubbed-in mixture, then mix with 1 egg yolk and enough water to make a stiff dough.

1. *In a mixing bowl, rubbing the margarine into the flour with the fingertips, until the mixture resembles fine breadcrumbs.*

2. *Adding the cold water to the mixture in the bowl.*

3. *Stirring the mixture into a dough, using a palette knife.*

4. *Kneading the dough lightly, so that the dough is not toughened, until smooth on a lightly floured board.*

7. *Easing and pressing the pastry carefully to line the flan tin.*

8. *Neatening the edge of the flan case with a rolling pin, to remove excess pastry.*

9. *Lining the unbaked flan case with greaseproof paper and then baking beans etc. ready to be baked blind.*

13

1. Dividing the margarine into four equal portions and adding a quarter to the sieved flour and salt in a mixing bowl.

2. Rubbing the margarine into the flour with the fingertips.

3. With the lemon juice and water added, mixing to a fairly soft dough using a palette knife.

4. Rolling out the dough on a lightly floured board into a 15- by 5-inch (38- by 13-cm.) oblong.

5. Dabbing the second quarter of margarine over the top two-thirds of the pastry, using a palette knife.

6. Folding the bottom third of the pastry up over the middle third.

7. Folding the top third of the pastry down to cover the first folding.

8. Sealing the open edges with a rolling pin. Then resting the pastry before repeating the rolling and folding three more times (see recipe).

9. Folding the rested and shaped dough cover over a chicken pie, with the aid of a rolling pin.

Flaky and rough puff pastry

Making this type of pastry is a most satisfying achievement. The idea is to introduce a thin layer of fat between the thinnest leaves of pastry dough and to do this the pastry is folded to trap the air which will cause it to puff in the oven when cooked. Follow the steps in the photographs making sure that the edges of the dough are sealed at each stage to capture as much air as possible. These layered pastries must be rested even more than the shortcrust and it is advisable for the pastry to have at least a 15- to 20-minute rest in the refrigerator between each rolling. This enables the fat to become firm again after being softened by the rolling. Always cover the dough before resting to avoid a skin forming, which will spoil the flakes. It is not necessary to grease the baking sheet for flaky pastry as it is already rich in fat and the fat on the sheet may hold back the rising during the first few minutes in the oven.

Flaky pastry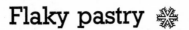

IMPERIAL/METRIC
6 oz./175 g. Stork margarine,
    straight from the refrigerator
8 oz./225 g. plain flour, sieved
pinch salt
2 teaspoons lemon juice
6–8 tablespoons cold water

Divide the margarine into four equal portions. Sieve the flour and salt and rub in a quarter of the margarine (see steps 1–2). Keep the remaining three-quarters in the refrigerator or cold place until required.

Pour the lemon juice and cold water into the flour mixture and mix to a fairly soft dough with the blade of a knife (step 3). Turn out on to a lightly floured worktop and knead for 2 minutes until smooth. Sprinkle with flour, place in a polythene bag and leave to rest for 15–20 minutes in the refrigerator or a cool place.

Roll out into a 15- by 5-inch (38- by 13-cm.) oblong (step 4). Brush off surplus flour. Divide another quarter of margarine into small knobs and dab evenly over the top two-thirds of the pastry (step 5).

Fold the bottom third up and the top third down to cover (steps 6–7). Seal the edges with a rolling pin (step 8). Cover as before and rest for 15–20 minutes in the refrigerator or a cool place. Turn the dough so the right hand now faces you and repeat the rolling and folding with the third and fourth quarters of margarine. Finally roll and fold once more and rest the dough in the refrigerator for 15 minutes before using.

Makes 8 oz. (225 g.) pastry
Freezing note Wrap well in cling wrap and foil.

Rough puff pastry

IMPERIAL/METRIC
6 oz./175 g. Stork margarine,
    straight from the refrigerator
8 oz./225 g. plain flour, sieved
pinch salt
2 teaspoons lemon juice
6 tablespoons cold water

Cut the margarine into walnut-sized pieces. Stir into the sieved flour and salt, keeping the margarine pieces whole. Mix the lemon juice and water and stir into the flour, using a palette knife to work to a soft dough. Add a little more water if necessary.

Gather the dough together with the fingertips and turn out on to a floured worktop. Shape into a small oblong and roll out carefully into a rectangle approximately 15 by 5 inches (38 by 13 cm.). Brush off any surplus flour and fold into three by folding the bottom third up and the top third down. Lightly seal the three open edges with a rolling pin. Turn the pastry round so that the right hand edge faces you and roll out as before into a rectangle. Fold again, seal the edges and rest in a polythene bag in a refrigerator or cold place for 20 minutes.

Repeat the rolling and folding twice more (if the dough becomes difficult to handle allow it to rest between times). Place in a polythene bag and chill for 15–20 minutes before using.
Makes 8 oz. (225 g.) pastry
Freezing note Wrap well in cling wrap and foil.

Hot water crust pastry

This type of pastry is associated with meat and game pies. It became popular in the Victorian era, as it was always connected with the hunt. Normally these pies are referred to as raised pies, because they are traditionally moulded over straight-sided containers. Today one can improvise using loaf or cake tins and jam jars, or if you feel extravagant you can buy special hinged moulds for the purpose. Hot water crust is an ideal pastry to make on a cold day as the dough is kneaded and moulded whilst it is still warm!

IMPERIAL/METRIC
10 oz./275 g. plain flour
½ teaspoon salt
1 egg yolk
3 oz./75 g. Stork margarine
¼ pint/150 ml. water

Sieve the flour and salt into a mixing bowl. Drop in the egg yolk and sprinkle with a little of the flour. Place the margarine and water in a saucepan over moderate heat and allow to melt, then bring rapidly to the boil. Pour on to the flour immediately and mix together with a wooden spoon. Turn out on to a floured worktop and knead until smooth. Sprinkle with flour, place in a polythene bag and rest for 30 minutes. Roll out on a floured worktop and use as required.
Makes 10 oz. (275 g.) pastry

Suet and pudding crust pastry

Basically these two pastries are the same except one uses suet and the other Stork margarine. They can be interchanged in any of the recipes calling for this type of pastry.

It is designed essentially for boiled and steamed puddings, but can be baked. This is the only pastry which requires extra raising agent to give a light, open sponge-like texture; this is because of the long moist cooking.

Usually suet or pudding crust pastry is used for steak and kidney puddings, jam roly-poly, spotted dick, etc. Always remember to make sure that the water in the steamer or saucepan is kept constantly boiling during cooking. Check the water level at intervals and refill with boiling water when necessary.

Suet pastry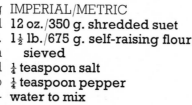

IMPERIAL/METRIC
12 oz./350 g. shredded suet
1½ lb./675 g. self-raising flour, sieved
¼ teaspoon salt
¼ teaspoon pepper
water to mix

Mix the suet, flour and seasonings with sufficient water to make a soft but firm dough. Knead and shape into a ball. Cover and leave to rest for 10 minutes. Use as required.
Makes 1½ lb. (675 g.) pastry
Freezing note Freeze the prepared pastry well wrapped in cling wrap and foil.

Variation
Savoury suet pastry Crumble one Red, Chicken or Curry Oxo cube into the dry ingredients.

Pudding crust pastry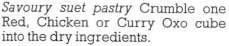

IMPERIAL/METRIC
8 oz./225 g. self-raising flour, sieved
½ teaspoon salt
4 oz./125 g. Stork margarine
5 tablespoons water

Sieve the flour and salt into a mixing bowl. Rub the margarine into the flour until the mixture resembles fine breadcrumbs. Add the water and using a palette knife mix to a soft dough. Knead lightly, then use as required.
Makes 8 oz. (225 g.) pastry
Freezing note Wrap well in cling wrap and foil.

Biscuit crust

Strictly speaking this is not a pastry, but it is used to line shallow pie dishes or flan cases to hold a filling. It is very quick to make and can be varied with the addition of mixed spices, lemon or orange rind. Use the back of a metal spoon to press the crumbs into the dish and chill in the refrigerator before filling. This will make the cutting easier.

IMPERIAL/METRIC
8 oz./225 g. digestive biscuits
1 teaspoon ground cinnamon
1 teaspoon ground nutmeg
½ teaspoon mixed spice or ground cloves
1 tablespoon castor sugar (optional)
3 oz./75 g. Stork margarine, melted

Put the biscuits in a polythene bag and crush them with a rolling pin, or use a blender. Mix the crushed biscuits with the spices and sugar, if used, and work in the melted margarine. Mix well, then press into the bottom and up the sides of an 8-inch (20-cm.) spring clip tin, cake tin or flan ring. Chill for 30 minutes to set the crust, then fill.
Makes 1 8-inch (20-cm.) flan case

Variation
Ginger biscuit flan Use ginger nuts, adding ½ teaspoon ground ginger instead of the spices, and 1 tablespoon castor sugar.

Choux pastry ❄

Choux pastry was so named because of its resemblance to a cabbage when baked – hence the French *choux* meaning cabbage. This type of pastry is made in a very different way from the other traditional pastries. The resulting mixture is more like a thick paste than the other pastry doughs with which we are more familiar.

Choux pastry can be used in many ways – its most popular use is for making éclairs, but it can be made into profiteroles, cream buns and gougère, or even deep-fried and served with sugar and cinnamon, or grated cheese. To vary savoury dishes, mashed potato or grated cheese can be added to the raw mixture before baking.

IMPERIAL/METRIC
2 oz./50 g. Stork margarine
¼ pint/150 ml. water
2½ oz./70 g. plain flour, sieved
2 standard eggs

Place the margarine and water in a saucepan over moderate heat and allow to melt (see step 1). Bring quickly to the boil, remove instantly from the heat and beat in the flour (step 2). Return to a low heat and beat for 1 minute until the mixture leaves the sides of the pan; cool slightly.

Lightly beat the eggs and add a little at a time to the mixture, beating well until all the egg is used and no traces remain. Use as required.
Makes ¼ pint (150 ml.) pastry
Freezing note Choux pastry freezes well. It can be frozen baked or unbaked. Leave unfilled and allow time to thaw before using.

Variations
Cheese choux pastry Before adding the eggs, beat in 1 oz. (25 g.) grated Cheddar cheese.
Choux fruit puffs Follow the recipe for Choux puffs with chocolate (see page 149), but pipe out in larger balls. Sprinkle over the flaked almonds and sugar and bake for 30–35 minutes. When cold, cut in half and fill with fresh whipped cream and fresh fruit in season. Dust the tops with icing sugar.
Illustrated on page 10

Eclairs filled with whipped fresh cream and covered with chocolate sauce (page 133)

1. *Melting the margarine and water in a saucepan over moderate heat.*

2. *Beating in the flour, off the heat. Return to heat for 1 minute. Remove and gradually beat in whisked eggs.*

3. *Filling a piping bag, fitted with a plain tube, with the completed choux paste.*

4. *Piping 3-inch (7½-cm.) lengths choux paste, for éclairs, on a greased and lightly floured baking sheet.*

Breakfast

No one would dream of trying to run a car without petrol and oil but many of us expect the body to work efficiently through the morning without fuel after many hours of sleep. Breakfast provides this fuel that we all need to keep us running well until lunchtime, so give the family a good start to the day with a really well-planned meal.

If mornings are a rushed affair then try a little forward planning. Set the table the night before and put the morning eggs, bacon or sausages on a plate at the front of the refrigerator. Some people find a liquid breakfast sufficient but do make sure it is a nourishing one. Try whisking up egg and milk with a little sugar and drink it while you are getting ready for work. A meal containing protein is an ideal way to start the day and eggs are good in this way and certainly more sustaining than toast and marmalade. Even in a rush it only takes a few minutes to boil an egg, or, even quicker, try some delicious muesli topped with fresh fruit, which you can make up in bulk to last the family for days (see page 21).

Grilled sausages are very simple and kippers can be prepared by standing them in a jug of boiling water for 5 minutes, which avoids the smell permeating the house first thing in the morning. In winter a bowl of porridge is just right for a cold morning and this can be made very quickly from instant porridge oats or by the traditional method, steeping the oatmeal overnight. If you feel that making tea or coffee takes too much time, why not have fruit juice or milk.

The weekend is the time to experiment, and if the family are late risers you can serve brunch – a combined breakfast and lunch which saves cooking two meals. Begin with fruit juice or grapefruit and then try a full-scale old-fashioned breakfast of bacon, eggs, kidney and mushrooms; or bacon, sausages and tomatoes with fried potatoes; or fish cakes with mushrooms and tomatoes, or our super kedgeree recipe (see page 20). As breakfast foods are no longer cheap remember that left-over potatoes or a slice of bread can be fried to make excellent fillers for hungry men and children. You will find enough ideas in this section to please everyone.

A final word to those people who are slimming: do make sure you have something to eat first thing otherwise you will be tempted to nibble during the morning – cut down on the other meals if necessary.

Breakfast: muesli (page 21) and kedgeree (page 20)

Kedgeree

IMPERIAL/METRIC
6 oz./175 g. long-grain rice
salt and pepper
8 oz./225 g. smoked haddock or cod
   fillet, skinned, or 7-oz./198-g.
   can tuna fish, flaked
2 oz./50 g. Stork margarine
2 hard-boiled eggs, chopped
1 tablespoon fresh chopped
   parsley (optional)
triangles of toast

Cook the rice in boiling salted water until tender – about 12 minutes – then drain thoroughly. Place the haddock or cod in a pan with a little water and simmer for about 10 minutes until tender. Drain and flake. Melt the margarine in a pan and add the cooked rice and cooked fish or tuna fish. Season well and heat gently, stirring carefully. Add the eggs, and parsley, if used, and continue to heat gently until piping hot. Serve on hot plates with triangles of toast.
Serves 4
Note The rice, fish and eggs can be cooked the night before, refrigerated overnight and quickly heated together in the morning.
Illustrated on page 19

Kipper toasts

IMPERIAL/METRIC
12 oz./350 g. kipper fillets, fresh
   or frozen
1 oz./25 g. Stork margarine
salt and pepper
2–3 tablespoons cream or top of the
   milk
4 slices toast or fried bread
1 lemon, quartered

Cook the kippers in a little boiling water for about 5 minutes until tender, or according to the directions on the pack. Drain well and flake, removing the biggest bones. Melt the margarine in a pan, then add the flaked kipper and seasoning to taste. Heat through, add the cream or milk and reheat until piping hot. Spoon on to the toast and serve garnished with lemon wedges.
Serves 4
Note These toasts also make a delicious supper snack.

Smoky fish cakes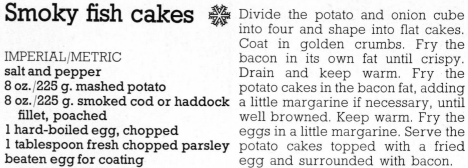

IMPERIAL/METRIC
salt and pepper
8 oz./225 g. mashed potato
8 oz./225 g. smoked cod or haddock
   fillet, poached
1 hard-boiled egg, chopped
1 tablespoon fresh chopped parsley
beaten egg for coating
golden breadcrumbs
2 oz./50 g. Stork margarine
fried tomatoes (optional)

Season the potatoes well then flake the fish into the potato. Add the chopped egg and parsley and mix thoroughly. Divide into four and shape into flat round cakes. Dip in beaten egg, then in golden breadcrumbs, pressing well in. Chill until required.
   Melt the margarine and sauté the fish cakes gently for 5–8 minutes on each side until golden brown. Drain on absorbent paper and serve, with tomatoes if liked.
Serves 4
Freezing note If freezing these fish cakes, omit the hard-boiled egg.

Fried cod's roe and tomatoes

IMPERIAL/METRIC
8–12 oz./225–350 g. boiled cod's roe
1½ oz./40 g. Stork margarine
4 tomatoes, halved

Cut the cod's roe into ½-inch (1-cm.) thick slices. Melt the margarine and sauté the roe until golden brown on each side. Drain on absorbent paper and keep warm. Fry the tomatoes in the fat remaining in the pan (or grill if preferred) and serve at once with the fried cod's roe, accompanied by brown bread and margarine.
Serves 4

Potato cake fry-up

IMPERIAL/METRIC
12 oz.–1 lb./350–450 g. mashed
   potato, mixed with 1 Onion Oxo
   cube, crumbled
golden breadcrumbs
8–12 rashers streaky bacon,
   derinded
1 oz./25 g. Stork margarine
4 eggs

Divide the potato and onion cube into four and shape into flat cakes. Coat in golden crumbs. Fry the bacon in its own fat until crispy. Drain and keep warm. Fry the potato cakes in the bacon fat, adding a little margarine if necessary, until well browned. Keep warm. Fry the eggs in a little margarine. Serve the potato cakes topped with a fried egg and surrounded with bacon.
Serves 4
Note This also makes a delicious lunchtime snack.

Kidney omelettes

IMPERIAL/METRIC
2 oz./50 g. Stork margarine
4 lambs' kidneys, skinned, cored
   and chopped
8 standard eggs
salt and pepper

Melt 1 oz. (25 g.) of the margarine and sauté the kidneys until sealed, then remove from the pan. Melt the remaining margarine in a small omelette or frying pan. Whisk 2 eggs with 1 tablespoon water and seasoning and pour into the pan. Add a quarter of the kidneys and cook gently pulling the edges of the omelette to the centre of the pan with a fork as it begins to set, and letting the liquid egg run out to the sides. When set loosen carefully with a palette knife, fold over and slide on to a plate. Serve at once. Make three more omelettes in the same way.
Serves 4

Variations
Fill omelettes with chopped cooked bacon or ham, sliced cooked mushrooms or chopped cooked tomatoes.

Baked eggs with bacon

IMPERIAL/METRIC
4 large eggs
salt and pepper
4 tablespoons single cream or top
of the milk
6 oz./175 g. bacon, derinded
and chopped, or 4 oz./100 g.
cooked ham, chopped
toast fingers

Break each egg carefully into an individual ovenproof dish and season lightly. Spoon 1 tablespoon cream or milk over each egg and cook in a moderately hot oven (375°F., 190°C., Gas Mark 5) for 5–10 minutes, until the eggs are just set. Meanwhile fry the bacon in its own fat until just beginning to brown, then drain off all the fat. Divide the bacon or ham among the four dishes, arranging it round the edge of each dish. Serve hot with fingers of toast.
Serves 4

Baked eggs with bacon

Spanish breakfast omelette

IMPERIAL/METRIC
2 oz./50 g. Stork margarine
4 oz./100 g. bacon, chopped
2 large potatoes, cooked and
chopped
2 tomatoes, chopped
4 tablespoons cooked peas
(optional)
6 eggs
4 tablespoons milk
1 Onion Oxo cube, crumbled
salt and pepper

Melt the margarine in a large frying pan and sauté the bacon until tender. Add the potatoes and continue to fry for a few minutes, stirring occasionally. Add the tomatoes and peas and mix thoroughly. Beat the eggs, milk, onion cube and seasoning together and pour into the pan. Mix lightly then cook over a low heat without stirring until the egg is almost set. Place under a hot grill just to set the top, cut into four and serve at once.
Serves 4
Note This omelette also makes a tasty lunchtime snack.

Cheesy poached eggs

IMPERIAL/METRIC
4 slices bread, toasted
Stork margarine for spreading
4 oz./100 g. Cheddar cheese, grated
4 eggs

Spread the toast lightly with margarine then cover with the grated cheese. Place under a moderate grill until just beginning to brown. Meanwhile poach the eggs until just set. Serve a poached egg on top of each slice of toasted cheese.
Serves 4
Note This recipe makes a tasty lunch or supper dish.

Variation
Poached eggs can also be served on portions of cooked smoked haddock or slices of cold ham.

Muesli

IMPERIAL/METRIC
1 lb./450 g. instant porridge oats
3 tablespoons wheatgerm
4 oz./100 g. cracked wheat, millet
flakes or other cereal
1–2 oz./25–50 g. soft brown sugar
4 oz./100 g. mixed chopped nuts
2 oz./50 g. raisins or sultanas
3 oz./75 g. dried apple rings,
chopped
3 oz./75 g. dried apricots, chopped

Place all the ingredients in a large bowl and mix well together. Store in an airtight jar. This quantity should last four people for about a week – it is very filling so you only need 3–4 dessertspoons per serving.

Serving suggestions
Serve with cream or top of the milk. Add a sliced banana, some strawberries or other fresh fruit, or stewed fruit in winter.
Illustrated on page 19

Soups & Starters

When planning a menu, whether it is to serve the family or for a dinner party or special occasion, the soup or starter plays an important role as it introduces the food which is to follow. Neither should be too highly flavoured or too filling.

There are all kinds of soups – thin and clear, thick and creamy, hot or cold. Therefore, remember that a thin soup would be more suitable served before a hearty casserole and a thicker soup would be ideal as the first course to a light steak and salad main course.

Soups

The basis of all soups is a tasty stock, but nowadays soup-making need not be a chore as there are so many ready-made stock preparations available, the most popular being Oxo cubes. These make a delicious stock and save an enormous amount of time and trouble. A good broth can be made with stock and root vegetables and any leftover boiled vegetables can be added just before serving. For example, chicken broth can be made with 2 pints (generous litre) chicken stock, 2 medium-sized diced carrots, 1 medium-sized diced onion and 1 leek and then either $1\frac{1}{2}$ oz. (40 g.) cooked rice with frozen peas or some chopped cooked chicken meat, and chopped parsley can be added before serving.

Remember that soups freeze well, so it's worth making double the quantity you need at any one time. When the soup is cool, pack in polythene or foil cartons in the individual portions you are likely to need.

Always garnish soups. Garnishes not only make the soup look attractive but they can also make it more nourishing. Here are a few ideas:

Croûtons Triangles or cubes of bread deep-fried until crisp and golden. Float them on top of soup to make it more substantial.

Cheese Sprinkle grated Cheddar or Parmesan on to some soups to add flavour and nourishment.

Chopped herbs Freshly chop to add colour and the finishing touch to the simplest of soups.

Cream A swirl of cream adds the final dash of sophistication to any strongly coloured soup.

Starters

Starters should be light and refreshing with just the right amount of flavour to interest family or guests. A mixed hors-d'œuvre makes an interesting starter with its varying textures and flavours. Choose from crisp fresh vegetables tossed in a dressing, cubes or slices of meat and fish, egg mayonnaise and try a few continental delicacies such as anchovies, olives and sliced cooked sausage.

Serve crudités as a first course or with drinks. They are crisp vegetables such as celery sticks, carrot sticks, cauliflower florets and cucumber wedges served with a cheese dip or garlic mayonnaise.

There are many interesting starters which, when in season, are reasonably priced. Try avocado pear, halved and served with French dressing or filled with mayonnaise and prawns, halved grapefruit cold or grilled with brown sugar, or simply serve melon.

Tuna and cucumber mousse (page 29), leek and bacon tartlets (page 26) and taramasalata (page 28)

Soups

Cream of mushroom soup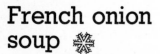

IMPERIAL/METRIC
1 oz./25 g. Stork margarine
1 oz./25 g. flour
3 Chicken Oxo cubes, crumbled
    and dissolved in 1 pint/575 ml.
    hot water
⅔ pint/400 ml. milk
2 tablespoons chopped parsley
salt and pepper
4 oz./100 g. mushrooms, chopped
    or sliced
juice of ½ lemon

Place all the ingredients, except the
lemon juice, in a saucepan. Bring to
the boil over a moderate heat,
whisking continuously. Simmer for
10 minutes. Just before serving, stir
in the lemon juice.
Serves 4
Freezing note Freeze, but omit
lemon juice.

French onion soup

IMPERIAL/METRIC
2 oz./50 g. Stork margarine
1 lb./450 g. onions, chopped
3 Red Oxo cubes, crumbled and
    dissolved in 1⅔ pints/1 litre hot
    water
½ oz./15 g. flour
1 teaspoon Worcestershire sauce
salt and pepper
4 slices French bread
2 oz./50 g. Cheddar cheese, grated

Melt the margarine and sauté the
onions until brown – about 12–15
minutes. Add the beef stock and
whisk in the flour. Continue to
whisk until the mixture comes to the
boil. Simmer for 20–30 minutes. Add
the Worcestershire sauce. Season.
Sprinkle each slice of bread with
½ oz. (15 g.) cheese and grill until
golden. Float a slice of the bread on
top of each bowl of soup.
Serves 4

Watercress soup

IMPERIAL/METRIC
2 bunches watercress
1 oz./25 g. Stork margarine
1 onion, chopped
1 potato, chopped
⅔ pint/400 ml. milk
2 Chicken Oxo cubes, crumbled and
    dissolved in ⅔ pint/400 ml. hot
    water
salt and pepper
4 tablespoons cream

Coarsely shred the watercress, keeping a few sprigs for garnish.

Melt the margarine and sauté the onion, potato and watercress for 5 minutes. Add the milk and chicken stock. Bring to the boil over a moderate heat, whisking continuously. Simmer for 10–15 minutes. Liquidise or sieve, return to a clean pan, season and reheat.

Serve hot or cold garnished with the reserved watercress and a swirl of cream.
Serves 4

Variation
Substitute 1 large lettuce, shredded, for the watercress.

Tomato and orange soup

IMPERIAL/METRIC
1-lb. 12-oz./794-g. can tomatoes
1 onion, chopped
1 carrot, chopped
1 bay leaf
4 Chicken Oxo cubes, crumbled
    and dissolved in 1⅓ pints/750 ml.
    hot water
½ oz./15 g. Stork margarine
½ oz./15 g. flour
rind and juice of ½ orange
pinch sugar
Garnish
chopped parsley
grated cheese

Place the tomatoes, onion, carrot, bay leaf, chicken stock and seasoning in a saucepan. Bring to the boil and simmer for 20–30 minutes.

Liquidise or sieve and return to a clean pan. Add the margarine and flour and bring to the boil over a moderate heat, whisking.

Shred and blanch the orange rind and stir into the soup with the juice and sugar. Garnish.
Serves 4

Spinach and lemon soup ❄

IMPERIAL/METRIC
1 oz./25 g. Stork margarine
1 small onion, finely chopped
8-oz./227-g. packet frozen spinach,
  thawed
2 Chicken Oxo cubes, crumbled
  and dissolved in ⅔ pint/400 ml. hot
  water
⅓ pint/200 ml. water
½ oz./15 g. flour
1 pint/575 ml. milk
¼ teaspoon ground nutmeg
salt and pepper
Garnish
thin lemon slices

Melt the margarine and sauté the
chopped onion for 5 minutes. Add
the spinach, chicken stock, water,
flour and milk. Bring to the boil over
moderate heat, whisking continuously. Season and cook for 10
minutes. Serve with lemon slices
floating on the surface.
Serves 4

Bone stock ❄

IMPERIAL/METRIC
meat bones or poultry carcass
For each 1 pint/575 ml. water
1 onion
1 carrot
bouquet garni

Cover the bones well, add the vegetables and cook for 2–3 hours
simmering gently. Strain and use as
required.

Vegetable stock ❄

IMPERIAL/METRIC
½ oz./15 g. Stork margarine
1 lb./450 g. carrots
1 lb./450 g. onions
few stalks celery
bouquet garni
6 peppercorns
2 teaspoons salt
6 pints/3½ litres boiling water

Melt the margarine in the saucepan
and add the peeled, washed and
roughly chopped vegetables. Shake
over moderate heat until the vegetables begin to brown. Add the
herbs and seasoning and finally the
boiling water. Cover with a lid and
simmer for 3 hours. Strain and use
as required.
Makes about 5 pints (3 litres)
Note Smaller quantities can be
made in the pressure cooker which
cuts cooking time to about 45
minutes.

Starters

Leek and bacon tartlets ❄

IMPERIAL/METRIC
8 oz./225 g. shortcrust pastry
  (see pages 12–13)
2 oz./50 g. Stork margarine
6 oz./175 g. bacon, diced
2 leeks, shredded
1½ oz./40 g. flour
1 Onion Oxo cube, crumbled
½ pint/275 ml. milk
¼ pint/150 ml. single cream
2 teaspoons chopped parsley
3 oz./75 g. cheese, grated
Garnish
8 rashers streaky bacon
sprigs parsley

Roll out the pastry on a floured worktop and use to line eight individual
tartlet tins. Prick the bases, line
with foil and bake blind in a moderate oven (350°F., 180°C., Gas Mark
4) for 15–20 minutes. Turn out and
place on a baking sheet.
  For the filling, melt ½ oz. (15 g.)
margarine and sauté the bacon until
it sizzles. Add the leeks and fry
gently until soft. To make the sauce,
put the remaining margarine, the
flour, onion cube and milk in a pan
over moderate heat and bring to
the boil, stirring continuously. Cook
for 1–2 minutes. Add the cream,
parsley, leeks and bacon.
  Divide the filling among the
tartlets. Sprinkle with the cheese
and return to the top shelf of the
oven for 10–15 minutes to brown or
brown quickly under the grill.
Garnish each tartlet with a bacon
roll and a sprig of parsley. To
make bacon rolls, spread the bacon
flat with the back of a knife, cut in
half, then roll up and grill or cook
in the oven until crisp.
Makes 8 tartlets
Illustrated on page 23

Stuffed baked avocados

IMPERIAL/METRIC
1 oz./25 g. Stork margarine
1 oz./25 g. flour
½ Onion Oxo cube, crumbled
½ Curry Oxo cube, crumbled
½ pint/275 ml. milk
6 oz./175 g. peeled prawns
2 ripe avocados
juice of ½ lemon
4 tablespoons dried breadcrumbs
1 oz./25 g. Stork margarine,
  melted
Anchovy toast
4 slices brown bread
2 oz./50 g. Stork margarine
4 anchovy fillets, chopped

Place the margarine, flour, onion
and curry cubes and milk in a
saucepan over moderate heat.
Bring to the boil, whisking continuously and cool for 5–7 minutes. Add
the peeled prawns.
  Cut the avocados in half. Remove
the stones and scoop out a little flesh.
Chop this and add to the sauce.
Sprinkle the lemon juice over the
cut surface of the avocados and add
any remaining juice to the mixture.
Spoon the mixture into the avocado
halves and pile up. Place on a baking sheet, sprinkle with the breadcrumbs and pour over the melted
margarine. Bake at the top of a
moderately hot oven (375°F., 190°C.,
Gas Mark 5) for 30 minutes. It may
be necessary to brown the tops
quickly under a hot grill.
  Serve with anchovy toast. To
make this, toast the slices of brown
bread. Spread with the margarine
mixed with the chopped anchovy
fillets. Place under the grill for a
few seconds.
Serves 4

Prawn and apple cocktail

Prawn and apple cocktail

IMPERIAL/METRIC
2 egg yolks
½ pint/275 ml. oil
1 tablespoon white wine vinegar
2 tablespoons double cream
2 dessert apples, peeled and cored
juice of ½ lemon
8 oz./225 g. peeled prawns
chopped lettuce or 4 oz./100 g.
 cooked rice
Garnish
chopped parsley

Make ½ pint (275 ml.) mayonnaise by whisking the egg yolks, then adding the oil very gradually, whisking all the time. Thin down with the white wine vinegar. Stir in the double cream. Chop the apples and mix with the lemon juice. Add the prawns, reserving four for garnish. Stir the apple and prawn mixture into the mayonnaise. Serve on a bed of lettuce in cocktail glasses, garnished with the reserved prawns and the parsley; or serve in scallop shells surrounded with 1 oz. (25 g.) cooked rice per portion, garnish with whole prawns and parsley.
Serves 4

Variation
Curried cocktail Add one Curry Oxo cube, crumbled, to the egg yolks for the mayonnaise and continue as before.

Stuffed aubergines au gratin

IMPERIAL/METRIC
2 aubergines
salt
5 oz./150 g. Stork margarine
2 onions, chopped
1 clove garlic, crushed
2 tomatoes, skinned, deseeded and
 chopped
4 oz./100 g. peeled prawns
½ teaspoon dried fennel
salt and pepper
2 tablespoons grated cheese
1 Onion Oxo cube, crumbled
¼ pint/150 ml. cheese sauce (see
 page 130)
2 tablespoons browned
 breadcrumbs
8 anchovy fillets, halved lengthways

Halve the aubergines. Score the flesh and sprinkle with salt. Leave for 30 minutes, rinse, drain and pat dry. Fry the aubergines gently on both sides in 3 oz. (75 g.) of the margarine. Remove. When cool, scoop out the flesh and chop it. Set aside. Place the aubergine shells in a greased dish. Fry the onions and clove of garlic in 1 oz. (25 g.) margarine until soft. Add the tomatoes, prawns and aubergine flesh. Mix in the fennel and seasoning to taste and spoon into the aubergine shells. Add the cheese and onion cube to the sauce and pour over the aubergines. Sprinkle with the breadcrumbs. Top with a lattice pattern of anchovy fillets. Melt the remaining margarine and spoon over. Reheat in the top of a moderate oven (350°F., 180°C., Gas Mark 4) for 15 minutes, or grill under a low heat for 10–15 minutes.
Serves 4

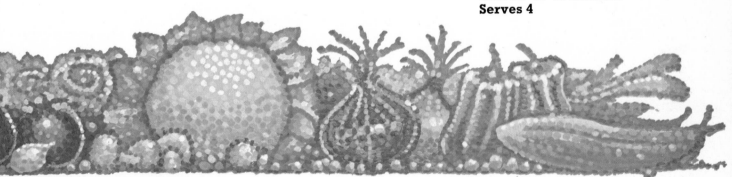

Chicken liver pâté ❄

IMPERIAL/METRIC
12 oz./350 g. chicken livers
1 oz./25 g. Stork margarine
1 small onion, finely chopped
1 clove garlic, crushed
1 tablespoon cream (optional)
2 tablespoons dry sherry or brandy
2 tablespoons tomato purée
salt and pepper to taste
4 oz./100 g. Stork margarine,
  melted
Garnish
parsley sprigs

Trim the chicken livers. Melt the margarine and sauté the livers gently until they change colour. Add the onion and garlic and cook for 5 minutes. Cool. Stir in the cream, if used, sherry or brandy, tomato purée and seasoning. Liquidise or sieve the mixture and divide among four individual dishes. Pour melted margarine over the top of each and chill. Garnish with parsley to serve.
Serves 4
Freezing note Pâté freezes well but it is best to store it for only 4–6 weeks as it loses texture and flavour if kept too long.

Tomato topknots

IMPERIAL/METRIC
1 oz./25 g. Stork margarine
1 small onion, finely chopped
1 small clove garlic, crushed
2 oz./50 g. mushrooms, finely
  chopped
2 oz./50 g. cooked ham, chopped
1 tablespoon tomato purée
½ oz./15 g. fresh white breadcrumbs
salt and pepper
4 tomatoes
lettuce

Melt the margarine and sauté the onion and garlic for about 5–10 minutes until tender. Add the mushrooms, ham and tomato purée and cook for 5 minutes. Stir in the breadcrumbs and season to taste.

Cut the top off each tomato and reserve. Scoop out the insides and fill each tomato generously with the mushroom mixture. Replace the tomato tops and arrange the tomatoes on a bed of lettuce. Chill.
Serves 4

Ham cornets

IMPERIAL/METRIC
4 oz./125 g. cream cheese
1 tablespoon mayonnaise
1 teaspoon tomato purée
1 teaspoon lemon juice
1 tablespoon chopped cucumber
4 thin slices cooked ham

Mix the cheese, mayonnaise, tomato purée and lemon juice together. Stir in the cucumber.

Mould the ham around a cream horn tin or shape into a cone and secure with a cocktail stick. Divide the cream cheese filling between the cornets and chill in the refrigerator. Serve on a bed of watercress.
Serves 4

Taramasalata ❄

IMPERIAL/METRIC
8 oz./225 g. smoked cod's roe
juice of 1 lemon
1 tablespoon fresh white
  breadcrumbs, soaked in a little
  water and squeezed
1 small potato, boiled and mashed
  (optional)
2 cloves garlic
1 tablespoon oil
Garnish
shredded lettuce
4–6 lemon slices
4–6 black olives

Put the cod's roe in a mortar or a blender and add a little of the lemon juice, the breadcrumbs, mashed potato, if used, and garlic. Mix together well, then work in the oil, remaining lemon juice and enough water to make a texture suitable for piping.

Place a little shredded lettuce in the bottom of four or six individual dishes and pipe the taramasalata in a swirl on top. Garnish with a slice of lemon and a black olive.

Serve with brown bread and Stork, or toast.
Serves 4–6
Freezing note Taramasalata can be frozen in several ways. Pipe large rosettes on to greaseproof paper and open freeze. Pack carefully into polythene bags or rigid containers.

Another way of freezing is to shape the taramasalata into individual portions and freeze separately or to shape into a roll, so that it can be sliced when required.
Illustrated on page 23

Curried jubilee eggs

IMPERIAL/METRIC
4 hard-boiled eggs, shelled
2 tablespoons mayonnaise or salad
  cream
2 teaspoons tomato purée
few drops lemon juice
freshly ground black pepper
pinch salt
½ Curry Oxo cube, crumbled
paprika pepper

Remove the top third of each egg. Carefully scoop out the yolks with a teaspoon. Place the yolks in a basin and add all the remaining ingredients except the paprika. Mix well until smooth. Either spoon the mixture into the egg whites or use a piping bag fitted with a large star tube. (If the eggs will not stand upright, cut a small slice from the base to make them stand flat.)

Replace the lid of each egg at an angle and sprinkle the tops with paprika. Serve on a bed of lettuce and watercress.
Serves 4
Freezing note Hard-boiled eggs become leathery when frozen so don't freeze dishes containing them.

Savoury bananas

IMPERIAL/METRIC
3 oz./75 g. Stork margarine
salt and pepper
cayenne pepper
4 firm bananas
1 oz./25 g. fresh breadcrumbs
1 oz./25 g. Parmesan cheese, grated
1 oz./25 g. Gruyère or Cheddar
  cheese, grated
Garnish
paprika pepper
chopped parsley

Melt the margarine with the seasoning and cayenne pepper in a frying pan. Add the peeled, whole bananas and toss in the margarine. Place in a gratin dish. Mix together the breadcrumbs, Parmesan and Gruyère or Cheddar cheese and sprinkle over the bananas. Spoon over any margarine left in the frying pan. Bake in a moderately hot oven (375°F., 190°C., Gas Mark 5) for 20 minutes until golden. Brown under the grill if necessary. Sprinkle with paprika and parsley, serve immediately.
Serves 4

Tuna and cucumber mousse ❄

IMPERIAL/METRIC
3½-oz./100-g. can tuna fish
¼ cucumber, peeled and diced
2 large eggs, separated
½ oz./15 g. gelatine
4 tablespoons cold water
Sauce
½ oz./15 g. Stork margarine
½ oz./15 g. flour
salt
freshly ground black pepper
1 tablespoon tomato purée
½ teaspoon anchovy essence
few drops lemon juice
¼ pint/150 ml. milk
Garnish
cucumber slices
watercress

For the sauce, place all the ingredients in a saucepan over a moderate heat. Bring to the boil, whisking continuously. Simmer for 2–3 minutes. Cool.

Bone and flake the tuna and add to the sauce with the cucumber and egg yolks. Dissolve the gelatine in the water over a pan of hot water (do not overheat). Stir into the sauce and when on the point of setting, whisk the egg whites until stiff and fold them into the mixture. Pour into a wetted mould and allow to set in a cool place. Dip the mould into hot water for 30 seconds. Turn out of the mould and garnish with cucumber and watercress.
Serves 4
Freezing note Freeze in the mould.
Illustrated on page 23

Avocado and grapefruit cups

IMPERIAL/METRIC
2 good-sized grapefruit
2 avocados
lemon juice
4 tablespoons ginger ale
Garnish
few sprigs mint

Halve the grapefruit and carefully remove the segments. Zigzag the edges of the grapefruit shells with a sharp knife. Peel the avocados and remove the stones. Chop the flesh roughly and sprinkle with a little lemon juice. Pile the halved grapefruit segments and avocado flesh back into the grapefruit shells and pour 1 tablespoon ginger ale over each. Garnish with mint.
Serves 4

Avocado and grapefruit cups

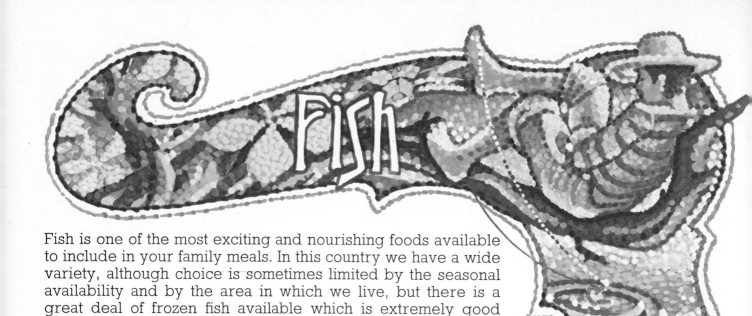

Fish

Fish is one of the most exciting and nourishing foods available to include in your family meals. In this country we have a wide variety, although choice is sometimes limited by the seasonal availability and by the area in which we live, but there is a great deal of frozen fish available which is extremely good value. As it is frozen when freshly caught it can be as fresh as the fish bought in a local shop, which has had to be transported from the fish market.

The different types of fish, white, oily and shellfish, are dealt with in charts on the following pages.

To choose fish

When you are buying from the fishmonger it is worth remembering the following points as an indication of freshness:

1 The flesh should feel firm and elastic and the tail quite stiff.
2 The gills should be red and the body should have firm scales.
3 The eyes of the fish should be bright and not sunken.

To scale and clean fish

Wash under a cold running tap and remove scales by scraping with the back of a sharp knife from tail to head, against the grain of scales. Pull off the gills and make a slit down the underside, pull out intestines. Now wash the inside of the fish under a cold running tap and dry on kitchen paper. Remove the head after skinning.

To skin fish

Round fish Hold the head firmly in one hand, grip the bony piece just under the gills and rip the skin on each side towards the tail.
Flat fish Place the fish, dark skin uppermost, on a board and then slit the skin just above the tail. Holding the fish firmly by the tail, pull the skin quickly towards the head. If necessary, hold a knife at an angle to the skin and, using a sawing motion, push the flesh away from the skin.

Methods of cooking fish

Poaching The fish is cooked in a liquid which is brought to the boil, but then only gently simmered for the remainder of the cooking time, allowing 10 minutes per lb. (450 g.) for white fish. The fish can be cooked in a saucepan on top of the cooker or in the oven in a casserole or covered in a fireproof dish. The cooking liquid for fish, if not water or milk, is known as a court bouillon and this can vary from plain salted water – ½ oz. (15 g.) salt to 2 pints (generous litre) water – to the court bouillon recipe on page 36. *Fish is cooked when the flesh flakes easily.*

Baking This method is suitable for whole fish which have been stuffed or cutlets or steaks. The fish should be basted frequently during cooking with hot oil or fat. Small whole fish can be baked in a piece of greaseproof paper or foil rubbed over with Stork margarine and wrapped round the fish. If this method is used then no basting is required. Bake fish in a moderate oven (350°F., 180°C., Gas Mark 4), allowing 25–30 minutes for small whole fish and about 20 minutes for fillets and steaks.

Frying (shallow) Small whole fish, fillets, cutlets and steaks can be shallow fried. The only preparation necessary is to dip the fish in seasoned flour or alternatively in beaten egg or milk and then toss it in breadcrumbs. Fry in hot fat for 5 minutes on each side or until cooked through. Strain the oil or fat after cooking if it is to be used again, and store, covered, in the refrigerator or cool larder.

Frying (deep) This method can be used for fillets, cutlets or steaks of fish and the fish should always be protected. Coat in batter (see page 110) or beaten egg or milk and breadcrumbs. Fry at 340–350°F., (175–180°C.) for 5–10 minutes, turning once.

Grilling This method is excellent for small oily fish such as herring and mackerel as the heat crisps the skin. It is also suitable for white whole fish such as plaice and sole, and for cuts of turbot, halibut, cod and hake, but for these fish the grid should be removed and the fish basted from time to time with oil or margarine.

Steaming Fillets of seasoned fish can be placed on a plate spread with margarine and milk and covered with greaseproof paper or wrapped in foil. A second plate can be placed on top and the fish steamed over a pan of gently simmering water. This method is specially suitable for invalids, babies or people with poor digestion.

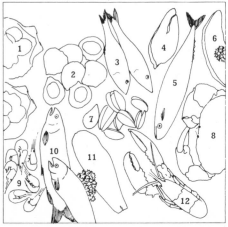

1 Scallops
2 Oysters
3 Red mullet
4 Salmon
5 Mackerel
6 Halibut
7 Mussels
8 Crab
9 Prawns
10 Trout
11 Whiting
12 Lobster

White fish

Fish	Season	Appearance	How to cook
Bass	May–July	Round silvery fish 2–6 lb. (1–2¾ kg.) with crisp firm flesh.	Small fish should be grilled or fried. Large fish cut into steaks and poached, served with a sauce.
Brill	All year round Best Jan.–April	Large flat fish with brown skin and creamy flesh, 2–6 lb. (1–2¾ kg.).	Bake filleted or whole with a sauce.
Cod	All year round Best Oct.–April	Large round fish with firm creamy flesh, weighing 1¼–20 lb. (600 g.–9 kg.).	Bake, steam, grill or fry. Larger fish are cut into steaks. Makes excellent fish cakes.
Coley	All year round	Dark skinned fish with rather grey flesh which whitens during cooking.	Sold in fillets. Fry and use as for haddock or cod.
Dab	April–Jan.	Small flat fish with rough scales.	Fry or grill.
Flounder	Sept.–Feb.	Small flat fish with light brown upper side.	Fry or grill.
Haddock	All year round	Large round fish with grey skin. Finger mark behind the gill known as St. Peter's mark.	Fry, bake or steam small fillets. Small fillets are also smoked as finnan haddock.
Hake	June–March	Long round silvery fish. Practically boneless.	Poach, steam, bake, grill or fry.
Halibut	Aug.–April	Largest of all flat fish.	Cook with care as flesh can be dry. Poach, steam, grill or bake in foil.
John Dory	June–Aug.	Ugly flat fish, blackish silver.	Cook as for sole.
Plaice	All year round	Flat fish with a browny grey skin and orange spots.	Fry fillets or poach and serve with a sauce as flesh tends to be tasteless.
Rock salmon	All year round	Usually sold skinned. Flesh is firm with a slight pink tinge.	Used extensively by the fried fish trade but can be used in fish stews or pies.
Skate	Oct.–April	Flat, ray-shaped fish. Only wings sold.	Deep fry, poach or grill.
Sole	All year round Best April–Jan.	Flat, oval fish. *Dover*, black skinned fish. *Lemon*, larger oval shape, brownish skin.	Skinned soles may be grilled whole, shallow fried or poached and served with a sauce.
Turbot	All year round Best May–July	Large oval flat fish with dark brown skin.	Do not skin or trim before cooking. Poach, steam, bake, grill or fry small fish or fillets.
Whiting	All year round	Round fish, belonging to the cod family. Weighs 6–8 oz. (175–225 g.) and about 9 inches (23 cm.) long. Delicate flesh.	Poach, bake, steam or fillet and shallow fry in egg and crumbs.

Fisherman's pie

IMPERIAL/METRIC
1 lb./450 g. cod or haddock
¼ pint/150 ml. water
½ pint/275 ml. milk
1½ oz./40 g. Stork margarine, beaten with 1 Onion Oxo cube
1½ oz./40 g. flour
2 oz./50 g. Cheddar cheese, grated
2 tablespoons chopped parsley
4-oz./113-g. packet frozen peas
2½-oz./71-g. packet instant potato
1 oz./25 g. Stork margarine
Garnish
tomato wedges, sprigs parsley

Place the cod or haddock with the water and milk in a saucepan and poach over a gentle heat for 10–15 minutes. Drain, reserving the liquor. Skin, bone and flake fish.

Place ¾ pint (425 ml.) of the fish liquor with the margarine and flour in a saucepan over moderate heat. Bring to the boil, whisking continuously. Cook for 2–3 minutes, whisking, until smooth.

Stir in the fish, seasoning, cheese, parsley and peas.

Make up the instant potato according to the instructions on the packet. Beat in the margarine. Place in a piping bag fitted with a large star tube and pipe a border around the edge of an ovenproof dish. Place the fish mixture in the centre. Bake in a fairly hot oven (400°F., 200°C., Gas Mark 6) for 15–20 minutes. Garnish.
Serves 4
Freezing note Freeze before baking.

Fishy florentine soufflés

IMPERIAL/METRIC
8 oz./225 g. cod or haddock
¼ pint/150 ml. milk
salt and pepper
8-oz./227-g. packet frozen spinach
½ oz./15 g. gelatine
4 tablespoons fish liquor
2 large eggs, separated
pinch nutmeg
few drops lemon juice
1 Onion Oxo cube, crumbled
¼ pint/150 ml. double cream

Place the fish, milk and seasoning in a saucepan and poach over a gentle heat for 10–15 minutes. Drain, reserving the liquor. Cook the spinach according to the instructions on the packet and drain well. Finely chop the fish or liquidise. Dissolve the gelatine in the 4 tablespoons fish liquor and add to the fish. Stir in the egg yolks, seasoning, nutmeg, lemon juice, onion cube and drained spinach.

Lightly whip the cream and stir into the mixture. Whisk the egg whites until fairly stiff and fold into the fish mixture. Pour into four individual dishes or a 5-inch (13-cm.) soufflé dish with a band of greased greaseproof paper tied round, standing 2 inches (5 cm.) above the rim of the dish. Leave to set in a cool place. Run a knife round the inside of the paper and carefully pull the paper away. Garnish with a twist of lemon and a sprig of parsley.
Serves 4

Fisherman's pie (page 32), fishy florentine soufflés (page 32) and whitebait with watercress dressing (page 37)

Haddock gougère

Fish with rich orange sauce

IMPERIAL/METRIC

4 medium-sized fillets white fish,
   e.g., whiting, plaice or haddock
1 lemon
3 egg yolks
3 tablespoons double cream
4 tablespoons white wine
2 oranges
salt and pepper
pinch cayenne pepper
4 oz./100 g. Stork margarine
1 tablespoon seasoned flour

Sprinkle the fish with the juice of
½ lemon. Beat together in a bowl the
egg yolks, cream, wine, juice of 1
orange and ½ lemon. Stand the bowl
over a pan of gently simmering
water and stir until thickened to the
consistency of thick pouring cream.
Add the seasoning and cayenne
then gradually beat in 1½ oz. (40 g.)
margarine in small pieces. Keep
warm without further cooking.
   Dip the fillets in seasoned flour.

Melt the margarine and fry the
fish for about 5 minutes on each
side until cooked through. Drain
and arrange on a serving dish
garnished with the remaining orange
cut into slices. Serve the orange
sauce separately.
Serves 4

Haddock gougère

IMPERIAL/METRIC

¼ pint/150 ml. cheese choux pastry
   (see page 17)
1 Onion Oxo cube
¼ pint/150 ml. milk
¼ pint/150 ml. water
12 oz./350 g. smoked haddock
1 oz./25 g. Stork margarine
1 oz./25 g. flour
2 hard-boiled eggs
grated rind of ½ lemon
1 tablespoon chopped parsley
salt and pepper
1 oz./25 g. cheese, grated
Garnish
parsley
tomato slices

Pipe or spoon the cheese choux
pastry round the sides of a greased
gratin dish or six individual dishes.
Crumble the onion cube into the
milk and water in a pan. Add the
smoked haddock, cover and bring
to the boil. Allow to stand for 10
minutes. Drain and flake the fish.
Reserve the cooking liquor.
   Make the sauce by placing the
margarine, flour and fish liquor in
a saucepan over moderate heat.
Bring to the boil, whisking continuously. Cook for 2–3 minutes,
still whisking, until thickened,
smooth and glossy. Add the chopped hard-boiled eggs. Stir in the
fish, lemon rind, chopped parsley
and seasoning. Spoon into the dish
and sprinkle the top with grated
cheese. Bake in a fairly hot oven
(400°F., 200°C., Gas Mark 6) for
20–40 minutes (depending on size)
until well risen and golden brown.
Garnish with parsley and tomato
slices and serve at once.
Serves 6
Note This dish is ideal for something
unusual to serve at suppertime.

Goujons of plaice with tartare sauce

IMPERIAL/METRIC
2 1¼-lb./575-g. whole plaice
little seasoned flour
2 standard eggs, beaten
golden breadcrumbs
1 oz./25 g. Stork margarine
1 onion, finely chopped
1 clove garlic, crushed
4 tablespoons thick mayonnaise
    (see page 132)
4 tablespoons soured cream
salt and pepper
1 tablespoon capers, chopped
1 tablespoon freshly chopped
    parsley
½ teaspoon grated lemon rind
3 gherkins, finely chopped
fat or oil for deep-frying
Garnish
1 lemon, quartered

Fillet and skin the plaice and cut the fillets into ¾- to 1-inch (2- to 2½-cm.) strips. Coat lightly in seasoned flour then dip in beaten egg and coat thoroughly in golden breadcrumbs. Chill until required.

Melt the margarine and sauté the onion and garlic for 10 minutes until golden brown. Drain off any excess fat and cool. Combine the mayonnaise, soured cream, seasoning, onion, garlic, capers, parsley, lemon rind and gherkins, mix well and chill until required.

Heat the fat to 360°F. (180°C.) or until a cube of bread browns in 1 minute. Fry the plaice strips (goujons) for 3–4 minutes until golden brown. Drain on absorbent paper. Serve at once garnished with lemon and with the tartare sauce served separately.

Serves 4

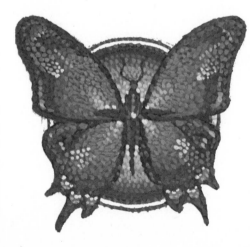

Curried fish balls

Curried fish balls ❄

IMPERIAL/METRIC
2 oz./50 g. Stork margarine
2½ oz./65 g. flour
2 Curry Oxo cubes, crumbled
¼ pint/150 ml. milk
12 oz./350 g. haddock or cod
    fillet, cooked and flaked
2 egg yolks, mixed
grated rind and juice of ½ lemon
1 tablespoon chopped parsley
salt and pepper
fat for deep-frying
lemon sauce for serving
    (see page 131)
Coating
flour
beaten egg
fresh white breadcrumbs
Garnish
watercress
lemon slices

Place the margarine, flour, crumbled curry cubes and milk in a saucepan over moderate heat. Bring to the boil, whisking continuously. Cook for 2–3 minutes, still whisking, until thickened, smooth and glossy. Add the fish, egg yolks, lemon rind and juice and parsley. Season to taste. Spread over a square tin and mark into eight portions. Leave to cool (refrigerate for 30 minutes if possible). Roll into balls on a floured worktop. Dip in the beaten egg and coat all over with breadcrumbs.

Heat the fat to 360°F. (180°C.) in a deep pan. Lower the fish balls gently into the fat and fry until crispy and golden. Drain on absorbent kitchen paper. Serve garnished with watercress and lemon. Hand lemon sauce separately.

Serves 4

Freezing note These may be frozen coated in the egg and breadcrumbs. Open freeze then pack in a polythene bag, excluding the air. Deep-fry from the frozen state.

Variations
Canned salmon or tuna fish may be used.

The fish balls may be made walnut-sized and served as cocktail snacks with a mayonnaise dip (see page 132).

35

Savoury fish pie ❄

IMPERIAL/METRIC
1½ lb./675 g. haddock, cod or hake,
    cut in 1½-inch (4-cm.) cubes
juice of ½ lemon
salt and pepper
2 oz./50 g. Stork margarine
1 onion, chopped
1 clove garlic, crushed
1½ oz./40 g. flour
1 Onion Oxo cube, crumbled and
    dissolved in ½ pint/275 ml. hot
    water
1 teaspoon tomato purée
7-oz./198-g. can sweetcorn
8 oz./225 g. tomatoes, skinned and
    chopped
pinch basil
1 tablespoon chopped parsley
6 oz./175 g. shortcrust pastry
    (see pages 12–13)
beaten egg or milk for glazing
1 Onion Oxo cube, crumbled
    (optional)

Place the cubes of fish, lemon juice and seasoning into a 2-pint (1-litre) pie dish and mix well. Melt the margarine and sauté the onion and garlic for 5 minutes until soft. Add the flour and onion stock to the saucepan over moderate heat. Bring to the boil, whisking continuously. Cook for 2–3 minutes, still whisking, until thickened and glossy. Stir in the tomato purée, sweetcorn, tomatoes, basil and parsley. Season to taste and pour on to the fish, mixing well.

Roll out the chilled pastry on a lightly floured worktop to 1 inch (2½ cm.) larger all round than the pie dish. Cut off narrow strips round the edge of the pastry. Damp the rim and line with the pastry strips. Damp the strips and cover the filling with the remaining pastry, pressing down gently to seal. Trim, flake and flute edges. Make a hole in the centre and decorate with pastry leaves made from the trimmings. Glaze with beaten egg or milk. Crumble the onion cube very finely over the surface. Bake in a moderately hot oven (375°F., 190°C., Gas Mark 5) for 45 minutes until the pastry is crisp and browned.
Serves 4–6
Freezing note This pie should be frozen covered with the raw pastry. Pack in a polythene bag, excluding the air. Bake after defrosting.
Illustrated on page 10

Scalloped fish pie

IMPERIAL/METRIC
1 lb./450 g. fresh cod or haddock
    fillet, skinned
¾ pint/425 ml. milk
salt and pepper
4 oz./100 g. streaky bacon rashers,
    derinded and chopped
1 onion, chopped
1 tablespoon freshly chopped
    parsley
1½ oz./40 g. Stork margarine
1½ oz./40 g. flour
½ teaspoon Worcestershire sauce
1 lb./450 g. boiled potatoes, sliced
1 tablespoon grated Parmesan
    cheese

Place the fish in a saucepan with the milk and seasoning. Bring to the boil, cover and simmer for 10 minutes. Strain off the liquor and reserve. Place the fish in a bowl and flake with a fork to remove any bones. Sauté the bacon and onion in the fat from the bacon until beginning to brown. Drain off any excess fat and mix the bacon and onion into the fish with the parsley.

Place the margarine, flour and fish liquor in a saucepan over moderate heat. Bring to the boil, whisking continuously. Cook for 2–3 minutes, still whisking, until thickened, smooth and glossy. Season well, add the Worcestershire sauce and simmer for 2 minutes. Stir half the sauce into the fish mixture and turn into an ovenproof dish. Cover with the sliced potatoes and then the remaining sauce. Sprinkle with the Parmesan cheese and cook in a fairly hot oven (400°F., 200°C., Gas Mark 6) for about 45 minutes until golden brown on top.
Serves 4

Stuffed baked haddock

IMPERIAL/METRIC
1½ lb./675 g. middle cut of fresh
    haddock
Stuffing
1 oz./25 g. Stork margarine
1 small onion, chopped
2 rashers streaky bacon, derinded
    and chopped
2 sticks celery, finely chopped
2 teaspoons chopped dill or fennel
salt and pepper
1 oz./25 g. fresh breadcrumbs
1 tablespoon lemon juice

Remove the backbone from the fish with a sharp knife. To make the stuffing, melt the margarine and sauté the onion, bacon and celery until soft. Add the dill, seasoning, breadcrumbs and lemon juice and mix well. Put the stuffing into the middle of the fish, fold over the flaps to enclose the stuffing and tie in place with string. Place the fish on a piece of well-greased foil and wrap loosely. Stand the foil parcel in a roasting tin and bake in a moderately hot oven (375°F., 190°C., Gas Mark 5) for 50–60 minutes until cooked through. Fold back the foil, remove the string and serve the fish with the juices spooned over.
Serves 4

Court bouillon ❄

IMPERIAL/METRIC
2 pints/generous litre water
2 small carrots
1 small onion
1 bay leaf
1 sprig thyme
½ oz./15 g. salt
2 tablespoons wine vinegar
few sprigs parsley
6 peppercorns

Place all the ingredients except the peppercorns in a saucepan. Cover and simmer for about 30 minutes. Add the peppercorns 15 minutes before the end of the cooking time. Strain, allow to cool and use for poaching fish.
Makes about 2 pints/1 litre
Freezing note Freeze in cubes or in a polythene container.

Oily fish

Type	Season	Appearance	How to cook
Carp	Mid June–March	Slightly oval freshwater fish with brownish skin.	Poach, bake, stuffed or fry.
Eel	All year round	Long black snake-like fish, up to 3 feet (92 cm.) in length. Conger eel is the sea fish. Common eel is the freshwater fish.	Fried in pieces. Poached and served in jelly.
Herring	All year round Best May–March	Small, silvery sea fish.	Grill, fry, bake, bone and souse in vinegar and water, or smoked.
Mackerel	All year round	Attractive striped silvery round sea fish.	Must be fresh – grill, fry, bake in foil, souse or smoked.
Mullet – grey	Aug.–Feb.	Silvery blue-skinned fish, fresh or coastal water.	Bake, poach or grill.
Mullet – red	May–Sept.	Bright pink sea fish, weighing 6–12 oz. (175–350 g.). Delicate white flesh.	Bake whole in paper or foil spread with margarine or shallow fry.
Pike	June–March	Long silvery freshwater fish with long mouth. Large fish having coarse flesh.	Most suitable baked and stuffed, and for quenelles (small savoury rounds made with fish, fat and egg which are then carefully boiled in water).
Pilchard	June–Sept. summer and autumn	Small, silvery sea fish.	Mainly canned. If fresh cook as for herring.
Salmon	Best May–July	Large silvery fish with pink flesh.	Poach to serve hot or cold. Steaks may be grilled or fried.
Sprat	Nov.–Feb. Best in winter	Small silvery sea fish of the herring family.	Bake, grill, fry or souse. Most delicious deep-fried. They are sometimes smoked.
Trout, rainbow	All year round	Pretty speckled silvery freshwater fish, with delicate white flesh.	Poach, bake, fry or grill.
Trout, sea (or salmon)	May–July	Pretty silvery fish with speckled marks. The flesh is delicate, pale and softer than salmon.	Poach to serve hot or cold. Steaks may be grilled or fried.
Whitebait	Feb.–July	Silvery in colour, about 1½ inches (4 cm.) long. Young of herring or sprat.	Coat in seasoned flour and deep-fry.

Whitebait with watercress dressing

IMPERIAL/METRIC
1 lb./450 g. whitebait, washed and
    dried (see note)
oil for deep-frying
Coating
1 egg, beaten
flour
Watercress dressing
½ bunch watercress, very finely
    chopped
¼ pint/150 ml. plain yogurt
Garnish
lemon wedges
sprig parsley

Coat the whitebait in the egg and
then toss in the flour. Heat the oil to
360°F. (180°C.) or when a cube of
day-old bread browns in 1 minute.
Fry the whitebait, a few at a time to
prevent sticking together, for 3–5
minutes. Drain well and keep hot.
Garnish with the lemon and parsley.
    For the dressing, combine the
watercress and yogurt.
Serves 4
Note Whitebait can be bought fresh
or frozen.
Illustrated on page 33

Fruity mackerel parcels

IMPERIAL/METRIC
4 mackerel
2 oz./50 g. Stork margarine
4 oz./100 g. celery, finely chopped
1 red eating apple, finely chopped
few drops lemon juice
pinch tarragon
2 tablespoons breadcrumbs
salt and pepper
Garnish
apple slices

Clean the mackerel, removing the
head, roe and fins. Remove the
backbone (see page 39). Cut each
fish in half to make two fillets.
    Melt the margarine and sauté the
celery and apple for 10 minutes.
Remove from the heat and add the
lemon juice, tarragon, breadcrumbs
and seasoning. Spread a little filling
on each fillet and fold in half carefully. Wrap each fillet in foil. Bake
in the middle of a moderate oven
(350°F., 180°C., Gas Mark 4) for
15–20 minutes.
    Serve cold on a bed of lettuce,
garnished with slices of apple.
Serves 4

Trout with almonds

IMPERIAL/METRIC
4 rainbow trout, cleaned
salt and pepper
3 oz./75 g. Stork margarine
2 oz./50 g. split blanched almonds
2 tablespoons lemon juice
1 tablespoon chopped parsley

Wipe the trout and season the
inside lightly. Place in a grill pan.
Melt 1 oz. (25 g.) margarine in a pan
and brush all over the trout inside
and out. Grill under a moderate
heat for about 5–7 minutes then turn
over carefully, brush again with
margarine and continue grilling for
about 5 minutes until cooked
through. Place on a hot serving
dish and keep warm.
    Meanwhile, melt the remaining
margarine and sauté the almonds
until pale golden brown, shaking
the pan frequently. Add the lemon
juice, remove from the heat and
stir well. Season to taste then spoon
over the trout. Sprinkle with parsley
and serve.
Serves 4

Salmon mousse

IMPERIAL/METRIC
½ pint/275 ml. all-in-one white sauce
  (see page 130)
½ teaspoon dry mustard
good pinch cayenne pepper
salt and pepper
2 tablespoons white wine vinegar
2 eggs, separated
8 oz./225 g. cooked salmon or
  7-oz./198-g. can salmon, flaked
4 tablespoons double cream
½-oz./15-g. packet gelatine
3 tablespoons water
Garnish
cucumber slices
twist of lemon
sprig parsley

Salmon mousse

To the white sauce add the mustard, cayenne, seasoning and vinegar and simmer for 2 minutes. Beat in the egg yolks and cook for 2 minutes. Remove from heat, add the flaked salmon and cream. Dissolve the gelatine in a small basin in the water over a pan of hot water, cool slightly then stir into the salmon mixture. Leave until on the point of setting then fold in the stiffly beaten egg whites. Pour into a bowl or greased mould and leave to set. Dip the base of the bowl or mould into hot water for a few seconds before turning out, to loosen the mousse. Garnish with the cucumber, lemon and parsley.
Serves 4–6

Soused mackerel

IMPERIAL/METRIC
4 mackerel
¼ pint/150 ml. vinegar
½ pint/275 ml. water
2 tablespoons lemon juice
few peppercorns
1 onion, sliced
bay leaf
few sprigs parsley
1 Onion Oxo cube, crumbled

Clean the mackerel, removing the head and backbone (see line drawings). Roll up, skin side outside, and secure with a wooden cocktail stick. Place in an ovenproof dish.
  Place the remaining ingredients in a saucepan and bring to the boil. Pour over the fish. Bake in a very moderate oven (325°F., 160°C., Gas Mark 3) for 40–45 minutes. Allow to become cold before serving.
Serves 4

Fresh sardines with cucumber sauce

IMPERIAL/METRIC
1 lb./450 g. fresh sardines (see note)
3 oz./75 g. Stork margarine, melted
freshly ground black pepper
few drops lemon juice
Cucumber sauce
½ pint/275 ml. white coating sauce
  (see page 130)
½ cucumber, peeled, deseeded and
  chopped
½ oz./15 g. Stork margarine
few drops lemon juice
Garnish
parsley

Make diagonal slits along each side of the sardines. Brush each sardine with the melted margarine. Sprinkle with black pepper and lemon juice. Place under a preheated grill for 3–4 minutes each side.
  To the sauce, add the cucumber which has been gently sautéed for 5 minutes in the margarine. Add the lemon juice just before serving. Garnish and serve sauce separately.
Serves 4
Note If fresh sardines are unobtainable, use four small mackerel.

Variation
Quick cucumber sauce To ¼ pint (150 ml.) plain yogurt, add 3 tablespoons chopped cucumber.

Boning a herring

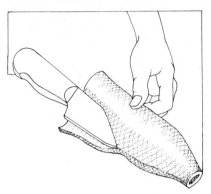

1. *Having removed the head and gutted the fish, slitting all along the underside with a sharp knife.*

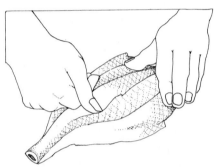

2. *With the fish flesh side down, pressing along the backbone to loosen it, using the thumb.*

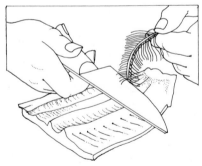

3. *After turning the fish over, lifting the backbone away from the flesh with the aid of a knife.*

Mustard herrings

IMPERIAL/METRIC
4 large herrings
1 oz./25 g. Stork margarine
salt and pepper
3–4 teaspoons made mustard
4 teaspoons tomato purée
4 tablespoons single or soured cream
Garnish
chopped parsley

Clean and fillet the herrings. Remove the backbone (see line drawings) and cut the fish into two fillets.

Place a little margarine on each fillet and roll up with the skin side outside. Place upright in a casserole and season well.

Mix together the mustard, tomato purée and cream until smooth and pour over the fish. Cover and bake in the middle of a moderate oven (350°F., 180°C., Gas Mark 4) for about 30 minutes. Garnish.
Serves 4

Herrings with herb dressing

IMPERIAL/METRIC
4 herrings, filleted
salt and pepper
6–8 tablespoons medium oatmeal or fresh breadcrumbs
2 oz./50 g. Stork margarine
Dressing
¼ pint/150 ml. thick mayonnaise
1 tablespoon finely chopped onion
1 tablespoon chopped chives
1 tablespoon freshly chopped dill or fennel
2 hard-boiled eggs, chopped
1 tablespoon lemon juice
Garnish
1 lemon, quartered

Season the herring fillets lightly and coat in either oatmeal or breadcrumbs, pressing well into the fish. Melt the margarine and sauté the fish for 5–6 minutes on each side. Drain and keep warm. Combine all the dressing ingredients and season well. Serve separately with the herrings, garnished with lemon.
Serves 4

Salmon cutlets with maître d'hôtel butter ❄

IMPERIAL/METRIC
4 salmon steaks
3 oz./75 g. Stork margarine, melted
salt and pepper
few drops lemon juice
Maître d'hôtel butter (see note)
4 oz./100 g. Stork margarine
1–2 tablespoons chopped parsley
salt and pepper
few drops lemon juice
Garnish
twists of lemon and cucumber

Brush the salmon with melted margarine, season and sprinkle with the lemon juice. Place the salmon under a preheated grill and allow 5–6 minutes on each side. Remove the skin and keep hot.

Mix all the ingredients for the maître d'hôtel butter together. Shape into a long roll and wrap in foil. Allow to harden in the refrigerator or freezer. Slice and serve on top of the salmon steaks. Garnish with the lemon and cucumber.
Serves 4
Note The maître d'hôtel butter should be made in advance to allow it to harden in the refrigerator.
Freezing note Salmon is ideally at its best if eaten fresh. It can be frozen raw, with a sheet of greaseproof paper between each cutlet for easy separation.

Maître d'hôtel butter freezes well. Cut off slices as required.

Salmon pie ❄

IMPERIAL/METRIC
8 oz./225 g. shortcrust pastry
  (see pages 12–13)
beaten egg or milk for glazing
Filling
2½ oz./65 g. Stork margarine
1½ oz./40 g. flour
¼ pint/150 ml. milk
¼ pint/150 ml. single cream
4 oz./100 g. mushrooms, sliced
8 oz./225 g. salmon, cooked and
  flaked
2 hard-boiled eggs, chopped
1 teaspoon dried fennel
1 tablespoon chopped parsley
½ teaspoon dried tarragon
salt and pepper
pinch nutmeg
2 tomatoes, skinned and sliced
4 oz./100 g. cheese, grated

Roll out half the pastry on a lightly floured worktop and line an 8-inch (20-cm.) flan tin. Place 1½ oz. (40 g.) of the margarine, flour and milk in a saucepan over moderate heat.

Bring to the boil, whisking continuously. Cook for 3 minutes, whisking, until thickened, smooth and glossy. Remove from the heat and stir in the cream. Cool. Melt the remaining margarine and sauté the mushrooms. Add the salmon and hard-boiled eggs. Mix this with the cold white sauce and add the fennel, parsley, tarragon, seasoning and nutmeg.

Spoon half the mixture into the pastry base. Cover with a layer of tomatoes and sprinkle on the cheese. Spoon over the remaining filling. Roll out the remaining pastry to make a lid. Damp the pastry base edge and cover with the pastry. Trim and pinch the edges well together and mark with a fork. Decorate with pastry leaves made from the trimmings. Glaze with beaten egg or milk and bake in a moderate oven (350°F., 180°C., Gas Mark 4) for 45 minutes.
Serves 4–6

Freezing note Do not add hard-boiled eggs. Freeze before baking.

Shellfish

Type	Season	Appearance	How to cook	Special points
Crab	May–Sept.	Rough shell with large claws.	Fresh – 15 minutes to 1 lb. (450 g.) in court bouillon (see page 36).	Always remove small sac at the top of large shell (see page 42) and spongy fingers round the shell.
Crawfish	May–Sept.	Rock lobster, no large claws, broad ugly head with rough dark shell.	Cook as for lobster.	Flesh is coarse in texture.
Crayfish	All year round Best March–Oct.	Freshwater shellfish like small lobster.	Bright pink in colour when cooked. Cook as for lobster.	
Lobster	All year round Best March–Oct.	Shell dark blue turning scarlet when boiled.	Plunge into boiling court bouillon (see page 36). 20 minutes – 1 lb. (450 g.) 30 minutes – 1½ lb. (675 g.) 45 minutes – 2 lb. (900 g.)	Remove small stomach bag in the head and dark line running down tail.
Mussels	Best Oct.–March	Blue-black shells. Must be alive with tightly closed shells before cooking.	Wash and scrub under a running tap. Remove beard and weed. Usually cooked in white wine with a little onion and pepper.	Examine carefully during first rinsing. Tap open ones with a sharp knife, if they do not close throw away.
Oysters	Sept.–April	Rough, grey shells which should be closed.	Larger ones for eating raw, small can be used in sauces. Serve with lemon, Tabasco sauce, brown bread and Stork margarine.	Open just before serving. To open, hold firmly in one hand and insert a ridged knife at the side of shell, just by the hinge.
Prawns	Available all the year round as they freeze well.	Soft-shelled grey crustaceans, turning bright red with pink flesh when boiled.	Cook fresh prawns in boiling water.	Use cooked and cold in hors-d'œuvres and salads. Delicious in hot savoury dishes.
Prawns – Dublin Bay (Scampi)	All year round Best May–Nov.	Largest British prawn. Pale pink with a hard shell. Pink when boiled.	As lobster.	
Scallops	Oct.–March. Available frozen.	White flesh and orange roe enclosed in a pinkish brown shell.	Mostly bought prepared but if alive put in a hot oven for a few minutes to open shells. Scrape away beard and black thread.	Use shells as serving dishes but scrub and rinse well first.
Shrimps	Intermittently all year round.	Brown – plentiful close to the shore. Pink – very good flavour.	1 pint (575 ml.) cooked in boiling salted water will serve two. Eat with brown bread and Stork, with lemon wedges. Use in paste, potted or as a garnish.	

Crab flan

Crab flan

IMPERIAL/METRIC
8 oz./225 g. shortcrust pastry (see
  pages 12–13)
little beaten egg or milk for glazing
1 oz./25 g. cheese, grated
Filling
1 oz./25 g. Stork margarine
¾ oz./20 g. flour
1 Onion Oxo cube, crumbled and
  dissolved in ¼ pint/150 ml. water
¼ pint/150 ml. single cream
8 oz./225 g. crabmeat
2 eggs, beaten
3 gherkins, chopped
½ teaspoon mustard
pinch cayenne pepper
juice of ½ lemon
salt and pepper
Garnish
gherkin slices

Roll out most of the pastry on a
lightly floured worktop and use to
line an 8-inch (20-cm.) flan ring,
keeping the remaining pastry for a
lattice decoration. Prick the base,
line with foil and bake in a fairly hot
oven (400°F., 200°C., Gas Mark 6)
for 15 minutes. Remove the foil from
the pastry case.

For the filling, place the margarine, flour and onion stock in a
saucepan over moderate heat. Bring
to the boil, whisking continuously.
Cook for 2–3 minutes, still whisking,
until thickened, smooth and glossy.
Stir in the cream and add the crabmeat, eggs, chopped gherkins, mustard, cayenne, lemon juice and
seasoning. Spoon into the partially
baked flan case. Use the remaining
pastry, cut into strips, to make a
lattice design on the flan. Glaze with
egg or milk. Sprinkle over the
grated cheese and bake at the same
temperature for 30–35 minutes until
firm and brown. Garnish with gherkins, placing them in the lattice
'windows'.
Serves 4–6

Scallop chowder

IMPERIAL/METRIC
1 oz./25 g. Stork margarine
1 onion, chopped
2 oz./50 g. mushrooms, chopped
1 oz./25 g. flour
⅔ pint/400 ml. milk
8 scallops, washed
1 Chicken Oxo cube, crumbled and
  dissolved in ⅓ pint/200 ml. hot
  water
3 tablespoons chopped parsley
few drops lemon juice
salt and pepper

Melt the margarine and sauté the
onion for 5 minutes until soft. Add
the mushrooms and cook for a
further 2–3 minutes. Stir in the flour
and cook for 1 minute. Add the milk,
stirring all the time, and bring to
the boil.

Poach the scallops in the chicken
stock for 10–15 minutes. Strain the
liquor and stir into the sauce. Chop
the scallops roughly and add to the
sauce with the parsley, lemon juice
and seasoning.
Serves 4

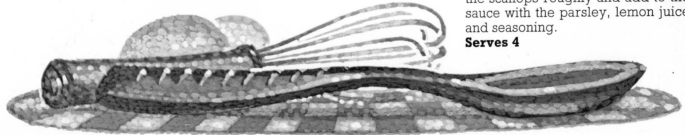

Creamed scallops

IMPERIAL/METRIC
6–8 large scallops
¼ pint/150 ml. dry white wine
¼ pint/150 ml. water
1 tablespoon lemon juice
salt and pepper
1½ oz./40 g. Stork margarine
1 onion, finely chopped
3 tablespoons flour
4 oz./100 g. button mushrooms,
 chopped
6 tablespoons double cream
2 tablespoons fresh breadcrumbs
2 oz./50 g. Cheddar cheese, finely
 grated

Ask the fishmonger to remove the scallops from their shells and give you the deep shells. Wash the scallops and cut into cubes. Place in a pan with the wine, water, lemon juice and seasoning. Bring to the boil, cover and simmer for about 10 minutes until tender. Drain and make the liquor up to ½ pint (275 ml.) with water if necessary.

Melt the margarine in a pan and sauté the onion gently for 5 minutes until soft. Add the flour and scallop liquor to the pan over a moderate heat. Bring to the boil, whisking continuously. Cook for 2–3 minutes, still whisking, until thickened, smooth and glossy. Stir in the mushrooms and scallops and season to taste. Simmer for 3 minutes. Stir in the cream and divide the mixture between the scallop shells or place in a shallow ovenproof dish. Mix the breadcrumbs and cheese together and sprinkle over the scallops. Place under a moderate grill for about 10 minutes until golden brown.
Serves 4

Scampi provençal

IMPERIAL/METRIC
1 lb./450 g. scampi
1 oz./25 g. Stork margarine
1 onion, chopped
1 clove garlic, crushed
15-oz./425-g. can tomatoes
pinch sugar
salt and pepper
1 Onion Oxo cube, crumbled and
 dissolved in ⅓ pint/200 ml. hot
 water
2 teaspoons cornflour
2 tablespoons chopped parsley

Wash the scampi and dry. Melt the margarine and sauté the onion and garlic for 5 minutes until soft. Stir in the scampi and sauté for a few minutes. Add the tomatoes, sugar, seasoning and onion stock, bring to the boil and simmer for 5 minutes.

Put a little liquid into a basin and blend with the cornflour until smooth. Return to the pan and stir continuously until thick. Add the parsley. Serve on a bed of rice.
Serves 4

Paella

IMPERIAL/METRIC
3 oz./75 g. Stork margarine
3 oz./75 g. lean bacon, cut in ½-inch
 (1-cm.) strips
2 chicken joints
1 onion, sliced
1 clove garlic, crushed
8 oz./225 g. long-grain rice
pinch powdered saffron or saffron
 threads soaked for 30 minutes in
 1 tablespoon water
2 Chicken Oxo cubes, crumbled and
 dissolved in 1½–2 pints/850 ml.–
 1 litre hot water
salt and pepper
4 oz./100 g. frozen peas
8 oz./225 g. whole shelled prawns
1 red or green pepper, sliced
lemon juice
Garnish
chopped parsley
lemon wedges

Melt the margarine in a large deep frying pan and sauté the bacon until it sizzles. Remove from the pan. Add the chicken joints to the pan and sauté until golden brown on both sides. Remove. When cool skin, bone and cut into 2-inch (5-cm.) pieces. Add the onion and garlic to the pan and sauté gently until soft. Stir in the rice and continue frying until the rice colours. Add the saffron (with water in which it was soaked if using saffron threads) and most of the chicken stock. Season to taste. Arrange the chicken and bacon in the pan with the peas, prawns and pepper. Cover and simmer gently on top of the cooker (or in a very moderate oven – 325°F., 160°C., Gas Mark 3 – if using an ovenproof pan) until the rice is cooked and all the liquid is absorbed – about 20–30 minutes. It may be necessary to add more stock during the cooking.

Remove the pan from the heat and leave to stand for 5 minutes before serving. Squeeze over a little lemon juice, sprinkle with parsley and garnish with lemon. Serve from the pan.
Serves 4

Variations
Use rabbit joints instead of chicken.

One pint (575 ml.) cooked mussels may be added and then use only 6 oz. (175 g.) prawns. To cook mussels, wash and scrub very thoroughly, removing the beards. Place in a colander or large metal sieve over a pan of boiling water. Cover and steam until the shells open. Break away half of the shell and keep the mussel in the remaining shell in which it is attached. Place on the rice 5 minutes before the end of the cooking time.

Crab au gratin

IMPERIAL/METRIC
1 large or 2 smaller crabs, cooked
2 oz./50 g. fresh white breadcrumbs
8 oz./225 g. Cheddar cheese, grated
salt and pepper
pinch dry mustard
pinch paprika pepper
½ teaspoon Tabasco sauce
4 tablespoons single cream

Wipe the crab with a damp cloth. Place on its back with the tail facing towards you and remove the claws and legs with a twisting movement. Carefully prise up the apron, remove the stomach bag and dead man's fingers. Scrape all the meat from the shell into a basin. Tap the inside edge of the shell to break it along the natural line. Wash the shell thoroughly and oil it lightly. Remove the meat from the claws, reserving the tiny claws for garnish.

Mix all the crabmeat together and stir in the breadcrumbs, cheese, seasonings, Tabasco sauce and cream, making a fairly soft consistency. Put this mixture back into the shell, place on a baking tray and cook in a fairly hot oven (400°F., 200°C., Gas Mark 6) for 20–25 minutes, until lightly browned and heated through. Serve garnished with the reserved claws and parsley.
Serves 4

Prawn puff pie

Prawn puff pie

IMPERIAL/METRIC
8 oz./225 g. flaky pastry, well chilled
   (see page 15)
beaten egg or milk for glazing
Filling
½ pint/275 ml. panada sauce, adding
   1 crumbled Onion Oxo cube to
   the flour (see page 130)
1 Chicken Oxo cube, crumbled
12 oz./350 g. peeled prawns
¼ pint/150 ml. single cream
1 teaspoon tomato purée
1 tablespoon chopped parsley
lemon juice
salt and pepper
Garnish
sprig parsley

Roll out the flaky pastry on a lightly floured worktop into two circles approximately 8 and 9 inches (20 and 23 cm.) in diameter. Place the smaller circle on a baking sheet.

Combine all the filling ingredients. Cool. Spoon the filling on to the circle of pastry to within 1 inch (2½ cm.) of the edge. Damp the pastry edges and cover with the larger pastry circle, pressing down gently to seal. Trim, flake and flute the edges. Decorate with pastry leaves made from the trimmings. Glaze with beaten egg or milk. Bake in a hot oven (425°F., 220°C., Gas Mark 7) for 45–50 minutes until well risen, crispy and golden. Garnish.

Serves 4–6
Freezing note Freeze unbaked.

Meat can make quite a hole in the family budget these days and the traditional roast joint at the weekend is rapidly becoming a luxury. It is therefore worth while doing a little homework to get to know all about meat and how to cook it well. There are charts for roasting times and detailed methods for each type of meat cookery. Always choose meat which is suitable for the method of cooking which you want to use.

It is a good idea to become familiar with the cheaper and less well known cuts which require long, slow cooking as these can produce really tasty meals providing they are cooked correctly. Minced beef seems to be a life saver these days as it can be made into so many dishes – add a meat extender (see notes on TVP on page 9) to make it go even further in shepherd's pie, bolognese sauces or served with savoury rice. Meat is one of our most valuable sources of body-building protein so choose wisely and make the most of your money.

Methods of cooking meat

Baking This term is used for all cooking in the oven by reflected heat, but when applied to meat it is usually known as roasting.

Boiling This method is used for tougher cuts of meat, offal and older birds. It is, as mentioned elsewhere, a misnomer because although the liquid is brought to the boil the remainder of the cooking is done at simmering point. For if meat is actually boiled, it is toughened rather than tenderised. Simmering softens the tissues in the meat, helping to tenderise tougher cuts. Larger pieces of meat or ham are more suitable for cooking by this method as small pieces lose their flavour into the cooking liquid. A few vegetables and herbs are usually added to the boiling water.

Braising This is an ideal method for using cheaper, tougher cuts of meat which can be full of flavour if properly cooked. Braise the trimmed meat in a heavy flameproof pan or casserole with a tight-fitting lid, in a very small quantity of liquid so that the meat, trimmed of excess fat, cooks in its own steam. Peel and dice or slice enough vegetables to cover the bottom of the pan. Melt a little cooking fat in the pan and heat until hot. Sear the meat on all sides. Remove the meat, add the vegetables and allow to sweat, covered, for a few minutes. Replace the meat on top of the vegetables and add enough stock to cover the vegetable layer. Add seasoning and herbs and cook in a very moderate oven (325°F., 160°C., Gas Mark 3) for about 2 hours until tender.

Casserole cooking This is cooking done in an ovenproof dish and is similar to pot roasting and braising, the main difference being that the meat and vegetables are cooked slowly in a sauce or liquid (the meat or poultry is cut into small pieces unlike the large joints used in pot roasting). The great joy of casserole cooking is that all the ingredients can be added at the beginning and little or no attention is needed after the initial preparation. A casserole serving four will take about 2 hours to cook.

Frying (shallow) This is a method used for tender steak or chops or to brown meat for a casserole. Use oil, margarine or cooking fat. Heat the fat quickly over high heat and fry the meat quickly on both sides to seal in the juices. If the meat is to be cooked through, reduce the heat and cook evenly on each side. Do use the meat juices left in the pan to make a tasty sauce or gravy.

Frying (deep) This is immersing the food in a pan a third full of cooking fat or oil heated to 360°F. (185°C.). Deep frying is most often used for cooking meat rissoles and some chicken dishes.

Grilling A fierce heat is required to grill meat successfully. Preheat the grill and sear the meat on both sides under the heat; further cooking can be done on a lower heat.

Only tender cuts can be grilled successfully and lean meat should be brushed over with oil or margarine before and during cooking.

Pressure cooking A good way of saving fuel on stews or pot roasts; however, do follow the manufacturer's instructions carefully for cooking times and pressure.

Roasting This is the most traditional and popular method of cooking in this country and one of the prime factors in a good roast is the quality of the meat. True roasting is done by radiant heat on a spit over an open fire and when we roast in our domestic ovens we are actually baking the meat. However, many modern cookers do have spits and this is an excellent way to roast; follow the manufacturer's instructions for cooking times. Research has proved that there is less shrinkage with the slower methods of roasting but you must experiment and decide how you like your meat cooked. See the chart below for roasting times.

Roasting (pot) A good alternative method to roasting if you do not want to use the oven, or for smaller joints which might shrink too much. Using a heavy saucepan or casserole, fry the meat or poultry in hot cooking fat on all sides, pour off excess fat, leaving a little in the bottom. Place whole small onions, carrots or celery around the meat and cover tightly with a lid. A 2½-lb. (1¼-kg.) piece of beef will require 2–3 hours on top of the cooker. You can also pot roast in a very moderate oven (325°F., 160°C., Gas Mark 3) allowing 45 minutes per lb. (450 g.).

Simmering This is mentioned in boiling. It is a method of cooking below boiling point at 185°F. (85°C.) compared to the boiling temperature of 212°F., (100°C.). Only an occasional bubble should show on the surface when food is being simmered.

Stewing This is a long, slow method of cooking meat in liquid with flavourings, such as herbs, spices and vegetables. A stew is one of the best methods of tenderising tougher cuts of meat. Stews are simmered, never boiled. An average size stew will take about 2 hours to cook.

To make gravy

Thin gravy Remove the roast to a heated dish to keep warm. Pour away the fat from the roasting tin but retain all the juices. Season and add ½ pint (275 ml.) Oxo stock, stir thoroughly until well mixed, then bring to the boil and simmer for 2–3 minutes. Strain and serve.

Thick gravy Leave 2 tablespoons fat in the roasting tin and stir in 1 tablespoon flour. Cook over a low heat until the mixture begins to brown, then gradually stir in ½ pint (275 ml.) stock. Bring to the boil and simmer for 2–3 minutes. Season to taste, strain and serve in a warmed gravy boat.

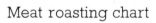

Meat roasting chart

To roast	Temperature	Cooking time	Cooking time in foil (see note)
	Put all meat into a very hot oven (450°F., 230°C., Gas Mark 8) for 10–15 minutes		Roast all foiled-wrapped meat in a hot oven (425°F., 220°C., Gas Mark 7)
Beef	Reduce to 350°F., 180°C., Gas Mark 4	15 minutes per lb. (450 g.) and 15 minutes over. Increase to 20 minutes per lb. (450 g.) for well done	*rare* 25–30 minutes per lb. (450 g.) *medium* 30–35 minutes per lb. (450 g.) *well done* 35–40 minutes per lb. (450 g.)
Veal	Reduce to 325°F., 160°C., Gas Mark 3	30 minutes per lb. (450 g.) and 30 minutes over	35–40 minutes per lb. (450 g.)
Lamb	Reduce to 350°F., 180°C., Gas Mark 4	25 minutes per lb. (450 g.) and 25 minutes over. For stuffed joints allow 35 minutes per lb. (450 g.) plus 30 minutes	30–35 minutes per lb. (450 g.)
Pork	Reduce to 350°F., 180°C., Gas Mark 4	30 minutes per lb. (450 g.) and 30 minutes over. For stuffed joints allow 40 minutes per lb. (450 g.) plus 40 minutes	35–40 minutes per lb. (450 g.)

Note When cooking meat in foil, fold back the foil for the last 15–20 minutes of cooking time to allow the meat to brown.

Roasting meat from the frozen state

Average size joints of meat from 2–8 lb. (1–3½ kg.) should be roasted for about 1 hour per lb. (450 g.). A meat thermometer is a must when cooking joints of meat from frozen. Any stuffing will need to be cooked separately.

Beef For the prime roasting cuts, preheat the oven to 400°F., 200°C., Gas Mark 6, and place the joint in a roasting tin, covered, for 10 minutes to seal the meat. Cover the meat loosely with foil and reduce the oven temperature to 350°F., 180°C., Gas Mark 4, allowing 1 hour per lb. (450 g.).

Check the joint with a meat thermometer: rare – 140°F. (60°C.), medium – 155°F. (68°C.), well done – 170°F. (76°C.).

Cook medium roasting cuts in a moderate oven (350°F., 180°C., Gas Mark 4).

Lamb Proceed as for the prime roasting cuts of beef, cooking the joint for 1 hour per lb. (450 g.). If using a meat thermometer, the lamb will be cooked when it registers 180°F. (82°C.).

Veal Follow the same instructions as for lamb.

Pork Place pork in a preheated oven (400°F., 200°C., Gas Mark 6) for 20 minutes then reduce the heat to 350°F., 180°C., Gas Mark 4 and calculate the cooking time at 1 hour per lb. (450 g.) from this point. Pork is fully cooked when a meat thermometer reads 190°F. (88°C.).

How to choose beef

Lean beef should be deep red in colour. Dry, dark red beef has been exposed to the air for too long.

The meat should have speckled fat, known as marbling, running through it; this gives the meat its flavour and tenderness. Beef fat should be creamy in colour.

Beef cuts

1 Leg of mutton cut
2 Top ribs
3 Brisket
4 Clod
5 Back rib
6 Bladebone steak
7 Fore rib
8 Neck
9 Shin
10 Flank
11 Chuck steak
12 Long fillet
13 Leg of beef
14 Flank
15 Sirloin
16 Top rump/thick flank
17 Undercut
18 Topside
19 Sirloin steak
20 Silverside
21 Rump (boneless)
22 Rump steak

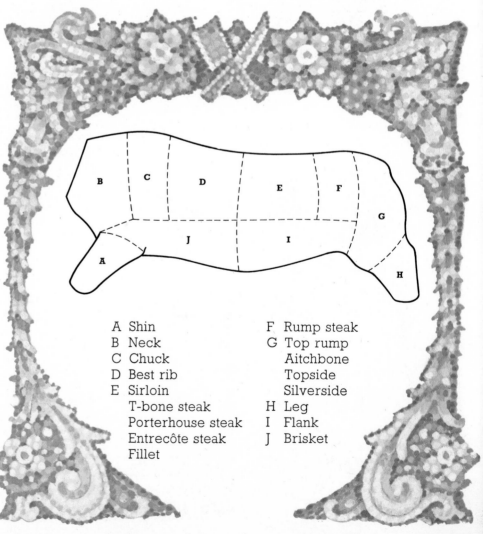

A Shin
B Neck
C Chuck
D Best rib
E Sirloin
  T-bone steak
  Porterhouse steak
  Entrecôte steak
  Fillet
F Rump steak
G Top rump
  Aitchbone
  Topside
  Silverside
H Leg
I Flank
J Brisket

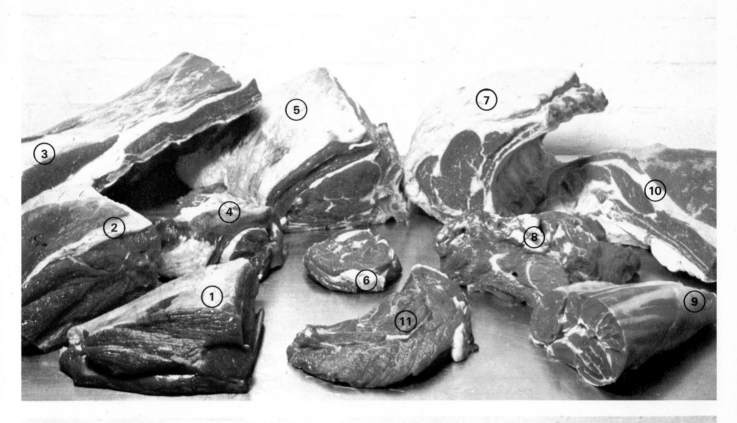

Carving beef

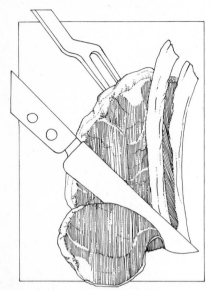

Rib *Carving the standing joint down to the bone in slices; if necessary cutting behind the ribs to free the meat.*

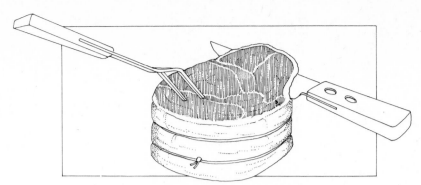

Sirloin *Carving the meat across the grain horizontally into thin slices.*

Nutty hamburgers ❄

IMPERIAL/METRIC
1 onion, grated
1 lb./450 g. minced beef
1 egg, lightly beaten
salt and pepper
1 oz./25 g. peanuts, chopped
2 teaspoons Worcestershire sauce
1 tablespoon oil
1 oz./25 g. Stork margarine

Mix the onion with the minced beef. Stir in the egg, seasoning, peanuts and Worcestershire sauce. Divide the mixture into eight portions and shape each into a round approximately $\frac{1}{4}$ inch ($\frac{1}{2}$ cm.) thick. If sticky add a little flour.

Melt the oil and margarine and fry the hamburgers until golden brown on both sides, approximately 3 minutes on each side. Serve with vegetables or in baps with French mustard.
Serves 4
Freezing note Can be frozen raw or cooked. Pack in a rigid polythene container with a piece of grease-proof paper or film between each hamburger.

Variation
Herby hamburgers In place of the peanuts, add a pinch of dried mixed herbs and 1 teaspoon dried parsley.

Goulash ❄

IMPERIAL/METRIC
1$\frac{1}{2}$ lb./675 g. stewing beef, cubed
$\frac{3}{4}$ oz./20 g. flour
salt and black pepper
2 oz./50 g. Stork margarine
2 large onions, chopped
1 small green pepper, deseeded and chopped
2 teaspoons paprika
$\frac{1}{4}$ pint/150 ml. tomato juice
1 Red Oxo cube, crumbled and dissolved in $\frac{1}{2}$ pint/275 ml. hot water

Coat the meat in the seasoned flour. Melt the margarine and sauté the meat for 10–15 minutes until well browned. Add the onions and green pepper and stir in the paprika. Cook for about 5 minutes then pour in the tomato juice and beef stock. Season to taste. Transfer to a casserole and cover. Bake in a very moderate oven (325°F., 160°C., Gas Mark 3) for 1$\frac{1}{2}$–2 hours or until the meat is tender.
Serves 4
Freezing note Freeze after 1 hour of the cooking time. Complete cooking time when the dish is required.

Variation
Goulash cobbler To make a scone topping for the goulash, make up the Oxo scone dough (see page 156) and cut into eight rounds. Ten minutes before the goulash is ready, remove from the oven, raise the heat to 425°F., 220°C., Gas Mark 7 and arrange the scone rounds on top of the goulash, slightly overlapping round the edge of the dish. Return to the oven and bake for 10 minutes until golden brown.

Beef and ale bake ❄

IMPERIAL/METRIC
$\frac{1}{2}$ oz./15 g. Stork margarine
1 lb./450 g. minced beef
8-oz./227-g. frozen stew pack or mixed vegetables
$\frac{1}{3}$ pint/200 ml. beef stock
$\frac{1}{2}$ pint/275 ml. brown ale
4 oz./100 g. mushrooms, chopped
salt and black pepper
Topping
1–2 tomatoes, skinned and sliced
salt and black pepper
1 lb./450 g. old potatoes, sliced thinly
1–2 oz./25–50 g. Stork margarine
$\frac{1}{2}$ pint/275 ml. natural yogurt
$\frac{1}{4}$ teaspoon ground nutmeg
2 oz./50 g. cheese, grated
Garnish
1 tomato
1 tablespoon chopped parsley

Melt the margarine and sauté the minced beef for 5–10 minutes. Add the vegetables, beef stock, brown ale and mushrooms. Season to taste and cook for about 30 minutes, then pour into an ovenproof dish. Place a layer of sliced tomatoes on top of the meat, season well, cover and place in a fairly hot oven (400°F., 200°C., Gas Mark 6) while you fry the potatoes in the margarine. Arrange over the tomatoes and pour over the yogurt mixed with the nutmeg. Sprinkle with grated cheese, garnish with tomato and return to the oven for 15–20 minutes until the cheese is browned. Just before serving sprinkle with chopped parsley.
Serves 4
Freezing note Freeze the minced beef base; assemble the pie with the topping after thawing.

Curried meatballs

Spaghetti bolognese ❄

IMPERIAL/METRIC
1½ oz./40 g. Stork margarine
1 medium-sized onion, chopped
1 clove garlic, crushed
1 lb./450 g. minced beef
4 oz./100 g. streaky bacon, chopped
2 Red Oxo cubes, crumbled and
    dissolved in 1 pint/575 ml. hot
    water
4 oz./100 g. mushrooms, chopped
2 tablespoons tomato purée
1 teaspoon oregano
salt and black pepper
2 teaspoons cornflour
1 lb./450 g. spaghetti
Parmesan cheese

Melt 1 oz. (25 g.) of the margarine
and sauté the onion and garlic for
5 minutes. Add the minced beef
and bacon and continue to fry for
about 10 minutes, until the meat is
browned. Stir in the beef stock,
mushrooms, tomato purée, oregano
and seasoning and simmer for
30–45 minutes. To thicken the sauce
blend the cornflour with a little cold
water and stir into the pan. Continue to cook for 5 minutes longer,
stirring.

Cook the spaghetti in boiling
salted water for 12–15 minutes or
according to the directions on the
packet. Drain well. Melt the remaining margarine in the pan and toss
the spaghetti in it, with a little black
pepper. Serve with the bolognese
sauce and hand Parmesan cheese
separately.

Serves 4

Freezing note Bolognese sauce
freezes well; pack in a rigid polythene container or foil bag. For a
richer sauce, on reheating add 3–4
tablespoons cream.

Variations

Use only 1 Red Oxo cube, crumbled
in ½ pint (275 ml.) water and ½ pint
(275 ml.) red wine.

Add a stick of chopped celery, a
chopped carrot and a small red
pepper, deseeded and chopped,
with the onion.

Curried meatballs ❄

IMPERIAL/METRIC
2 oz./50 g. Stork margarine
1 tablespoon cooking oil
Meatballs
1 onion, finely chopped
1 lb./450 g. minced beef
1 teaspoon chopped parsley
2 Curry Oxo cubes, crumbled
½ teaspoon ground nutmeg
salt and black pepper
1 egg
Coating
2 oz./50 g. wholemeal flour
1 Curry Oxo cube, crumbled
salt and black pepper
1 egg, beaten

Melt a little of the margarine and
sauté the onion gently for 5 minutes
until soft. Add to the minced beef

and the remaining ingredients for
the meatballs. Mix well and form
into small balls about 1 inch (2½ cm.)
in diameter. Combine the flour,
curry cube and seasoning for the
coating. Dip each meatball in beaten
egg then roll in the coating. Melt
the remaining margarine with the
oil and fry the meatballs for 10–15
minutes.

Serve with boiled rice, mango
chutney and other curry accom-
paniments, such as sliced bananas
sprinkled with lemon juice, desiccated coconut, slices of tomato and
cucumber, and peanuts. To add
colour, a pinch of saffron could be
added to the rice.

Serves 4

Freezing note Freeze raw or
cooked, in a rigid polythene container.

Somerset beef casserole ❄

IMPERIAL/METRIC
1½ lb./675 g. stewing beef, cubed
1 oz./25 g. flour
salt and pepper
1 oz./25 g. Stork margarine
3 medium-sized onions, sliced
4 sticks celery, sliced
½ pint/275 ml. cider
1 Red Oxo cube, crumbled and
    dissolved in ½ pint/275 ml. hot
    water
1 tablespoon black treacle
1 large cooking apple, peeled,
    cored and thickly sliced
8 oz./225 g. canned or frozen
    sweetcorn with peppers
½–1 teaspoon dried rosemary
Crispy dumplings
4 oz./100 g. self-raising flour
1 Onion Oxo cube, crumbled
2 oz./50 g. beef suet
salt and pepper
Garnish
1 red dessert apple, sliced and
    dipped in lemon juice
parsley

Coat the meat in seasoned flour. Melt the margarine and sauté the meat for 10 minutes until well browned. Put the meat into a casserole. Fry the onions and celery until browned. Stir in any remaining seasoned flour and blend in the cider and beef stock. Add the remaining ingredients, pour over the meat and cover the dish. Bake in a very moderate oven (325°F., 160°C., Gas Mark 3) for 1½–2 hours.

Turn the oven up to 425°F., 220°C., Gas Mark 7. To make the dumplings, sieve the flour into a bowl. Add the crumbled onion cube, suet, seasoning and enough water to make a soft dough. Divide into nine and shape into balls. Place on top of the meat in the casserole and bake for 15–20 minutes until the dumplings are golden brown and crisp. Garnish with sliced apple and parsley.
Serves 4
Freezing note Freeze the casserole after cooking but before adding the dumplings, which should be added on reheating. Freeze the dumplings in a polythene container with a piece of greaseproof paper separating each dumpling.

Variation
Replace the celery with two sliced leeks.

Minced beef pasties ❄

IMPERIAL/METRIC
8 oz./225 g. shortcrust pastry,
    well chilled (see pages 12–13)
beaten egg or milk for glazing
Filling
½ oz./15 g. Stork margarine
1 small onion, chopped
2 oz./50 g. streaky bacon, chopped
6 oz./175 g. minced beef
¼ pint/150 ml. beef stock
salt and black pepper
1–2 fresh or canned tomatoes
3 oz./75 g. cooked diced potato

To make the filling melt the margarine and sauté the onion, bacon and meat for 5–10 minutes. Add the stock, seasoning and tomatoes. Simmer for 30 minutes until the meat is tender. Add the cooked potato.

Divide the pastry into four and roll each quarter out on a lightly floured worktop large enough to make a circle 6 inches (15 cm.) in diameter. Use a saucer or small plate to mark out the circle. Place a quarter of the filling in the centre of each circle. Damp the edges of the pastry and lift them so that they can be joined in the centre to make a pasty shape. Pinch the join to seal well and flute. Glaze with beaten egg or milk. Bake in a hot oven (425°F., 220°C., Gas Mark 7) for 15–20 minutes.
Makes 4 pasties
Freezing note Freeze cooked or raw; open freeze then wrap in cling wrap and pack in a rigid polythene container.

Variation
Pasties are a good way of using up the meat left over from the week-end joint. Sauté the onion and bacon, add the left over minced meat and remaining ingredients except the stock. Add sufficient stock to bind the filling.

Lamb paprika (page 65), Somerset beef casserole (opposite) and osso buco (page 59)

Beef bourguignonne

IMPERIAL/METRIC
1½ lb./675 g. stewing beef, cubed
¾ oz./20 g. flour
salt and black pepper
1 oz./25 g. Stork margarine
12 button onions
4 oz./100 g. streaky bacon, chopped
1 Red Oxo cube, crumbled and
　dissolved in ½ pint/275 ml. hot
　water, and ½ pint/275 ml. red wine
½ teaspoon ground nutmeg
pinch thyme
pinch sage
4 oz./100 g. whole button
　mushrooms
1 clove garlic, crushed
Garnish
triangles of fried bread
chopped parsley

Coat the meat in seasoned flour. Melt the margarine and sauté the meat with the whole onions and bacon for 10 minutes until well browned. Stir in any remaining flour and blend in the beef stock and the wine. Add the remaining ingredients and season to taste. Pour into a casserole and cover. Cook in a very moderate oven (325°F., 160°C., Gas Mark 3) for 1½–2 hours. Garnish with fried bread triangles with one corner dipped in chopped parsley.
Serves 4
Freezing note If to be frozen, reduce the cooking time by 30 minutes. Freeze the bourguignonne in a rigid polythene container.

Beef provençal

IMPERIAL/METRIC
1½ lb./675 g. stewing beef, cubed
¾ oz./20 g. flour
salt and black pepper
1 oz./25 g. Stork margarine
2 large onions, sliced
1 large clove garlic, crushed
14-oz./397-g. can tomatoes
4 oz./100 g. mushrooms, chopped
1 Red Oxo cube, crumbled and
　dissolved in ½ pint/275 ml. hot
　water
1 teaspoon sugar
½ teaspoon oregano
16 black olives (optional)
Garnish
chopped parsley

Coat the meat in seasoned flour. Melt the margarine and sauté the meat for 10 minutes until browned. Place in a casserole. Sauté the onions and garlic for 5 minutes, then add the tomatoes and juice, mushrooms, beef stock, sugar, oregano and salt and pepper. Pour over the meat and cover. Bake in a very moderate oven (325°F., 160°C., Gas Mark 3) for 1½–2 hours. Just before serving stir in the stoned black olives.

Serve on a bed of cooked noodles and garnish with chopped parsley.
Serves 4
Freezing note If to be frozen reduce the cooking time by 30 minutes. Add the olives on reheating. Freeze in a rigid polythene container.

Chunky meatballs

IMPERIAL/METRIC
1 lb./450 g. minced beef
1 onion, finely chopped
2 oz./50 g. fresh breadcrumbs
6 tablespoons chunky pickle
salt and pepper
1 egg, beaten
1 oz./25 g. Stork margarine
8-oz./227-g. can tomatoes
1 Red Oxo cube, crumbled and
　dissolved in ½ pint/275 ml. hot
　water
1 large onion, sliced
2 cloves garlic, crushed
1 teaspoon Worcestershire sauce

Combine the mince, onion, breadcrumbs, 2 tablespoons pickle and seasoning and bind together with the egg. Divide into 16 pieces and shape into small balls. Melt the margarine in a frying pan and fry the meatballs for about 10 minutes until browned all over. Transfer to an ovenproof casserole. Place the tomatoes, beef stock, onion and garlic in a liquidiser and blend until smooth, or sieve. Put the mixture in a pan with the remaining pickle, Worcestershire sauce and seasoning and bring to the boil. Pour over the meatballs, cover and cook in a very moderate oven (325°F., 160°C., Gas Mark 3) for about 45 minutes. Adjust seasoning and serve with boiled rice or pasta.
Serves 4
Freezing note Freeze the meatballs in a foil bag or rigid polythene container.

Country beef olives

Country beef olives ❄

IMPERIAL/METRIC
parsley and thyme stuffing (see
    page 89)
salt and pepper
4 4-oz./100-g. slices topside of beef,
    beaten flat
1 tablespoon fat
1 onion, peeled and sliced
4 teaspoons flour
1 Red Oxo cube, crumbled and
    dissolved in ½ pint/275 ml. hot
    water
1 teaspoon Worcestershire sauce
2 teaspoons mixed herbs
4 tablespoons tomato ketchup
4 oz./100 g. mushrooms, sliced
    (optional)
Garnish
parsley

Make the parsley and thyme stuffing. Season the slices of beef and
spread a little stuffing over each
slice. Roll each up carefully and
secure with wooden cocktail sticks.
Melt the fat in a pan and brown the
beef olives all over. Transfer to a
shallow ovenproof dish. Sauté the
onion in the same fat for 5 minutes
until browned, then stir in the flour
and cook for 1 minute. Add the beef
stock, Worcestershire sauce, herbs
and ketchup. Bring to the boil, stirring, season and add mushrooms,
if used. Pour over the olives, cover
and cook in a moderate oven (350°F.,
180°C., Gas Mark 4) for about 1 hour
or until tender. Remove the cocktail sticks before serving. Garnish
with parsley.
Serves 4
Freezing note Freeze before cooking.

Spicy meat on skewers

IMPERIAL/METRIC
8 oz./225 g. rump steak
4 oz./100 g. streaky bacon
8 pickled onions
8 button mushrooms
1 tomato, cut into 8 pieces
4 frankfurters, cut into 8–12 pieces
1 kidney, cored and cut into small
    pieces
1 oz./25 g. Stork margarine
Marinade
4 tablespoons wine or malt vinegar
2 teaspoons Worcestershire sauce
½ teaspoon chilli powder
½ teaspoon allspice
salt and black pepper
Garnish
chopped watercress or parsley

Cut the meat into small cubes.
Combine all the ingredients for the
marinade and marinate the meat in
this for 2–3 hours.

Meanwhile remove the rind and
bone from the bacon, flatten each
rasher with the back of a knife and
cut in half. Roll up the pieces tightly.
Drain the meat, reserving the marinade, and thread a selection of the
foods on eight skewers. Melt the
margarine and pour into the remaining marinade. Use this to brush
the food on the skewers. Cook
under a preheated grill for about
10 minutes until well cooked, basting continually with the marinade.
Serve with rice coloured with saffron and garnish with watercress or
parsley.
Serves 4

Variation
Use an alternative marinade – 4
tablespoons oil, 2 teaspoons wine
vinegar, 1 tablespoon freshly chopped mint, pinch garlic salt and
freshly ground black pepper.

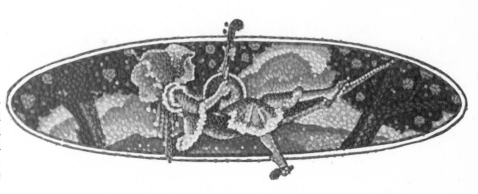

Steak and kidney pudding

IMPERIAL/METRIC
8 oz./225 g. pudding crust pastry
   (see page 16)
Filling
1 lb./450 g. stewing steak, cut into
   1-inch (2½-cm.) cubes
4–6 oz./100–175 g. ox kidney,
   cored and sliced
4 oz./100 g. mushrooms,
   chopped
1 tablespoon flour
salt and pepper
3 tablespoons chopped parsley
1 onion, chopped
1 Red Oxo cube, crumbled and
   dissolved in ¼ pint/150 ml. hot
   water

Make the pastry and roll out on a lightly floured worktop to a round 3 inches (7 cm.) larger than the diameter of a 1½-pint (1-litre) basin. Cut out a quarter of the dough and reserve for the lid. Fold the remainder of the circle into three and place inside the greased basin, unfolding and easing it in carefully. Press the join together to seal.

Mix all the filling ingredients together and place in the lined basin. Fold the edge of the pastry in over the filling. Brush with water. Roll out the remaining quarter of the dough into a circle large enough to fit the top of the basin. Damp the edges and cover with the pastry, pressing down gently to seal well. Cover with foil or greaseproof paper and secure with string. Place the pudding inside a steamer over a saucepan two-thirds full of fast boiling water, or in a saucepan of fast boiling water coming halfway up the basin. Steam for 2½–3½ hours. Check the water level at regular intervals and top up when necessary.
Serves 4

Variation

When making the pudding crust pastry, crumble an Onion Oxo cube into the flour.

Steak and kidney pie

IMPERIAL/METRIC
8 oz./225 g. flaky or rough puff
   pastry (see page 15)
beaten egg or milk for glazing
Filling
1½ lb./675 g. stewing steak
8 oz./225 g. ox kidney
seasoned flour
1 onion, sliced
4 oz./100 g. mushrooms
1 Red Oxo cube, crumbled and
   dissolved in ½ pint/275 ml. hot
   water

Trim the stewing steak and cut into cubes. Wash the kidney in salt water, remove the core and cut into small pieces. Toss the meat and kidney in seasoned flour. Place in a large saucepan with the onion, mushrooms and beef stock. Season. Cover, bring to the boil and simmer for 1½–2 hours. Allow to cool.

Fill a 1½-pint (1-litre) oval pie dish with the cooked meat and vegetables. Roll out the chilled pastry on a lightly floured worktop to an oval 1 inch (2½ cm.) larger all round than the pie dish. Cut off narrow strips round the edge of the pastry. Damp the rim and line with the pastry strips. Damp the strips and cover the filling with the remaining pastry, pressing down gently to seal. Trim, flake and flute the edges. Cut three slits in the centre and decorate the centre of the pie with pastry leaves and a rose made from trimmings. Mark the top of the pie in a diamond pattern using the point of a knife. Glaze with beaten egg or milk. Bake on the second shelf from the top of a hot oven (425°F., 220°C., Gas Mark 7) for 35–45 minutes.
Serves 4

Variations

Beef and frankfurter pie Substitute 8 oz. (225 g.) frankfurters, sliced, for the kidney, but add 30 minutes before end of simmering time.
Beef and mussel pie Use only 1 lb. (450 g.) stewing steak. Omit the kidney and add 1 pint (575 ml.) mussels, washed and scrubbed. Steam the mussels over a pan of boiling water until the shells open. Remove from the shells and add to the meat 30 minutes before the end of the simmering time.

Steak and kidney pie

Beef and aubergine pie

Beef and aubergine pie ❄

IMPERIAL/METRIC
2 aubergines, sliced
salt and pepper
5 oz./150 g. Stork margarine
2 onions, chopped
1 lb./450 g. minced beef
1 Red Oxo cube, crumbled and
   dissolved in ⅓ pint/200 ml. hot
   water
1 oz./25 g. flour
8 oz./225 g. cheese all-in-one
   pastry (see page 12)
8 oz./225 g. tomatoes, skinned and
   sliced
pinch oregano
beaten egg or milk for glazing
2 oz./50 g. cheese, grated
Garnish
sprig parsley

Sprinkle the aubergines with salt, leave 30 minutes. Rinse and dry. Melt 4 oz. (100 g.) of the margarine and sauté the aubergine slices until brown on both sides. Drain on absorbent kitchen paper. Melt the remaining 1 oz. (25 g.) margarine and sauté the onions and minced beef gently for 15 minutes. Add the beef stock and seasoning and cook for 15 minutes. Make a paste with the flour and a little stock and add to the mixture.

Roll out two-thirds of the pastry on a lightly floured worktop and line a deep 8-inch (20-cm.) round flan dish. Cover the base of the flan case with half the aubergines. Top with half the mince mixture and half the sliced tomatoes. Sprinkle with oregano and repeat the layers. Roll out the remaining pastry to make a lid. Cut out a 3½-inch (9-cm.) circle from the centre of the pastry lid. Damp the flan case edge and cover with the pastry. Trim, flake and flute the edges. Decorate with pastry leaves made from the trimmings. Glaze with beaten egg or milk. Bake in a moderately hot oven (375°F., 190°C., Gas Mark 5) for 40 minutes. Sprinkle the grated cheese into the centre hole. Bake for a further 15 minutes in the top of the oven until the cheese is melted and browned. Garnish with parsley.
Serves 4–6
Freezing note Freeze the prepared pie before baking.

Variation
Use four large courgettes instead of the aubergines, but omit sprinkling them with salt.

55

Roast beef with individual Yorkshire puddings (see page 111)

56

Spiced beef and walnut pie ❄

IMPERIAL/METRIC
1 oz./25 g. flour
1 Curry Oxo cube, crumbled
¼ teaspoon mixed spice
¼ teaspoon paprika pepper
salt and pepper
1½ lb./675 g. chuck steak, cut
   in 1-inch/2½-cm. cubes
2 oz./50 g. Stork margarine
2 onions, sliced
1 clove garlic, crushed
1 small head celery, thinly sliced
2 Red Oxo cubes, crumbled and
   dissolved in ¾ pint/425 ml. hot
   water
2 tablespoons Worcestershire
   sauce
1 bay leaf
1 tablespoon chopped parsley
1½ oz./40 g. broken walnuts
Topping
8 oz./225 g. pudding crust pastry
   (see page 16)
2 oz./50 g. walnuts, finely chopped
beaten egg or milk for glazing

Mix the flour with the curry cube,
spices and seasoning and toss the
meat in this to coat. Melt the margarine and sauté the onion and
garlic for 5 minutes. Add the celery
and fry for 5 minutes. Remove
the vegetables. Add the meat to
the pan and brown well. Replace
the celery and onion mixture, then
add the beef stock, Worcestershire
sauce, bay leaf, parsley and seasoning to taste. Cover and simmer in a
moderately hot oven (375°F., 190°C.,
Gas Mark 5) for 1½ hours or continue cooking very slowly on top
of the cooker. Remove the bay leaf,
add the broken walnuts and turn
the mixture into a shallow oval
ovenproof dish. Cool.
   Make up the pastry adding 1½ oz.
(40 g.) of the walnuts with the flour.
Roll out on a lightly floured worktop to about ½-inch (1-cm.) thickness.
Cut into 2-inch (5-cm.) rounds and
place overlapping on top of the
meat around the edge of the dish.
Glaze with the beaten egg or milk
and sprinkle over the remaining
walnuts. Bake in a hot oven (425°F.,
220°C., Gas Mark 7) for 20–25
minutes until golden brown.
Sprinkle with parsley, if liked.
Serves 4–6
Freezing note Freeze the meat
mixture and topping separately.

Steak in peppered sauce

IMPERIAL/METRIC
2 oz./50 g. Stork margarine
4 6–8-oz./175–225-g. rump steaks
1 small onion, finely chopped
1 oz./25 g. plain flour
4 tomatoes, skinned and deseeded
1 green pepper, deseeded and
   sliced
2 tablespoons capers
pinch mixed herbs
1 tablespoon tomato purée
2 tablespoons sherry (optional)
2 tablespoons chopped parsley
1 Red Oxo cube, crumbled and
   dissolved in ¼ pint/150 ml. hot
   water
salt and pepper

Melt the margarine in a frying pan
and fry the steaks and onion. Turn
the steaks once and fry to personal
taste. Remove the meat and keep
hot.
   Stir the flour into the remaining fat
in the frying pan and cook, stirring
all the time, for 1 minute. Chop the
tomatoes and add with the pepper
to the pan. Add the remaining ingredients. Bring to the boil, stirring
all the time, and then simmer for 5
minutes. Return the steak to the pan
and reheat in the sauce. Serve at
once.
Serves 4

Variation
Use braising steak instead of the
rump steaks, adding red wine
instead of sherry. Cook in a covered
casserole in a moderate oven
(325°F., 160°C., Gas Mark 3) for
2–2½ hours or until the meat is
tender. Check the liquid at intervals,
adding more stock when necessary.

Spiced beef and walnut pie

How to choose veal

There are two kinds of veal, one of which is fed entirely on milk, and the other on grass. Calves fed on milk have very tender flesh, and they are generally considered to be the best, hence the high price. Grass feeding a calf produces less tender meat, but it is thought by some to have more flavour.

Veal is not always easy to obtain, as it does not keep longer than three or four days after slaughtering. Butchers are therefore less inclined to stock veal unless they have a good demand for it.

The flesh should be firm and moist, never flabby and wet. As veal is a very young animal it has a higher water content than beef. Look for a finely textured flesh, off-white for milk fed calves and pale pink for those fed on grass. Staleness is indicated by a mottled appearance with a dry, brownish flesh.

The bones of veal are pinkish white and fairly soft. The young bones produce a large amount of jelly when boiled.

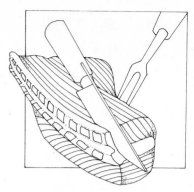

Carving loin *Carving slices down the length of the backbone, turning the knife to follow the bone in order to release the slices. Then turning the joint over and carving at an angle to the bone.*

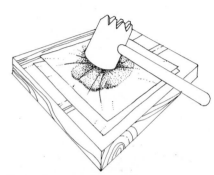

Preparing a veal escalope *Placing the veal on a board between two sheets of greaseproof paper and flattening with a steak basher or rolling pin.*

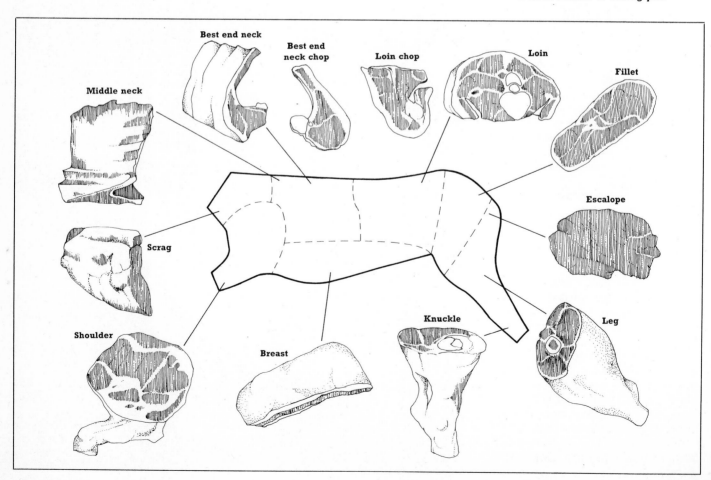

Veal escalopes in a creamy mushroom sauce

IMPERIAL/METRIC
4 veal escalopes
salt and pepper
2 oz./50 g. Stork margarine
2 tablespoons brandy (optional)
4 oz./100 g. mushrooms, sliced
¼ pint/150 ml. single cream
Garnish
watercress

Sprinkle the veal with seasoning. Melt 1 oz. (25 g.) of the margarine and sauté the escalopes quickly until tender – 1–2 minutes on each side. If using the brandy pour it over and ignite with a lighted match. When the flames have died down remove the veal and keep warm.

Melt the remaining margarine and sauté the mushrooms for 1–2 minutes. Return the veal to the pan and stir in the cream. Simmer for 5 minutes. Serve immediately, garnished with watercress.
Serves 4

Veal estrella

IMPERIAL/METRIC
4 5-oz./150-g. pieces pie veal
salt and pepper
1 oz./25 g. Stork margarine
1 large onion, peeled and sliced
2 tablespoons flour
15-oz./425-g. can tomatoes
1 Chicken Oxo cube, crumbled and dissolved in ⅓ pint/200 ml. hot water
1 tablespoon tomato purée
1 tablespoon capers
1 tablespoon caper liquor
Garnish
chopped parsley

Season the veal with salt and pepper. Melt the margarine in a pan and brown the pieces of veal all over. Transfer to a casserole. Brown the onion in the same pan then stir in the flour and cook for 1 minute. Add the tomatoes, chicken stock, tomato purée, salt and pepper and capers and liquor, bring to the boil. Pour over the veal, cover and cook in a moderate oven (350°F., 180°C., Gas Mark 4) for about 1¼ hours or until tender. Garnish.
Serves 4

Osso buco

IMPERIAL/METRIC
1 oz./25 g. Stork margarine
2 onions, sliced
4 thick slices shin of veal or 1½ lb./ 675 g. stewing veal, cut into small pieces
3 carrots, sliced
2 sticks celery, diced
3 tomatoes, skinned and quartered
salt and pepper
1 oz./25 g. flour
grated rind and juice of 1 lemon
3 Chicken Oxo cubes, crumbled and dissolved in 1 pint/575 ml. hot water
1 tablespoon tomato purée
1 teaspoon thyme
4 oz./100 g. mushrooms
Garnish
chopped parsley

Melt the margarine and sauté the onions for 2–3 minutes. Add the veal, carrots, celery, tomatoes and seasoning and cook for 2–3 minutes. Blend in the flour then stir in the lemon rind and juice, chicken stock, tomato purée and thyme. Bring to the boil and simmer, covered, for 2–2½ hours until the meat is tender. Add the mushrooms 30 minutes before the end of the cooking time. Sprinkle with parsley. Serve with rice.

Serves 4

Note This dish can be cooked in a moderate oven (350°F., 180°C., Gas Mark 4) for 2–2½ hours.

Freezing note Reduce cooking time to 2 hours. When required, cook for remaining time or until the meat is tender.

Illustrated on page 51

Veal estrella

Veal cutlets Corsican style

Veal and ham pie

IMPERIAL/METRIC
1¼ lb./575 g. hot water crust pastry
  (see page 16)
beaten egg white for glazing
Filling
1¾ lb./800 g. pie veal, cut in small
  pieces
6 oz./175 g. ham, chopped
pinch tarragon
2 tablespoons chopped parsley
grated rind of 1 lemon
salt and pepper
2 hard-boiled eggs
Jelly
½ oz./15 g. gelatine
1 Chicken Oxo cube, crumbled and
  dissolved in ⅓ pint/200 ml. hot
  water

Roll out two-thirds of the pastry
on a lightly floured worktop into a
round 14 inches (35 cm.) in diameter. Grease a 6- to 7-inch (15- to
18-cm.) cake tin. Lift in the pastry
and mould it into the tin with your
fingertips. Chill in a cool place.

To make the filling, mix together
all the ingredients except the eggs.
Half fill the pie with filling, place the
eggs in the centre and cover with
the remaining filling.

Roll out the remaining pastry to
a circle 1 inch (2½ cm.) larger all
round than the diameter of the pie.
Damp the rim of pastry, place the
lid on top of the pie and pinch the
edges well together. Trim the edges
and snip with a pair of scissors to
give a decorative edge. Make a
hole in the top. Use the pastry
trimmings to make a decorative
'rose' and lay over the hole. Chill
for 30 minutes before baking.

Brush the pie with egg white.
Bake in a fairly hot oven (400°F.,
200°C., Gas Mark 6) for 30 minutes,
then reduce the temperature to
350°F., 180°C., Gas Mark 4 for a
further 30–45 minutes. When the
pastry has set turn the pie carefully
out of the tin and set on a greased
baking sheet. Brush the sides with
egg white and return to the oven
to complete cooking – about 30–45
minutes.

Dissolve the gelatine in the chick-
en stock and leave to cool. Remove
the decoration from the centre of
the pie and pour the jelly into the
pie through a funnel. Replace the
decoration and allow the jelly to
set. Serve cold with salad.
Serves 6

Veal cutlets Corsican style

IMPERIAL/METRIC
4 veal cutlets
salt and pepper
1 oz./25 g. Stork margarine
1 Onion Oxo cube, crumbled
2 tomatoes, sliced
2 teaspoons dried basil
1 small green pepper, deseeded,
  sliced and blanched
1½ oz./40 g. Cheddar cheese, finely
  grated (optional)

Place the cutlets in a grill pan and
season well. Dot with margarine.
Cook under a moderate heat for
about 10 minutes, then turn over,
sprinkle with the crumbled onion
cube and continue for a further
10–15 minutes until cooked through.
Cover with the sliced tomato, basil,
sliced pepper and finally the grated
cheese if used. Return to the grill
for 5 minutes or until the cheese is
golden brown. Serve hot.
Serves 4

Escalopes of veal

IMPERIAL/METRIC
4 veal escalopes
salt and pepper
1 beaten egg
2 oz./50 g. Stork margarine
few drops lemon juice
thinly pared rind of ½ lemon, cut into
  julienne strips
Garnish
lemon wedges
parsley

Lightly flatten the escalopes and
season. Coat each one in beaten
egg. Melt the margarine and sauté
the escalopes for 1–2 minutes on
each side. Remove from the pan,
add a few drops of lemon juice and
the lemon strips to the remaining
margarine and reheat. Pour over
the escalopes and garnish with
wedges of lemon and parsley. Serve
escalopes of veal with a tossed
green salad or peas, and duchesse
potatoes (see page 178) halving the
recipe.
Serves 4

Escalopes of veal

How to choose lamb

Lamb is available nearly all the year round from various parts of the world. English lamb is available from June–September, Welsh lamb from July–August, and Scotch lamb towards the end of the year to the beginning of April. New Zealand lamb comes in after Christmas and is available up until June.

A blue tinge in the knuckle bones and a light coloured flesh indicates a young animal. The flesh should be a light pink, but as the animal gets older the flesh becomes light to dark red. The fat should be firm and white. The fat of imported lamb varies from that of home produced. The former being white and firm and the latter being creamy white. A yellowish tinge indicates old age. Always avoid brittle fat as this indicates that the animal has been kept too long in the freezer. When choosing lamb always look for plumpness in the legs and shoulders.

Lamb cuts
1 Neck cutlets
2 Shoulder
3 Leg (long cut) haunch
4 Best end neck
5 Breast
6 Chops
7 Middle neck and scrag
8 Loin
9 Leg
10 Neck cutlets (Frenched)
11 Lamb kidney

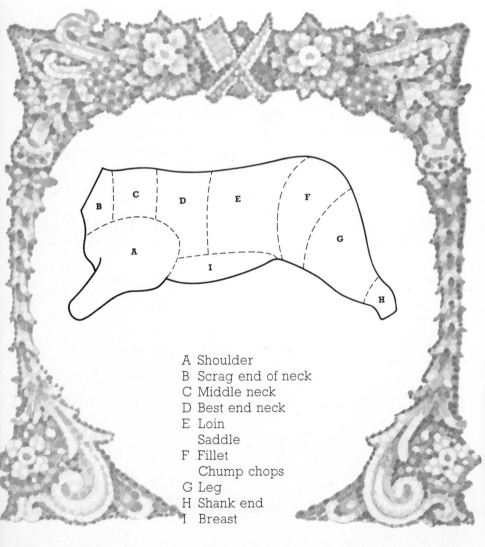

A Shoulder
B Scrag end of neck
C Middle neck
D Best end neck
E Loin
  Saddle
F Fillet
  Chump chops
G Leg
H Shank end
I Breast

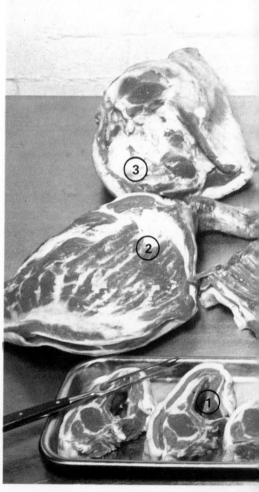

Carving lamb

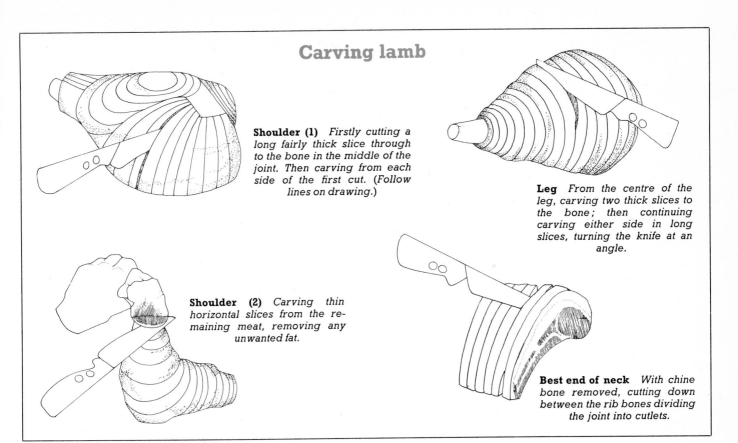

Shoulder (1) *Firstly cutting a long fairly thick slice through to the bone in the middle of the joint. Then carving from each side of the first cut. (Follow lines on drawing.)*

Leg *From the centre of the leg, carving two thick slices to the bone; then continuing carving either side in long slices, turning the knife at an angle.*

Shoulder (2) *Carving thin horizontal slices from the remaining meat, removing any unwanted fat.*

Best end of neck *With chine bone removed, cutting down between the rib bones dividing the joint into cutlets.*

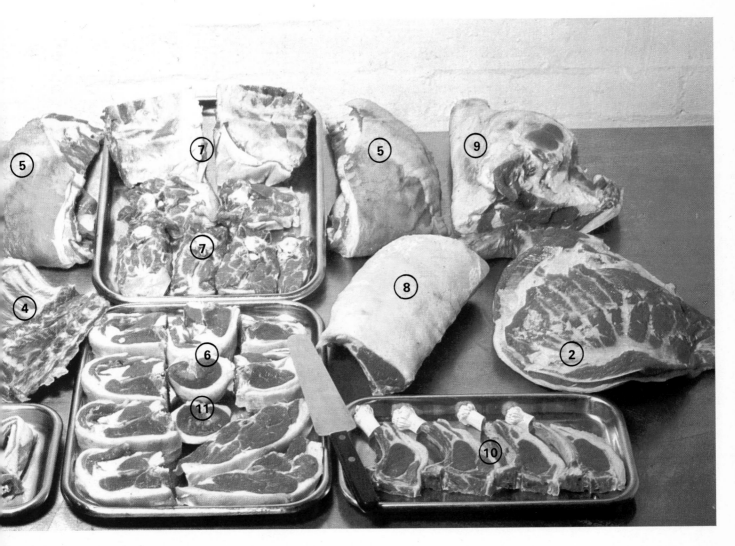

Potato moussaka

IMPERIAL/METRIC
1½ oz./40 g. Stork margarine
1 large onion, finely chopped
1 lb./450 g. minced lamb
1 clove garlic, crushed
1 Chicken Oxo cube, crumbled and
    dissolved in ⅓ pint/200 ml. hot
    water
2 tablespoons tomato purée
salt and pepper
1½ lb./675 g. potatoes
1 oz./25 g. flour
½ pint/275 ml. milk
pinch nutmeg
2 oz./50 g. Cheddar cheese, grated
Garnish
tomato slices

Melt 1 oz. (25 g.) of the margarine and sauté the onion until golden. Add the lamb and garlic and stir in the chicken stock, tomato purée and seasoning. Peel and slice the potatoes. Place in boiling water and simmer for 5–10 minutes. Drain well.

Place the remaining margarine, the flour, milk and nutmeg in a saucepan over moderate heat. Bring to the boil, whisking continuously. Cook for 2–3 minutes, then add 1 oz. (25 g.) of the grated cheese.

Lightly grease a casserole dish and line the base with a layer of the potatoes. Next add half the meat mixture, followed by half the remaining potatoes. Spread a little sauce on top and repeat the layers finishing with the sauce. Sprinkle the cheese on top. Bake in the middle of a moderately hot oven (375°F., 190°C., Gas Mark 5) for 40–45 minutes. Garnish with the tomato slices.
Serves 4

Variations

Substitute aubergines for the potatoes. Slice the aubergines and sprinkle with salt. Leave for 30 minutes, then rinse well, pat dry and sauté in 2 tablespoons oil and 1 oz. (25 g.) Stork margarine until lightly browned. Proceed as above.

Thatched shepherd's pie

IMPERIAL/METRIC
1 oz./25 g. Stork margarine
1 onion, chopped
1 oz./25 g. plain flour
1 Red Oxo cube, crumbled and
    dissolved in ⅓ pint/200 ml. hot
    water
1 lb./450 g. minced lamb
salt and pepper
1 tablespoon Worcestershire sauce
pinch nutmeg
¼ teaspoon curry powder
8-oz./227-g. can baked beans
Topping
1 lb./450 g. potatoes, cooked
1 oz./25 g. Stork margarine
1 Onion Oxo cube, crumbled
    (optional)
2 tablespoons milk
Garnish
parsley

Melt the margarine and sauté the onion for 5–8 minutes. Stir in the flour and cook for 1 minute. Remove from the heat and stir in the beef stock, lamb, seasoning, Worcestershire sauce, nutmeg and curry powder. Bring to the boil and simmer for 30 minutes. Add the baked beans and cook for a further 3–4 minutes. Place in an ovenproof dish.

For the topping, mash the potatoes, adding the margarine, crumbled onion cube and milk. Place in a piping bag with a large star tube and pipe lines of potato across the meat. Alternatively, spread the potato on top and mark with a fork. Place under a hot grill until golden brown. Garnish with parsley.
Serves 4
Freezing note This can be frozen, after placing the potato on top of the meat but before grilling. Make it up in a foil dish with a lid.

Variations
Substitute an 8-oz. (225-g.) can tomatoes and a pinch of basil for the baked beans.

Use leftover cooked lamb. Mince the meat and prepare the mixture as above but cook for only 10 minutes before adding the beans.

Thatched shepherd's pie

Traditional lamb hot pot

IMPERIAL/METRIC
1½ lb./675 g. middle neck lamb
  chops
1 tablespoon flour
1 Chicken Oxo cube, crumbled
1½ oz./40 g. Stork margarine
2 onions, sliced
8-oz./227-g. can tomatoes
pinch mixed herbs
salt and pepper
1½ lb./675 g. potatoes, sliced
1 Chicken Oxo cube, crumbled and
  dissolved in ⅓ pint/200 ml. hot
  water
Garnish
watercress

Trim the chops and toss in the flour
and chicken cube. Melt 1 oz. (25 g.)
of the margarine and sauté the
chops quickly on both sides – about
2–3 minutes. Place in a casserole
dish. Sauté the onions in the fat left
in the frying pan for 3–5 minutes and
then place in the casserole with the
tomatoes, herbs and seasoning.

Parboil the potatoes for 5 minutes
and drain well. Arrange the potatoes neatly on top of the meat. Stir
any leftover flour into the fat in the
frying pan and cook for 1 minute.
Stir in the chicken stock and bring
to the boil. Pour over the potatoes.
Dot with the remaining margarine
and cover. Bake in the middle of a
moderately hot oven (375°F., 190°C.,
Gas Mark 5) for 1 hour. Remove the
lid and cook for a further 30 minutes
to brown the potatoes. Garnish with
watercress.
Serves 4

Rice-stuffed lamb

IMPERIAL/METRIC
2 lb./1 kg. best end neck of lamb
Stuffing
½ oz./15 g. Stork margarine
1 onion, chopped
2 tomatoes, skinned and chopped
1 oz./25 g. long-grain rice
1 tablespoon chopped mint
salt and pepper
1 Red Oxo cube, crumbled and
  dissolved in ⅓ pint/200 ml. hot
  water

Bone the lamb. Melt the margarine
and sauté the onion and tomato for
2–3 minutes. Stir in the rice and

remaining ingredients. Bring to the
boil and simmer for 15–20 minutes.
Cool.

Spread the stuffing over the meat
(boned side uppermost), roll up and
tie with string. Place in a roasting
tin. Bake in the middle of a moderate
oven (350°F., 180°C., Gas Mark 4)
for 1¼–1½ hours. Remove the string
and serve.

If liked serve with heated condensed tomato soup as a sauce, or
with tomato sauce (see page 131).
Serves 4

Lamb paprika ❄

IMPERIAL/METRIC
1½ lb./675 g. boned leg of lamb
1 oz./25 g. flour
1 oz./25 g. Stork margarine
1 large onion, chopped
1 clove garlic, crushed
7-oz./198-g. can pimentos
  (optional)
8-oz./227-g. can tomatoes
1 heaped tablespoon paprika
  pepper
pinch brown sugar
1 teaspoon Worcestershire sauce
2 bay leaves
1 teaspoon celery salt
salt and pepper
¼ pint/150 ml. plain yogurt
Garnish
chopped parsley

Cut the lamb into 1-inch (2½-cm.)
cubes and toss in the flour. Melt the
margarine and sauté the onion,
meat and garlic for 5 minutes. Drain
and slice the pimentos, if used, add
to the meat with all the remaining
ingredients, except the yogurt, and
cover. Bake in an ovenproof casserole in the middle of a moderate
oven (350°F., 180°C., Gas Mark 4)
for 1½–2 hours. Just before serving,
pour over the yogurt and garnish
with the parsley.
Serves 4
Freezing note Freeze after 1¼ hours
of the cooking time. Complete the
cooking time when the dish is
required.
Illustrated on page 51

Noisettes of lamb with tomato sauce

IMPERIAL/METRIC
4 noisettes (see note)
Tomato sauce
½ oz./15 g. Stork margarine
1 small onion, chopped
½ oz./15 g. cornflour
8-oz./227-g. can tomatoes
garlic salt to taste
pinch rosemary
salt and pepper
pinch sugar
Minted dressing
2 oz./50 g. Stork margarine
2 tablespoons chopped mint

Place the noisettes under a preheated grill for 10–15 minutes on
each side.

To make the sauce, melt the margarine and sauté the onion for 2–3
minutes. Blend the cornflour with a
little of the tomato juice and stir into
the onion with the remaining ingredients. Bring to the boil and
simmer for 5–10 minutes. Strain or
liquidise.

Mix the margarine and mint
together for the dressing and form
into a roll. Wrap in foil and freeze.
Serve the noisettes with the sauce
poured around and a slice of minted
dressing on top of each.
Serves 4
Note Noisettes are boned, rolled
and tied lean best end neck of lamb
chops.

Variation
Use four lamb chops instead of the
noisettes.

Cabbage parcels

IMPERIAL/METRIC
8 cabbage leaves
Filling
½ oz./15 g. Stork margarine
1 small onion, chopped
2 oz./50 g. mushrooms, chopped
2 oz./50 g. long-grain rice
1 Red Oxo cube, crumbled and
    dissolved in ⅓ pint/200 ml. hot
    water
1 tablespoon tomato purée
8 oz./225 g. cooked lamb, minced
½ teaspoon basil
tomato sauce (see page 131)

Cook the cabbage leaves in boiling salted water for 5 minutes. Drain.

Melt the margarine and sauté the onion for 2 minutes. Stir in the mushrooms and rice. Cook for a further minute. Add the beef stock and bring to the boil. Simmer for 10 minutes. Stir in the lamb, tomato purée and basil.

Place a little filling in the centre of each cabbage leaf and wrap up like a parcel. Place in an ovenproof dish and pour over the tomato sauce. Cover and bake in the middle of a moderate oven (350°F., 180°C., Gas Mark 4) for 20 minutes. Serve with creamed potatoes and a tomato and cress salad, if liked.
Serves 4
Illustrated opposite

Shish kebabs ❄

IMPERIAL/METRIC
1 lb./450 g. boned leg of lamb
4 small courgettes, sliced diagonally
8 bay leaves
4 small tomatoes
1 banana, sliced into 1-inch/2½-cm.
    lengths
Marinade
¼ pint/150 ml. plain yogurt
1 clove garlic, crushed
2 teaspoons lemon juice
pinch dried mint
1 tablespoon tomato purée
salt and pepper

Cut the lamb into 1-inch (2½-cm.) cubes. Mix the ingredients for the marinade together in a bowl. Add the meat and marinate overnight.

Blanch the courgettes in boiling water for 2–3 minutes and drain. Remove the meat from the marinade. Thread the meat, bay leaves, vegetables and fruit on to eight skewers. Brush well with the marinade. Place under a preheated grill for 15–20 minutes, turning occasionally and brushing with the marinade. Serve with boiled rice and a salad.
Serves 4
Freezing note Freeze the prepared meat cubes in the marinade.

Savoury lamb bake

IMPERIAL/METRIC
1 oz./25 g. Stork margarine
1 large onion, sliced
1 lb./450 g. minced lamb
1 Red Oxo cube, crumbled and
    dissolved in ½ pint/275 ml. hot
    water
salt and pepper
2 tablespoons tomato purée
8 oz./225 g. long-grain rice
½ pint/275 ml. white sauce (see
    page 130)
3 oz./75 g. Cheddar cheese, grated

Melt the margarine in a pan and sauté the onion until soft. Add the lamb and cook gently for 5 minutes. Add the beef stock to the pan with the seasoning and tomato purée. Bring to the boil and simmer for 10 minutes.

Meanwhile cook the rice in boiling salted water until just tender – about 12 minutes – then drain thoroughly. Put a layer of rice in the base of an ovenproof dish and cover with half the meat. Repeat the layers of rice and meat and finish with a layer of rice.

Bring the sauce to the boil, season well, add 2 oz. (50 g.) of the cheese and stir until melted. Pour over the rice, sprinkle with the remaining cheese and cook in a fairly hot oven (400°F., 200°C., Gas Mark 6) for about 45 minutes or until the top is golden brown.
Serves 4

Variation
Used minced leftover cooked lamb.

Stuffed shoulder of lamb ❄

IMPERIAL/METRIC
1 oz./25 g. Stork margarine
1 onion, finely chopped
1 clove garlic, crushed
4 oz./100 g. lamb's liver, chopped
1½ teaspoons dried mixed herbs
salt and pepper
2 oz./50 g. long-grain rice, cooked
3½-lb./1½-kg. shoulder of lamb,
    boned and rolled
cooking fat
4 teaspoons flour
1 Red Oxo cube, crumbled and
    dissolved in ½ pint/275 ml. hot
    water
1 tablespoon tomato purée

Melt the margarine and sauté the onion and garlic until soft. Add the liver and continue cooking gently for 5 minutes, stirring frequently. Add the herbs, seasoning and cooked rice and mix thoroughly. Leave to cool.

Unroll the lamb, spread the stuffing over the meat then re-roll carefully to enclose the stuffing. Secure with string and weigh the joint. Stand in a roasting tin, season lightly and add a little cooking fat to the pan. Cook in a fairly hot oven (400°F., 200°C., Gas Mark 6) for about 1¾ hours, allowing 35 minutes per lb. (450 g.) plus 30 minutes over. Baste several times during cooking. Remove the joint and keep warm. Stir the flour into 1 tablespoon pan drippings then gradually add the beef stock, tomato purée and seasoning. Bring to the boil and simmer for 2 minutes. Strain and serve with the joint.
Serves 5–6
Freezing note Freeze the stuffed joint before cooking.

Cabbage parcels

Hidden cutlets

Irish-style stew

IMPERIAL/METRIC
1½ lb./675 g. scrag or middle neck
    of lamb
1 lb./450 g. potatoes, sliced
8 oz./225 g. onions, sliced
2 tablespoons chopped parsley
8 oz./225 g. carrots, chopped
2 sticks celery, chopped
salt and pepper
1 Red Oxo cube, crumbled and
    dissolved in ⅓ pint/200 ml. hot
    water
¼ teaspoon celery salt
dash Worcestershire sauce

Trim the meat and cut into pieces,
leaving the meat on the bones. Put
a layer of potatoes at the bottom of a
greased casserole. Add a layer of
meat and vegetables. Season well.
Repeat these layers finishing with
potato slices. Pour over the beef
stock with the celery salt and Worcestershire sauce added. Cover
and bake in a very moderate oven
(325°F., 160°C., Gas Mark 3) for
2–2¼ hours. When cooked, remove
the lid and brown the potatoes
under the grill for 5 minutes.
Serves 4

Hidden cutlets

IMPERIAL/METRIC
8 oz./225 g. shortcrust pastry
    (see pages 12–13)
1 Curry Oxo cube, crumbled
salt
4 large lamb cutlets, untrimmed
beaten egg or milk for glazing
Garnish
sprigs watercress

Roll out the pastry thinly on a
floured worktop. Brush the pastry
lightly with water and sprinkle all
over first with the crumbled curry
cube and then lightly with salt. Cut
the pastry into 1-inch (2½-cm.) wide
strips. Carefully wrap the strips
of pastry around the cutlets, damp-
ing the edges where necessary to
make them stick, until completely
enclosed. Place the cutlets on a
lightly greased baking sheet and
glaze with beaten egg or milk. Cook
in a fairly hot oven (400°F., 200°C.,
Gas Mark 6) for about 40 minutes
until golden brown. Garnish with the
watercress.
Serves 4
Freezing note Freeze wrapped
cutlets before cooking.

Variation
Mix 2 teaspoons made mustard with
1 teaspoon brown sugar and spread
over the chops before wrapping in
the pastry.

68

Curried lamb pie ✳ Spring lamb pie ✳

IMPERIAL/METRIC
Marinade
1 Curry Oxo cube, crumbled and
    dissolved in ¼ pint/150 ml. hot
    water
¼ teaspoon ground ginger
¼ teaspoon cayenne pepper
¼ teaspoon turmeric
grated rind and juice of 1 lemon
salt and pepper
1 onion, finely chopped
1 clove garlic, crushed
Filling
1½ lb./675 g. boned shoulder or leg
    of lamb, cut into 1-inch (2½-cm.)
    cubes
2 oz./50 g. Stork margarine
1 onion, chopped
1 oz./25 g. flour
1 Red Oxo cube, crumbled and
    dissolved in ½ pint/275 ml. hot
    water
1 cooking apple, peeled, cored and
    coarsely chopped
2 oz./50 g. raisins, stoned
2 oz./50 g. cashew nuts
2 tablespoons chutney
salt and pepper
8 oz./225 g. pudding crust pastry
    (see page 16)
beaten egg or milk for glazing

Mix the ingredients for the marinade
together, add the lamb and leave
overnight. Drain the lamb thoroughly, reserving the marinade. Melt
the margarine and sauté the meat
for 10 minutes until browned. Remove. Sauté the onion in the remaining margarine in the pan until soft
and add the flour, beef stock, apple,
raisins, nuts, chutney and reserved
marinade liquid. Season to taste.
Place in a casserole with the meat,
cover and cook at 350°F., 180°C.,
Gas Mark 4 for 45 minutes until
tender. Remove from the oven.
Turn the oven temperature up to
425°F., 220°C., Gas Mark 7.

Roll out the pudding crust pastry
on a lightly floured worktop to
¼-inch (½-cm.) thickness. Cut out
2-inch (5-cm.) circles and arrange
on top of the casserole slightly overlapping. Glaze with beaten egg or
milk and bake for 20–25 minutes
until well risen and golden in
colour.
Serves 4–6
Freezing note Freeze the meat
filling and pastry separately.

IMPERIAL/METRIC
3 oz./75 g. Stork margarine
2 onions, chopped
8 oz./225 g. new carrots, cut into
    ½-inch (1-cm.) pieces
1½ lb./675 g. boned shoulder of
    lamb, cut into 1-inch (2½-cm.)
    cubes
1 oz./25 g. seasoned flour
1 clove garlic, crushed
2 Red Oxo cubes, crumbled and
    dissolved in 1 pint/575 ml. hot
    water
1–2 tablespoons fresh chopped
    mint
1 teaspoon vinegar
juice of ½ lemon
4 oz./100 g. frozen peas
salt and pepper
6 oz./175 g. rough puff or flaky
    pastry (see page 15), well chilled
beaten egg or milk for glazing

Melt 2 oz. (50 g.) of the margarine in
a saucepan and gently sauté the
onion for 5 minutes until soft. Add
the carrots and cook for 5 minutes.
Remove the onions and carrots. Add
the remaining margarine to the pan.
Toss the lamb in seasoned flour and
fry in the hot fat with the garlic until
well browned. Return the onion and
carrots to the pan, add the stock,
mint, vinegar and lemon juice and
simmer for 40 minutes. Add the
peas and adjust the seasoning.
Place the mixture in a 2-pint (1-litre)
pie dish and leave to cool.

Roll out the pastry on a lightly
floured worktop to 1 inch (2½ cm.)
larger all round than the pie dish.
Cut off narrow strips round the edge
of the pastry. Damp the rim of the
pie dish and line with the pastry
strips. Damp the strips and cover
the filling with the remaining pastry,
pressing down gently to seal. Trim,
flake and flute the edges. Cut three
slits in the centre and decorate with
pastry leaves made from the trimmings. Glaze with beaten egg or
milk. Bake in a fairly hot oven
(400°F., 200°C., Gas Mark 6) for 45
minutes until the pastry is crisp, well
risen and golden brown.
Serves 4–6
Freezing note Freeze the meat
filling and pastry separately.

How to choose pork

With the advent of home freezing, pork can now be eaten at any time of the year; although it is wise in hot weather to avoid buying pork that has been kept in an unrefrigerated shop window.

As the animal is slaughtered at a young age, all cuts are very tender and the whole carcass is suitable for roasting unlike beef or lamb. The flesh should be firm and smooth with hardly any gristle. There should be small flecks of fat in the flesh, known as 'marbling'. This increases the tenderness and flavour of the meat. The fat should be firm and white. If it is grey and soft it is of poor quality. A good quality animal should have a good layer of fat on the outside.

In a young animal the rind or skin should be thin, if it is rough and thick then the animal is old. The bones should be small and pink, becoming white with old age. The flesh should be fine in texture and pink, becoming a deeper pink with maturity. A brownish dry look indicates staleness. Pork crackling is always popular, so always ask the butcher to leave the skin on joints and to score it for you.

The cuts featured in the photograph below are wholesale ones and include some smoked as well as fresh pork joints.

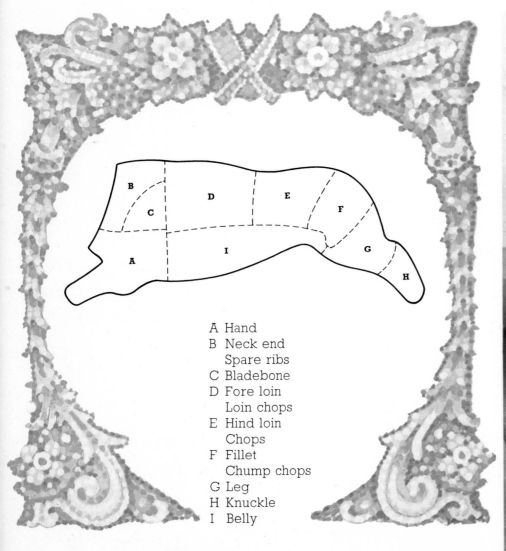

A Hand
B Neck end
  Spare ribs
C Bladebone
D Fore loin
  Loin chops
E Hind loin
  Chops
F Fillet
  Chump chops
G Leg
H Knuckle
I Belly

Pork cuts
1 Fore end of pork (boneless)
2 Fore end of bacon
3 Belly pork
4 Back bacon
5 Pig's head

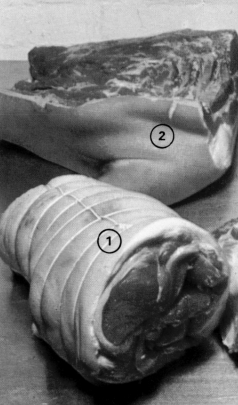

Carving pork

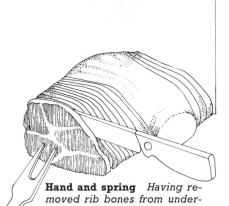

Hand and spring *Having removed rib bones from underside, turn joint back over and start carving slices from both ends, working towards the centre bone. It is easier to carve if the crackling is first removed.*

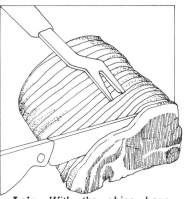

Loin *With the chine bone removed, carving slices down the loin. Carving is easier if the crackling is removed in sections. Carve pork thicker than beef.*

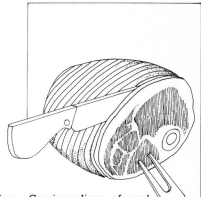

Leg *Carving slices of pork at the broad end, moving back towards the thick end of the bone. Carve over the top of the bone.*

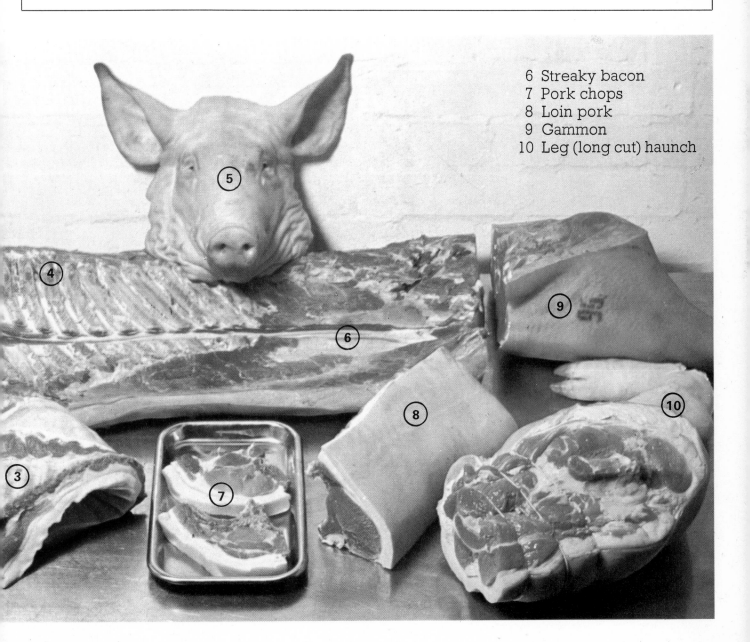

6 Streaky bacon
7 Pork chops
8 Loin pork
9 Gammon
10 Leg (long cut) haunch

Spicy spareribs

IMPERIAL/METRIC
1 oz./25 g. Stork margarine
1 onion, sliced
1 clove garlic, crushed
3 tablespoons lemon juice
2 oz./50 g. brown sugar
3 tablespoons Worcestershire
  sauce
3 tablespoons tomato purée
1 Curry Oxo cube, crumbled and
  dissolved in ⅓ pint/200 ml. hot
  water
½ teaspoon sage
few drops soy sauce (optional)
1 lb./450 g. pork spareribs or
  sparerib chops
Garnish
chopped parsley

Melt the margarine and sauté the
onion and garlic for 3–4 minutes.
Add the remaining ingredients except the spareribs, and simmer for
10 minutes. Place the spareribs in a
casserole and pour the sauce over.
Cover. Bake in the middle of a fairly
hot oven (400°F., 200°C., Gas Mark
6) for 50–60 minutes. Sprinkle with
chopped parsley.
Serves 4

Sweet and sour pork ❄

IMPERIAL/METRIC
1 oz./25 g. Stork margarine
1½ lb./675 g. boneless pork, cubed
2 oz./50 g. spring onions, sliced
8-oz./227-g. can pineapple cubes
4 tablespoons pineapple juice from
  the can, blended with
  1 tablespoon cornflour
1 tablespoon vinegar
1 tablespoon tomato purée
good pinch ground ginger
1 teaspoon lemon juice
1 Red Oxo cube, crumbled and
  dissolved in ½ pint/275 ml. hot
  water
1 tablespoon soy sauce
salt and black pepper
4-inch/10-cm. piece cucumber,
  diced
Garnish
cucumber slices

Melt the margarine and sauté the
meat over high heat for 10 minutes
until well browned. Place in a
casserole. Pour away some of the
fat in the pan and use the remainder
to fry the spring onions for 2
minutes. Add the remaining ingredients except the cucumber,
bring to the boil, stirring continuously, and cook for 5–10 minutes.
Pour over the meat and cover.
Cook in a moderate oven (350°F.,
180°C., Gas Mark 4) for about
30–45 minutes or until the meat
is tender. Then add the diced
cucumber and return to the oven
for a further 15 minutes.
  Serve with bean sprouts and
boiled rice; garnish.
Serves 4
Freezing note Freeze before adding the cucumber. Add the cucumber when reheating so that it
stays crisp.

Minced pork balls with curry cream sauce ❄

IMPERIAL/METRIC
1 oz./25 g. Stork margarine
2 oz./50 g. bacon, diced
1 small onion, chopped
1 lb./450 g. lean pork, minced
salt and black pepper
1 egg, lightly beaten
1 tablespoon cooking oil
Sauce
½ oz./15 g. Stork margarine
1 very small onion, finely chopped
4 oz./100 g. button mushrooms,
  sliced
2 Curry Oxo cubes, crumbled and
  dissolved in ¼ pint/150 ml. hot
  water
¼ pint/150 ml. single cream
salt and pepper
1 tablespoon chopped parsley

To make the meatballs, melt a little
of the margarine and sauté the
bacon and onion until tender. Place
the minced pork in a bowl and add
the bacon, onion, seasoning and
egg. Mix well then form into small
balls about 1 inch (2½ cm.) in diameter. Fry in the oil and remaining
margarine until brown and cooked
through – about 10–15 minutes.
Drain on absorbent paper and keep
hot while making the sauce.
  Melt the margarine and sauté the
onion until soft, then add the sliced
mushrooms and the curry stock.
Simmer for 5 minutes until the
mushrooms are cooked. Stir in the
cream and season to taste. Return
to the boil and stir in the chopped
parsley, reserving some for garnish.
  To serve, pile the meatballs on a
bed of cooked noodles and serve
the sauce separately. Garnish with
parsley.
Serves 4
Freezing note Freeze the meatballs and make the sauce when
required.

Stuffed pork roll ❄

IMPERIAL/METRIC
2–2½ lb./about 1 kg. boned belly
  of pork
Stuffing
½ oz./15 g. Stork margarine
1 small onion, finely chopped
1 oz./25 g. porridge oats
½ egg, lightly beaten
½ Onion Oxo cube, crumbled
salt and black pepper
grated rind of ½ lemon
1 teaspoon chopped fresh or dried
  sage
1 teaspoon chopped fresh parsley
15-oz./425-g. can apricot halves,
  drained
Coating
½ Onion Oxo cube, crumbled with
  1 oz./25 g. dried breadcrumbs
Garnish
sprigs watercress

Melt the margarine and sauté the onion until soft but not brown. Mix with the oats, egg, onion cube, seasoning, lemon rind, sage, parsley and half the apricots, drained and finely chopped. Allow to stand until some of the liquid is absorbed by the oats. Spread over the piece of belly of pork, then roll up and tie tightly. Roast in a moderate oven (350°F., 180°C., Gas Mark 4) for 30 minutes per lb. (450 g.) and 30 minutes over or until the meat is cooked through.

Allow to cool then remove the outer rind from the meat and roll the joint in the breadcrumbs and crumbled onion cube. Serve cold, garnished with the remaining apricots and watercress.
Serves 6
Freezing note Freeze after cooking and deriding but before rolling in breadcrumbs.

Stuffed pork roll

Pork chops with apple and raisin sauce ❄

IMPERIAL/METRIC
4 pork chops
Sauce
1 oz./25 g. Stork margarine
½ green pepper, deseeded and
  diced
½ pint/275 ml. stock
2 oz./50 g. raisins
2 large cooking apples, peeled,
  cored and thickly sliced
1 teaspoon grated lemon rind
1 bay leaf
salt and pepper
1–2 tablespoons tomato purée
Garnish
watercress

Grill the pork chops gently for 5–10 minutes on each side. Meanwhile prepare the sauce. Melt the margarine and sauté the green pepper for 5 minutes until soft. Add the remaining ingredients and simmer for 10 minutes or until the apple is cooked. Remove the bay leaf and pour the sauce over the chops in a serving dish. Garnish with watercress. Pipe a border of mashed potato round the edge if liked.
Serves 4
Freezing note The sauce can be frozen.

Crispy pork chops

IMPERIAL/METRIC
4 pork chops
3 oz./75 g. white breadcrumbs
1 tablespoon chopped parsley
1 standard egg
3 oz./75 g. Stork margarine
2 tablespoons cooking oil
Garnish
1 bunch spring onions
tomatoes

Trim the chops, cutting away the fat from the end of the bone. Mix the breadcrumbs and parsley together. Beat the egg and coat the chops in egg and breadcrumbs, pressing on well.

Melt the margarine with oil and gently fry the chops for 15–25 minutes, turning once, until crisp and golden. If you like, serve in a napkin-lined basket, and garnish with spring onions and tomatoes.
Serves 4

73

Pork chops with orange stuffing

IMPERIAL/METRIC
4 pork chops
Stuffing
½ onion, finely chopped
½ oz./15 g. Stork margarine
1 oz./25 g. fresh white breadcrumbs
grated rind of 1 orange
1 tablespoon orange juice
¼ pint/150 ml. chicken stock
pinch celery salt
pinch dried or chopped fresh thyme
1 teaspoon grated lemon rind
few drops lemon juice
2 oz./50 g. sweetcorn, cooked
Garnish
½ orange, sliced

Mix all the ingredients for the stuffing and allow to stand until the liquid has been absorbed.

Slit each pork chop horizontally through the middle, almost to the bone. Fill the slit with the stuffing so that the chop is forced to stay open and spear with a wooden cocktail stick to hold it. Place in an oven-proof dish. Bake the chops in a moderate oven (350°F., 180°C., Gas Mark 4) for 45–60 minutes.

Garnish with orange slices speared on to the cocktail sticks.
Serves 4

Pork rashers with barbecue sauce ❄

IMPERIAL/METRIC
8 thick pork rashers
salt and pepper
Barbecue sauce
1 oz./25 g. Stork margarine
1 onion, chopped
1 rasher streaky bacon, chopped
1 tablespoon tomato purée
½ pint/275 ml. dry cider
1 oz./25 g. demerara sugar
1 tablespoon Worcestershire sauce

Snip the rind on the pork rashers using a pair of scissors. Season and cook under a preheated grill for 10–15 minutes until golden and crisp, turning once.

To make the barbecue sauce, melt the margarine and sauté the onion and bacon for 4–5 minutes until soft. Add the remaining ingredients and bring to the boil. Simmer for 15 minutes. Liquidise or sieve and serve with the pork rashers.
Serves 4
Freezing note Barbecue sauce can be frozen; reheat while grilling the pork.

Pork stroganoff

IMPERIAL/METRIC
1 oz./25 g. Stork margarine
1 large onion, peeled and thinly sliced
1 lb./450 g. pork fillet or slices, cut into thin strips
4 oz./100 g. button mushrooms, sliced
4 tomatoes, peeled and sliced
salt and pepper
½ pint/275 ml. chicken stock
¼ pint/150 ml. soured cream

Melt the margarine in a pan and sauté the onion gently until soft. Add the pork and cook gently for 10 minutes, stirring frequently. Add the mushrooms, tomatoes, seasoning and chicken stock. Bring to the boil, cover and simmer very gently for 15–20 minutes. Stir in the soured cream, adjust the seasoning and reheat to just below boiling point.
Serves 4

Honey pork with orange

IMPERIAL/METRIC
1 Onion Oxo cube, crumbled
1 oz./25 g. flour
4 pork chops
1½ oz./40 g. Stork margarine
1 onion, chopped
1 tablespoon clear honey
1 Chicken Oxo cube, crumbled and dissolved in ⅓ pint/200 ml. hot water
pinch nutmeg
juice of 1 orange
4 oz./100 g. button mushrooms
Garnish
1 orange, sliced
watercress

Mix the crumbled onion cube with the flour. Trim the fat from the chops and toss them in the flour. Melt the margarine and sauté the chops on both sides with the onion until golden – about 5 minutes. Remove the meat and onion and place in a casserole. Add any remaining flour to the fat in the pan and cook for 1 minute. Stir the honey and chicken stock into the pan and bring to the boil. Pour over the chops and add the nutmeg, orange juice and seasoning. Cover. Bake in the middle of a moderate oven (350°F., 180°C., Gas Mark 4) for 40 minutes. Stir in the mushrooms and cook for a further 5 minutes. Place on a serving dish. Arrange the orange slices on top of the chops. Garnish.
Serves 4

Pork and tarragon pie

Pork and tarragon pie ❄

IMPERIAL/METRIC
1 tablespoon cooking fat
1 onion, peeled and chopped
3 oz./75 g. bacon, derinded and
   chopped
1 lb./450 g. minced pork
1 Chicken Oxo cube, crumbled and
   dissolved in ⅓ pint/200 ml. hot
   water
salt and pepper
1 teaspoon dried tarragon
6 oz./175 g. shortcrust pastry
   (see pages 12–13)
beaten egg or milk for glazing
Garnish
tomato wedges
sprig parsley

Melt the fat and sauté the onion and bacon for 5 minutes until soft. Add the pork and cook gently for 5 minutes, stirring occasionally. Stir in the chicken stock, bring to the boil, cover and simmer for 10 minutes. Season well, add the tarragon and mix thoroughly. Leave to cool.

Roll out two-thirds of the pastry on a lightly floured worktop and use to line an 8½-inch (21-cm.) shallow fluted flan tin or pie plate with a removable base. Fill with the pork mixture. Roll out the remaining pastry to make a lid. Damp the edges of the pie and cover with the lid. Press the edges well together and trim. Cut a slit in the centre and decorate with pastry leaves cut from the trimmings. Glaze with egg or milk and bake in a hot oven (425°F., 220°C., Gas Mark 7) for 15 minutes. Reduce the heat to 350°F., 180°C., Gas Mark 4 and continue for 30–40 minutes until golden brown. Serve hot or cold. Garnish with the tomato and parsley.
Serves 4–6

Variations
Omit the tarragon and the onion, and add 1 tablespoon dried sage and onion stuffing mix to the pork before adding the chicken stock.

Omit the bacon and add an apple, peeled and thinly sliced. Place the apple slices on top of the filling before covering with the pastry lid.

Toad in the hole

IMPERIAL/METRIC
1 quantity Yorkshire pudding
  batter (see page 111)
1 lb./450 g. pork sausages
cooking oil
Garnish
parsley

Make up the Yorkshire pudding batter. Pour sufficient oil to cover the base of a 10- by 8-inch (26- by 20-cm.) deep baking tin or oven-proof dish and heat in a hot oven (425°F., 220°C., Gas Mark 7) for 5 minutes. Place the sausages in the hot oil, arranging neatly in rows. Pour over the batter. Bake for 40–45 minutes. Garnish with sprigs of parsley.
Serves 4

Variation
Use 1 lb. (450 g.) pork sausage meat instead of the sausages. Mix 1 tablespoon tomato purée, ¼ teaspoon mixed herbs and a few drops of Worcestershire sauce into the sausage meat and roll into balls. Continue recipe as above.

Shooters' pie ❄

IMPERIAL/METRIC
2 lb./900 g. pork sausage meat
8 oz./225 g. streaky bacon rashers,
  derinded and chopped
1 onion, chopped
6 oz./175 g. mushrooms, chopped
salt and pepper
2 teaspoons dried sage
10 oz./275 g. flaky or rough puff
  pastry (see page 15)
beaten egg or milk for glazing
Garnish
parsley sprigs
tomato wedges

Combine the sausage meat, bacon, onion, mushrooms, seasoning and sage and form into a brick shape. Roll out the pastry large enough to enclose the sausage meat mixture completely. Place the sausage meat in the centre of the pastry and brush the edge with beaten egg or milk. Fold over the pastry, tucking in the ends. Place on a dampened baking sheet with the pastry join underneath. Decorate with pastry leaves made from the trimmings and make two slashes in the top. Glaze with the beaten egg or milk and bake in a hot oven (425°F., 220°C., Gas Mark 7) for

Toad in the hole

15–20 minutes until beginning to brown. Reduce the oven temperature to 350°F., 180°C., Gas Mark 4 and continue cooking for 30–40 minutes until browned and cooked through. Drain off any fat or juices and cool on a wire rack. To serve, cut into 20 slices and arrange on a dish garnished with parsley and tomato wedges.
Serves 10–20 (depending on appetite)
Illustrated on page 172

Savoury roll ❄

IMPERIAL/METRIC
8 oz./225 g. flaky pastry (see page
  15)
12 oz./350 g. pork sausage meat
1 teaspoon mixed herbs
1 standard egg
1 tablespoon tomato purée
1 Onion Oxo cube, crumbled
beaten egg or milk for glazing
Garnish
tomato slices
parsley

Roll the pastry out on a lightly floured worktop to an 11- by 7-inch (28- by 18-cm.) rectangle. Mix the sausage meat, herbs, egg, tomato purée and onion cube. Place the filling down the centre of the pastry and fold the pastry over to form a roll. Cut the pastry trimmings into thin strips the same length as the roll and plait them. Damp the top of the roll and lay the decoration on top. Brush the roll with beaten egg or milk and bake near the top of a hot oven (425°F., 220°C., Gas Mark 7) for 10 minutes. Cover with foil and reduce the temperature to 375°F., 190°C., Gas Mark 5 for a further 15–20 minutes. Garnish with tomato slices and parsley.
Serves 4–6
Freezing note Wrap in foil without garnishing.

Variation
Instead of rolling the pastry into a rectangle, roll into a 10-inch (25-cm.) square. Place the filling in the centre and damp the pastry edges. Bring the edges together to form a parcel, sealing well. Cut any pastry trimmings into leaves and decorate the top. Continue as above.

How to choose bacon, ham and gammon

Bacon is the salted or salted, dried and smoked flesh of the bacon pig. Green bacon is brine-cured but not smoked. It has a pale-coloured rind, whilst smoked has a deep brown rind.

Ham, from the hind leg of the pig, is removed before salting and cured locally.

Gammon is the hind leg of the bacon pig, cut square off the side of bacon and not rounded like a ham. It is cured before being taken off the carcass.

Freshly cut bacon and joints should have a pleasant aroma. The lean should be firm and deep pink in colour, without any yellow or greenish marks. A dark, dry appearance on the outside of a cut surface indicates long exposure to the air. The fat should be white and firm with a thin rind. Choose a ham with a thin rind · and not too fatty. Sliced ham should look fresh with white fat and pink flesh.

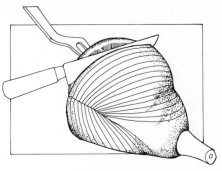

Hock *Carving slices from uppermost side. Because of the bone, the joint should then be turned over and carved from the other side.*

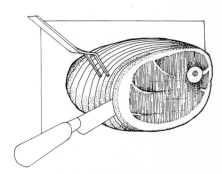

Middle cut *Carving thin slices right across the joint, making the slices wider at the outside to avoid ending up with an odd-shaped fatty piece.*

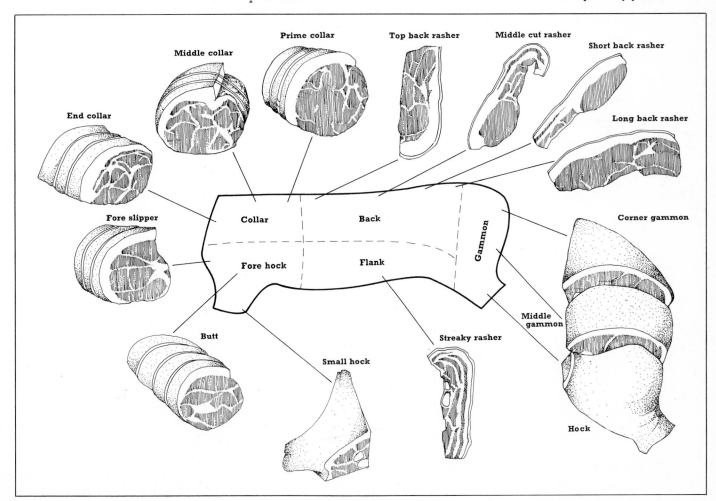

Provençal bacon

Provençal bacon

IMPERIAL/METRIC
2½-lb./1¼-kg. joint prime collar
   bacon, boned and rolled
1 oz./25 g. Stork margarine
8 oz./225 g. button onions, peeled
4 large tomatoes, skinned and
   quartered
1½ teaspoons dried oregano
¼ pint/150 ml. dry white wine or
   dry cider
salt and pepper
2 cloves garlic, crushed
1 Onion Oxo cube, crumbled
2 tablespoons white breadcrumbs
Garnish
chopped parsley
watercress sprigs

Soak the joint in cold water overnight. Drain. Place the bacon in a
saucepan and cover with fresh cold
water. Bring to the boil, cover and
simmer for 1 hour. Remove the
bacon joint and strip off the skin.
Place the joint in a casserole or
small roasting tin.

Melt the margarine and sauté the
onions for 5 minutes until just

beginning to brown then add the
tomatoes, oregano, wine or cider
and a little seasoning. Bring to the
boil and spoon around the bacon.
Mix together the garlic, onion cube
and breadcrumbs and sprinkle over
the bacon fat. Cook, uncovered, in
a fairly hot oven (400°F., 200°C.,
Gas Mark 6) for ½–¾ hour until
tender. Garnish.
Serves 5–6

Boiled bacon with sage and onion sauce

IMPERIAL/METRIC
2 knuckles boiling bacon
1 tablespoon sugar
1 bay leaf
2 oz./50 g. Stork margarine
1 large onion, chopped
1½ oz./40 g. flour
1 Onion Oxo cube, crumbled
½ pint/275 ml. milk
1 tablespoon freshly chopped sage
   leaves or 2 teaspoons dried sage
salt and pepper

Place the bacon knuckles in a saucepan with the sugar and bay leaf and
cover with water. Bring to the boil,
cover and simmer for about 1½
hours or until tender. Remove the
bacon, strip off the skin and keep
warm. Reserve the bacon stock.

Melt the margarine in a saucepan
and sauté the onion gently for 5
minutes until soft but not coloured.
Add the flour, onion cube, ⅓ pint
(200 ml.) of reserved stock and milk
and bring to the boil over a moderate heat, whisking continuously.
Cook for 2–3 minutes, still whisking,
until thickened and smooth. Add the
sage and seasoning and simmer for
3 minutes. Either serve the sauce
separately with the boiled bacon or
strip the flesh from the knuckles,
add to the sauce and serve in a
casserole.
Serves 4

Bacon and spinach quiche ❄

IMPERIAL/METRIC
6 oz./175 g. shortcrust pastry
   (see pages 12–13)
Filling
3 oz./75 g. streaky bacon
2 large eggs, beaten
1 Onion Oxo cube, crumbled
salt and pepper
¼ pint/150 ml. single cream or top
   of the milk
3 oz./75 g. Cheddar cheese, grated
6-oz./170-g. packet frozen spinach
¼ teaspoon nutmeg

Make up the pastry and roll out on
a lightly floured worktop into a
round large enough to line an
8-inch (20-cm.) flan ring. Line the
flan ring, trim the edges and chill
for 20 minutes.

Make three bacon rolls and reserve them for the garnish, grill the
remainder of the bacon and chop
or crumble. Drain and sprinkle on
the base of the flan case. Beat the
remaining ingredients together and
pour into the flan case. Bake in a
fairly hot oven (400°F., 200°C., Gas
Mark 6) for 20 minutes then lower
the heat to 350°F., 180°C., Gas Mark
4 for a further 10–20 minutes.
Garnish with grilled bacon rolls.
Serves 4
Freezing note This quiche may be
frozen but for best results freeze
the unbaked pastry case only.

Bacon surprise

IMPERIAL/METRIC
1 oz./25 g. Stork margarine
1 lb./450 g. pork sausages
1 onion, chopped
8 oz./225 g. back bacon rashers, chopped
1 Red Oxo cube, crumbled
8-oz./227-g. can baked beans
13-oz./350-g. can tomatoes
salt and pepper
3 medium-sized potatoes, peeled and thinly sliced
Topping
¼ pint/150 ml. plain yogurt
1 egg, beaten
Garnish
chopped parsley

Melt the margarine in a frying pan and fry the sausages, onion and bacon for 5–8 minutes, turning the sausages frequently. Crumble in the beef cube. Place layers of sausage mixture, alternating with beans and tomatoes, in a casserole dish. Season and top with the thinly sliced potatoes. Bake in a moderate oven (350°F., 180°C., Gas Mark 4) for 40–50 minutes.

Mix the yogurt and beaten egg together and pour over the casserole. Return to the oven for a further 20–30 minutes. Garnish with chopped parsley.
Serves 4
Freezing note Freeze without the topping.

Apricot bacon

IMPERIAL/METRIC
4 bacon chops (¾-inch/2-cm. thick slices back bacon)
7-oz./198-g. can apricot halves
2 teaspoons dry mustard
1 Onion Oxo cube, crumbled
2 tablespoons demerara sugar

Remove the rind from the bacon then slash the fat at ½-inch (1-cm.) intervals to prevent it from curling up. Place in a grill pan and cook under a moderate heat for about 5 minutes until the fat is golden brown. Turn the chops. Mix 1 tablespoon apricot juice with the mustard, onion cube and demerara sugar and spread over the uncooked side of the chops. Grill for a further 3–4 minutes then place the drained apricot halves on top of the bacon. Return to the grill for 1–2 minutes and serve at once.
Serves 4

Sausages in bacon with noodles

IMPERIAL/METRIC
16 thin streaky bacon rashers, derinded
1 lb./450 g. sausages
1 oz./25 g. Stork margarine
1 tablespoon oil
1 clove garlic, crushed
1 large onion, chopped
1 red pepper, deseeded and sliced
16-oz./454-g. can tomatoes
2 tablespoons tomato purée
salt and pepper
½ teaspoon sugar
12 oz./350 g. noodles
Garnish
sprigs parsley

Wrap two streaky bacon rashers around each sausage. Place in a grill pan. Melt the margarine and oil and sauté the garlic and onion for 5 minutes until soft. Add the pepper, tomatoes and tomato purée, bring to the boil and simmer gently for about 10 minutes, until the sauce is thick. Season and add the sugar.

Cook the sausages under a pre-heated grill for about 10 minutes on each side. Cook the noodles in plenty of boiling salted water according to the directions on the packet or for 12–15 minutes until *al dente*. Drain well and arrange on a flat dish. Spoon the tomato mixture down the centre and arrange the sausages on top.
Serves 4

Sausages in bacon with noodles

Roast gammon with honey and orange glaze

IMPERIAL/METRIC
2-lb./1-kg. gammon joint
2 oz./50 g. demerara sugar
12 cloves
1–2 tablespoons honey
2–3 tablespoons orange juice
Garnish
1 orange, sliced

Soak the gammon in cold water overnight. Drain. Place the joint in a saucepan, cover with water and add half the sugar. Bring to the boil and remove the scum. Simmer for 30 minutes.

Remove the joint and carefully strip off the rind. Score the fat and stud with cloves. Place in a baking tin.

Blend the remaining sugar, honey and orange juice and pour over the joint. Bake in a moderate oven (350°F., 180°C., Gas Mark 4) for the remaining 45 minutes. Baste during the cooking; 15 minutes before the end of cooking increase the temperature to 425°F., 220°C., Gas Mark 7. Serve hot and garnish with orange slices.
Serves 4

Variation
Use lemon or grapefruit juice instead of the orange for the glaze.

Bacon fricassée

IMPERIAL/METRIC
1 lb./450 g. cooked bacon, from hock or knuckle joint
¾ pint/425 ml. white pouring sauce (see page 130)
grated rind and juice of 1 orange
few drops lemon juice
1 teaspoon chopped parsley or 4 oz./100 g. cooked peas
salt and pepper
Garnish
4 slices bread from a large white loaf, crusts removed
1 oz./25 g. Stork margarine
finely chopped parsley
grilled bacon rolls (optional)

To make the fricassée, cut the bacon into small cubes and add to the white sauce with the remaining ingredients. Mix well and season to

taste. Heat thoroughly. Pour into a serving dish and keep hot.

Cut the bread into small triangles and fry in the melted margarine until golden brown. Dip one corner of each triangle in the parsley and place round the edges of the dish. Put the bacon rolls, if used, in the centre of the fricassée.
Serves 4

Bacon brochettes with Cumberland sauce

IMPERIAL/METRIC
8 rashers bacon, derinded
4 lambs' kidneys, skinned and cored
8 medium-sized mushrooms
8 cocktail sausages
8 bay leaves
2 oz./50 g. Stork margarine, melted
Cumberland sauce
2 tablespoons redcurrant jelly
shredded rind of ½ orange
juice of 1 orange
juice of ½ lemon
¼ pint/150 ml. red wine or Red Oxo stock

Stretch the bacon with the back of a knife and cut each rasher in half. Roll up. Cut each kidney into four pieces. Thread two bacon rolls, two pieces of kidney, a mushroom, a sausage and a bay leaf on to eight small skewers. Place under a pre-heated grill for 10–15 minutes, brushing with the melted margarine and turning frequently.

To make the sauce, melt the red-currant jelly and add the remaining ingredients; reheat. Serve with the bacon brochettes.
Serves 4

Devilled ham bouchées ❄

IMPERIAL/METRIC
8 oz./225 g. rough puff or flaky pastry, chilled (see page 15)
beaten egg or milk for glazing
Filling
¼ pint/150 ml. white coating sauce (see page 130)
4 oz./100 g. cooked ham, chopped
½ Onion Oxo cube, crumbled
½–1 teaspoon Worcestershire sauce
½–1 teaspoon French mustard
salt and pepper
Garnish
parsley

To make the bouchées, roll out the pastry to ½-inch (1-cm.) thickness and, using a 2-inch (5-cm.) round cutter, cut out 20–24 pastry rounds. Using a smaller cutter, approximately 1 inch (2½ cm.) in diameter, cut out the centres of half the rounds. Place the rings over the complete pastry rounds, using water to seal. Knock up the edges and glaze with beaten egg or milk. Place these and the removed centres, glazed, on a baking sheet. Bake in a hot oven (425°F., 220°C., Gas Mark 7) for about 10 minutes until well risen and golden brown.

Mix together all the ingredients for the filling and allow to cool slightly. Remove any raw pastry from the centre of the cooked bouchées and fill. Place the centre pieces of cooked pastry on top. Serve hot or cold, garnished with parsley.
Makes 10–12 bouchées
Freezing note Unfilled bouchée cases may be frozen raw or cooked. Open freeze and pack in rigid-based containers. Freeze the filling separately.
Illustrated on page 10

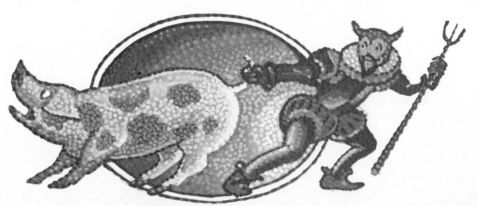

Bacon, onion and apple loaf ❄

IMPERIAL/METRIC
12 oz./350 g. shortcrust pastry (see pages 12–13)
beaten egg or milk for glazing
Filling
1 lb./450 g. collar bacon or gammon, minced
¼ pint/150 ml. cider
½ oz./15 g. Stork margarine
2 onions, finely chopped
2 cooking apples, peeled, cored and finely chopped
1 Chicken Oxo cube, crumbled
2 egg yolks
1 tablespoon chopped parsley
salt and pepper
8 oz./225 g. streaky bacon, derinded

Soak the bacon in the cider overnight. Melt the margarine and sauté the onion, apple and chicken cube for a few minutes until soft, then remove from the heat. Add the bacon and cider and mix well. Stir in the egg yolks and parsley and season to taste.

Line a 7-inch (18-cm.) square or an 8-inch (20-cm.) round cake tin with a removable base with three-quarters of the pastry, pressing it firmly into the corners. Stretch the bacon rashers with the back of a knife and use 6 oz. (175 g.) to line the pastry base and sides. Spoon half the filling mixture into the prepared tin. Make a layer of the remaining bacon rashers over the mixture and spoon in the remaining bacon mixture. Press down gently and smooth the surface. Fold in any bacon rasher ends. Roll out the remaining pastry to make a lid. Damp the pastry edges and cover with the pastry. Pinch the edges well together and mark with a fork. Make a slit in the centre and decorate with pastry leaves made from the trimmings. Glaze with the beaten egg or milk. Bake in a moderate oven (350°F., 180°C., Gas Mark 4) for 1 hour. Push the loaf carefully out of the tin and, leaving the base intact, brush the sides and top of the loaf with beaten egg. Turn the oven up to 400°F., 200°C., Gas Mark 6 and cook for a further 15 minutes until crisp and browned. Serve hot or cold.
Serves 4–6
Note This loaf is suitable for taking on a picnic. Serve with a salad.

Leek and bacon pie

IMPERIAL/METRIC
8 oz./225 g. all-in-one cheese pastry (see page 12)
beaten egg or milk for glazing
grated Parmesan cheese
Filling
1-lb./450-g. bacon joint, boned
2 oz./50 g. Stork margarine
1 lb./450 g. leeks, halved and sliced
2 green peppers, thinly sliced
¾ oz./20 g. flour
1 Onion Oxo cube, crumbled and dissolved in ¼ pint/150 ml. hot water
⅓ pint/200 ml. double cream
2 egg yolks
pepper

Soak the bacon overnight. Drain and cut into cubes. Melt the margarine and sauté the bacon for 10 minutes until lightly browned. Add the leek and pepper and cook for 5–7 minutes until soft. Remove the bacon, leek and pepper. Add the flour to the remaining fat and cook for a few minutes before adding the onion stock and cream. Cook until thick. Return the leek and bacon mixture to the pan. Add the egg yolks and pepper to taste. Cool.

Roll out two-thirds of the pastry on a lightly floured worktop and line an 8-inch (20-cm.) flan tin. Pour the filling into the flan case. Roll out the remaining pastry to make a lid. Damp the flan case edges and cover with the pastry. Pinch the edges well together and mark with a fork. Bake in a moderate oven (350°F., 180°C., Gas Mark 4) for 45 minutes. Brush the top with beaten egg or milk, sprinkle with the grated cheese and return to the top shelf of the oven for a further 15 minutes to brown.
Serves 4–6

Variation
When leeks are not available, 1 lb. (450 g.) sliced onions may be used.

Bacon plait ❄

IMPERIAL/METRIC
12 oz./350 g. flaky pastry, well chilled (see page 15)
beaten egg or milk for glazing
Filling
1½ oz./40 g. Stork margarine
2 onions, chopped
8 oz./225 g. gammon or collar bacon, cut in ¼-inch (½-cm.) thick slices and finely diced
4 oz./100 g. mushrooms, thinly sliced
8 oz./225 g. sausage meat
1 standard egg, beaten
½ teaspoon thyme
1 tablespoon chopped parsley
2 teaspoons snipped chives
1 teaspoon fresh chopped sage
salt and pepper

For the filling, melt the margarine and sauté the onion for 2–3 minutes until soft. Add the gammon and fry gently for 10 minutes, then add the mushrooms and continue to fry for 5 minutes. Mix with the sausage meat, egg and herbs and season to taste.

Roll out the pastry on a lightly floured worktop to an oblong approximately 12 by 8 inches (30 by 20 cm.). Fold in half lengthways and make diagonal cuts 2 inches (5 cm.) in from the edge of the pastry. Place on a dampened baking sheet and open out the pastry. Spoon the prepared filling in a roll shape down the length of the pastry. Fold over the pastry strips in a lattice design. Dampen the ends to fix securely. Glaze with beaten egg or milk and bake in a hot oven (425°F., 220°C., Gas Mark 7) for 30–40 minutes until cooked, crisp and golden. Serve garnished with parsley sprigs, if liked.
Serves 4–6
Freezing note Wrap the cooked, cooled plait in foil and freeze.
Illustrated on page 10

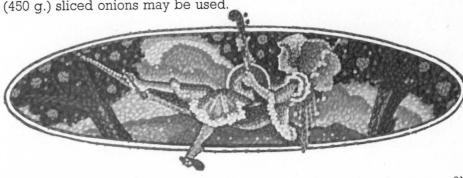

It is a pity that offal is so called because this is rather an unattractive name for what can make very tasty, nutritious and often economical dishes. The Americans call offal 'variety meats', and the different types can certainly add variety and interest to your menu for both family and special meals.

Apart from sweetbreads and calves' liver most offal is not expensive and there is very little waste. Offal contains the same food elements as red meats, and many kinds are excellent sources of vitamins and minerals, e.g., liver is rich in iron.

Described opposite are the different types of offal and some cooking suggestions; do try not to be put off by the unappetising appearance of some offal in its raw state because it makes a valuable contribution to the diet.

Brains

Calf's All brains should be fresh and used quickly. Calves' brains are considered the best and these are usually poached and served with a sauce, although they may be fried.

Lamb's Most frequently cooked with the head for stews and broths but may be cooked as calves' brains.

Feet

Calf's Can be used for making calf's foot jelly for invalids, and aspics for cold meats. Used cooked with other meats to give a delicious jelly-type stock, e.g. in a pot au feu.

Pig's trotters Can be boiled or stewed. After boiling they may be boned and stuffed, and then grilled or fried.

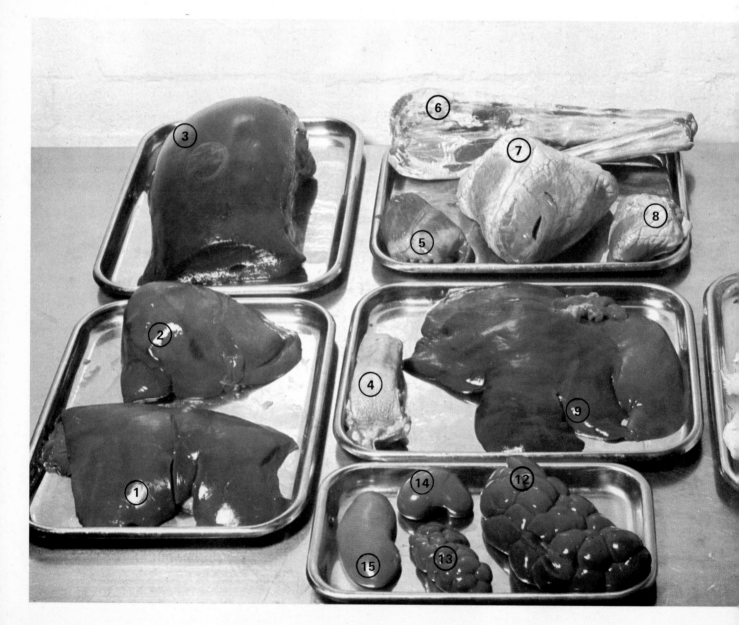

Head

Ox cheek A very economical cut of meat which must be cooked slowly as a stew or casserole.

Calf's Boil and serve with sauce or make into a brawn.

Sheep's May be split in half and boiled for broth, but may be used as a separate dish.

Pig's Can be boiled and used for brawn. The cheek is treated in brine, boned and boiled, and is known as Bathchap. It can be sliced and served hot, or cold with salad.

Heart

Ox This is large and has strong muscles which can be tough unless carefully cooked. Slice or chop then stew or braise with gravy.

Calf's This is more tender; may be roasted, braised or stewed.

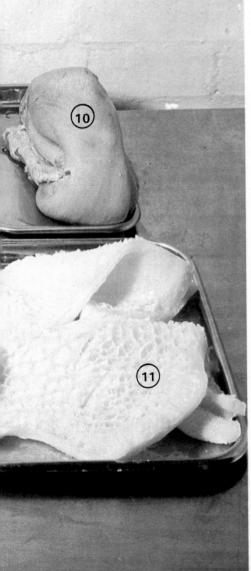

Sheep or lamb's Very small and can be stuffed, then roasted or braised.

Kidneys

Ox Strong flavour, requires careful cooking to tenderise; stew and use in pies and puddings.

Calf's Tender, use as ox kidneys.

Sheep or lamb's Small and excellent for grilling or frying. To prepare, steep in salt water, remove the skin and core before using.

Pig's Use as for lamb; can also be chopped for stews.

Liver

Ox This has a strong flavour and is coarse in texture and most suitable for braising with steak.

Calf's Considered to be the finest liver and is now very expensive. Fry gently and don't over-cook.

Sheep or lamb's This has a fairly strong flavour and is suitable for frying, grilling or braising.

Pig's This has a strong flavour and is more suitable for pâtés, meat loaves and stews.

Oxtail

Excellent for stews and soup; should have creamy white fat and bright coloured meat.

Sweetbreads

These are the pancreas and the thymus glands. They should only be

Types of offal

1 Calf liver
2 Lamb/sheep liver
3 Ox liver
4 Pig tongue
5 Pig heart
6 Oxtail
7 Ox heart
8 Lamb/sheep heart
9 Pig liver
10 Ox tongue
11 Tripe – smooth and honeycomb
12 Ox kidney
13 Calf kidney
14 Lamb kidney
15 Pig kidney

bought when fresh and must be used up quickly. 1 lb. (450 g.) is enough for 3–4 portions. Calves' and lambs' sweetbreads are the most tender and delicately flavoured, so choose these where possible.

Tongue

Ox Excellent flavour; avoid over-cooking, and remember to check with the butcher to see if the tongue has been salted or not.

Calf's Delicious in flavour and texture, weighing 1–2 lb. (450–900 g.) and are usually unsalted. Press into a tin or ovenproof bowl and add jellied stock.

Lamb's Weigh 8–10 oz. (225–275 g.) each and are usually boiled or braised but must be cooked until the skin comes away easily. Serve lambs' tongues hot or cold, jellied as above.

Tripe

This is the lining of an ox stomach. There are several different varieties – honeycomb, blanket, monk's head and book. Tripe is considered a great delicacy in the North and it is a light, easily digested meal but requires careful preparation. It is usually sold partly cooked and blanched, therefore the final cooking time varies according to how well the tripe has previously been prepared.

Points to remember when buying offal

Offal must be eaten fresh. If bought prepacked from a supermarket, unwrap immediately you reach home and store in the refrigerator if not being used at once. Place the offal in a dish or on a plate and cover lightly. Do not store in an airtight polythene container.

Liver and bacon kebabs

IMPERIAL/METRIC
1 lb./450 g. lambs' liver
10 rashers streaky bacon, derinded
½ oz./15 g. Stork margarine
2 cloves garlic, crushed
2 teaspoons flour
⅓ pint/200 ml. stock
4 tablespoons tomato ketchup
4 tablespoons red wine
salt and pepper

Cut the liver into 20 even-sized pieces. Stretch the bacon with the back of a knife and cut each rasher in half. Wrap a piece of bacon around each piece of liver and thread on four long skewers. For the sauce, melt the margarine and sauté the garlic for 2–3 minutes until golden brown, then add the flour, stock and ketchup to the pan over moderate heat. Bring to the boil, whisking continuously. Cook for 2–3 minutes, still whisking, until thickened, smooth and glossy. Add the wine and seasoning and simmer gently, uncovered, for about 10 minutes, stirring occasionally.

Grill the kebabs under a moderate heat for 5–8 minutes on each side until just cooked through. Serve with the sauce and plain boiled rice.
Serves 4

Kidney and butter bean casserole

IMPERIAL/METRIC
1 oz./25 g. Stork margarine
1 onion, sliced
2 rashers bacon, chopped
1 lb./450 g. ox kidney, skinned, cored and thickly sliced
½ oz./15 g. flour
1 Red Oxo cube, crumbled and dissolved in ½ pint/275 ml. hot water
salt and pepper
2 teaspoons Worcestershire sauce
1 tablespoon tomato purée
8-oz./227-g. can butter beans, drained
Garnish
croûtes of fried bread
parsley

Melt the margarine and sauté the onion and bacon for 5 minutes. Add the sliced kidney to the pan and cook for 1–2 minutes. Place in a casserole dish. Stir the flour and beef stock into the fat remaining in the pan over moderate heat. Bring to the boil, whisking continuously. Cook for 2–3 minutes, still whisking, until thickened, smooth and glossy. Season and add the Worcestershire sauce and tomato purée. Bring back to the boil, pour over the kidneys and cover.

Bake in a very moderate oven (325°F., 160°C., Gas Mark 3) for 30 minutes. Stir in the butter beans and return to the oven for a further 5 minutes. Garnish with croûtes of fried bread and parsley.
Serves 4

Braised ox heart with orange

IMPERIAL/METRIC
1 oz./25 g. Stork margarine
1 large onion, sliced
1 lb./450 g. ox heart
2 tablespoons flour
1 Red Oxo cube, crumbled and dissolved in ½ pint/275 ml. hot water
2 oranges
1 teaspoon tomato purée
salt and pepper
4 carrots, peeled and sliced

Melt the margarine and sauté the onion for 5 minutes until pale brown. Cut the heart into ½-inch (1-cm.) thick strips, add to the pan and fry until browned. Stir in the flour and cook for 1 minute, then gradually add the beef stock and bring to the boil. Grate the rind from the orange and add to the pan. Squeeze the juice from both oranges and make it up to ¼ pint (150 ml.) with water if necessary. Add to the pan with the tomato purée, seasoning and carrots. Bring back to the boil, transfer to a casserole and bake in a moderate oven (350°F., 180°C., Gas Mark 4) for 1½–2 hours until tender.
Serves 4

Stuffed hearts

IMPERIAL/METRIC
4 lambs' hearts, fat removed
1 oz./25 g. flour
2 oz./50 g. Stork margarine
2 sticks celery, sliced
2 onions, sliced
2 Red Oxo cubes, crumbled and dissolved in ⅔ pint/400 ml. hot water
Stuffing
1 onion, chopped
grated rind of 1 lemon
1 Onion Oxo cube, crumbled
2 oz./50 g. fresh breadcrumbs
1 tablespoon chopped parsley
¼ teaspoon basil
1 standard egg
salt and pepper
Garnish
parsley

Slit each heart lengthways and open out. Remove the blood vessels and divide the wall of each to make a cavity for the stuffing. Soak in cold water for 30 minutes. Dry well.

To make the stuffing, mix all the ingredients together and fill each heart. Secure with string and dust with flour.

Melt the margarine and sauté the celery and onion for 2–3 minutes until soft. Place them in a casserole. Fry the hearts in the remaining fat for about 5 minutes until golden. Place the hearts on top of the vegetables and pour over the beef stock. Bake in the middle of a moderate oven (350°F., 180°C., Gas Mark 4) for 1½–2 hours. Garnish with parsley.
Serves 4

Kidneys in wine sauce

IMPERIAL/METRIC
1 oz./25 g. Stork margarine
1 onion, sliced
1 clove garlic, crushed
8 lambs' kidneys, halved, skinned and cored
1½ tablespoons flour
4 tablespoons dry white wine
1 Red Oxo cube, crumbled and dissolved in ⅓ pint/200 ml. hot water
salt and pepper
4 oz./100 g. mushrooms, halved
4 tablespoons soured cream
Garnish
1 tablespoon chopped parsley

Melt the margarine in a pan and sauté the onion and garlic gently for 5 minutes until soft. Add the kidneys and fry until well sealed all over. Stir in the flour and cook for 1 minute, then gradually add the wine, beef stock and seasoning. Bring to the boil, cover and simmer for 10 minutes. Add the mushrooms and continue cooking for 5–10 minutes until tender. Stir in the soured cream, adjust the seasoning and reheat without boiling. Sprinkle with parsley. Serve with boiled rice.
Serves 4

Chicken liver risotto

IMPERIAL/METRIC
2 oz./50 g. Stork margarine
1 lb./450 g. chicken livers, trimmed
2 rashers streaky bacon, cut in strips
1 onion, chopped
4 oz./100 g. long-grain rice
1 Chicken Oxo cube, crumbled
10¼-oz./291-g. can vegetable juice or ½ pint/275 ml. seasoned tomato juice
1 teaspoon tarragon
2 bay leaves
salt and pepper
4-oz./113-g. packet frozen peas
6½-oz./184-g. can pimentos (optional)
Garnish
chopped parsley

Melt the margarine and sauté the chicken livers, bacon, onion and rice for 5–8 minutes. Stir in the chicken cube, vegetable or tomato juice, herbs and seasoning. Bring to the boil and simmer gently for 20 minutes. Add the peas and sliced pimentos if used, and cook for a further 5 minutes. Garnish.
Serves 4

Variation
For a special occasion, use ¼ pint (150 ml.) red wine and ¼ pint (150 ml.) vegetable juice.

Oxtail casserole ❄

IMPERIAL/METRIC
1 oxtail, cut into joints
2 Red Oxo cubes, crumbled and dissolved in 2 pints/generous litre hot water
bouquet garni
2 onions, peeled and sliced
2 carrots, peeled and sliced
1 oz./25 g. Stork margarine
1 oz./25 g. flour
salt and pepper
2 tablespoons tomato purée
4 oz./100 g. mushrooms
Garnish
chopped parsley

Place the oxtail in a saucepan with the beef stock and bouquet garni. Bring to the boil and simmer gently for 1½–2 hours. Strain the liquor and skim off the fat when cold. Make up to 1 pint (575 ml.) with water if necessary.

Place the vegetables in a casserole with the oxtail on top.

Place the margarine, flour and reserved liquor in a saucepan over moderate heat. Bring to the boil, whisking continuously. Cook for 2–3 minutes, still whisking, until thickened, smooth and glossy. Season and add the tomato purée. Pour over the oxtail and cover. Bake in a very moderate oven (325°F., 160°C., Gas Mark 3) for 1½ hours. Add the mushrooms and continue to cook for a further 20–30 minutes. Garnish with chopped parsley.
Serves 4
Freezing note If freezing, reduce the cooking time by 30 minutes. Freeze in a rigid polythene container.

Variation
Add a can of red kidney beans to the casserole 15 minutes before the end of the cooking time.

Kidneys in wine sauce

Casserole of lambs' tongues

IMPERIAL/METRIC
4–6 lambs' tongues
1 oz./25 g. Stork margarine
1 stick celery, sliced
4 carrots, sliced lengthways
1 turnip, cut into cubes
1 onion, sliced
bay leaf
1 tablespoon chopped parsley
½ teaspoon dried thyme
freshly ground black pepper
1 Red Oxo cube, crumbled and
    dissolved in ¾ pint/425 ml. hot
    water
Garnish
chopped parsley

Soak the lambs' tongues in salt water for 2 hours. Drain, cover with fresh cold water and bring to the boil. Drain and dry thoroughly.

Melt the margarine in a flame-proof casserole and sauté the prepared vegetables for 5 minutes. Add the herbs and seasoning. Place the tongues on top of the vegetables and pour over the beef stock. Cover and simmer very gently for 1½–2 hours, until the tongues are tender. Sprinkle with chopped parsley before serving.
Serves 4

Casserole of lambs' tongues

Liver provençal

IMPERIAL/METRIC
1 lb./450 g. lambs' liver
2 oz./50 g. flour
2 oz./50 g. Stork margarine
4 oz./100 g. streaky bacon, chopped
1 onion, sliced
1 clove garlic, crushed
8-oz./227-g. can tomatoes
1 tablespoon Worcestershire sauce
⅓ pint/200 ml. stock
salt and pepper
2 bay leaves
few black olives (optional)
Garnish
chopped parsley

Wash, dry and slice the liver. Toss in the flour. Melt the margarine and sauté the liver, bacon, onion and garlic for 5–8 minutes. Remove and place in a casserole. Stir the remaining flour into the fat in the pan and cook for 1 minute. Add the tomatoes, Worcestershire sauce, stock, seasoning and bay leaves. Bring to the boil, pour over the liver and cover the dish. Bake in a slow oven (300°F., 150°C., Gas Mark 2) for 1 hour. Stir in the olives just before the end of the cooking time and garnish with parsley. Serve with noodles.
Serves 4
Freezing note Add the olives on reheating. Cook the dish for 45 minutes only before freezing. Pack in a rigid polythene container.

Creamed sweetbreads

IMPERIAL/METRIC
1 lb./450 g. calves' sweetbreads
½ pint/275 ml. liquor from
    sweetbreads
2 oz./50 g. Stork margarine
2 oz./50 g. flour
½ pint/275 ml. milk
salt and pepper
1 Onion Oxo cube, crumbled
few drops lemon juice
Garnish
chopped parsley
croûtes of fried bread

Soak the sweetbreads for 2 hours in cold water. Drain, cover with cold water and bring slowly to the boil. Simmer for 10 minutes. Plunge into cold water, then remove any skin or gristle.

Place the sweetbreads in 1 pint (575 ml.) cold salted water and bring to the boil. Simmer gently for 1 hour or until tender. Remove the sweetbreads and keep hot; reserve ½ pint (275 ml.) liquor. Place the margarine, flour, milk and liquor in a saucepan over moderate heat. Bring to the boil, whisking continuously. Cook for 2–3 minutes, still whisking, until thickened, smooth and glossy. Season; add the onion cube and lemon juice to taste. Add the sweetbreads to the sauce. Pour into a dish and garnish with parsley and croûtes of fried bread.
Serves 3–4

Variation
Creamed sweetbreads make a good filling for vol au vents, either on their own or with a few sliced mushrooms, sautéed in margarine, added.

Sweetbread and mushroom pie ❄️

IMPERIAL/METRIC
1½ lb./675 g. calves' sweetbreads
3 oz./75 g. Stork margarine
8 oz./225 g. flat mushrooms, peeled and destalked (reserve stalks)
2 onions, chopped
1 oz./25 g. flour
1 Chicken Oxo cube, crumbled and dissolved in ½ pint/275 ml. hot water
¼ pint/150 ml. single cream
juice and grated rind of ½ lemon
1 tablespoon chopped parsley
salt and pepper
6 oz./175 g. flaky pastry (see page 15), well chilled
beaten egg or milk for glazing

Soak the sweetbreads for 2 hours in cold water. Drain, cover with cold water and bring slowly to the boil. Simmer for 10 minutes. Plunge into cold water, then remove any skin or gristle. Cut into ½-inch (1-cm.) slices. Melt 2 oz. (50 g.) of the margarine and sauté the sweetbreads for 10 minutes. Remove from the pan. Add the whole mushrooms and the stalks halved lengthways and sauté for a few minutes on either side. Remove from the pan and layer with the sweetbreads in a 2-pint (1-litre) pie dish.

Melt the remaining margarine in a pan, add the onion and sauté for 2–3 minutes until soft. Add the flour and chicken stock to the pan over moderate heat. Bring to the boil, whisking continuously. Cook for 2–3 minutes, still whisking, until thickened. Add the cream, lemon juice and grated rind, parsley and seasoning to taste. Pour over the sweetbreads and mushrooms in the pie dish.

Roll out the chilled pastry on a lightly floured worktop to 1 inch (2½ cm.) larger all round than the pie dish. Cut off narrow strips round the edge of the pastry. Damp the rim and line with the pastry strips. Damp the strips and cover the filling with the remaining pastry, pressing down gently to seal. Trim, flake and flute the edges. Cut three slits in the centre. Cut the pastry trimmings into strips and make a pastry lattice on top. Glaze with beaten egg or milk. Bake in a hot oven (425°F., 220°C., Gas Mark 7)

until well risen and golden brown – about 30–40 minutes.
Serves 4–6
Freezing note Freeze before baking.

Lambs' kidney pie ❄️

IMPERIAL/METRIC
6 lambs' kidneys, skinned, halved and cored
1 tablespoon seasoned flour
2 oz./50 g. Stork margarine
1 onion, sliced
8 oz./225 g. button mushrooms, sliced
¾ oz./20 g. flour
1 Red Oxo cube, crumbled and dissolved in ⅓ pint/200 ml. hot water
3 tablespoons sherry
8 oz./225 g. cooked ham, cut in ¼-inch/½-cm. slices and diced
1 teaspoon made mustard
chopped parsley
salt and pepper
10 oz./275 g. all-in-one rich flan pastry, omitting sugar (page 12)
beaten egg or milk for glazing

Toss the kidneys in seasoned flour. Melt the margarine and sauté the kidneys until they change colour. Remove from the pan. Add the onion to the pan and sauté for 5 minutes until soft. Add the mushrooms and cook quickly for a few minutes, add the flour, beef stock and sherry to the pan over a moderate heat. Bring to the boil, whisking continuously. Cook for 2–3 minutes, still whisking, until thickened. Finally add the ham, mustard, parsley and seasoning to taste.

Roll out two-thirds of the pastry on a lightly floured worktop and line a deep 8-inch (20-cm.) flan tin. Fill with half the mushroom and ham mixture. Arrange the kidneys on top and cover with the remaining mushroom and ham mixture. Roll out the remaining pastry to make a lid. Damp the flan case edges and cover with the pastry. Trim and pinch the edges well together and mark with a fork. Make a slit in the centre and decorate with pastry leaves made from the trimmings. Glaze with beaten egg or milk. Bake in a fairly hot oven (400°F., 200°C., Gas Mark 6) for 40–50 minutes.
Serves 4–6
Freezing note Freeze the prepared pie before baking.

Liver and bacon puffs ❄️

IMPERIAL/METRIC
8 oz./225 g. calves' liver, thinly sliced and cut in fine strips
1 oz./25 g. seasoned flour
2 oz./50 g. Stork margarine
4 oz./100 g. back bacon, cut in fine strips
1 onion, finely chopped
1 oz./25 g. flour
1 Red Oxo cube, crumbled and dissolved in ½ pint/275 ml. hot water
1 tablespoon tomato ketchup
good pinch sage
chopped parsley
salt and pepper
12 oz./350 g. flaky pastry, well chilled (see page 15)
beaten egg or milk for glazing

Toss the liver in seasoned flour. Melt 1½ oz. (40 g.) margarine and sauté the liver slowly for 10–15 minutes. Remove from the pan. Add the remaining margarine and sauté the bacon. Add the onion and cook until soft. Add the flour, beef stock, ketchup and herbs to the pan over a moderate heat. Bring to the boil, whisking continuously. Cook for 2–3 minutes, still whisking, until thickened. Season. Return the liver to the pan and simmer gently for 10 minutes. Leave to cool.

Roll the pastry out very thinly on a lightly floured board and cut out eight 3½-inch (9-cm.) circles and eight 4-inch (10-cm.) circles. Place the eight smaller circles on a dampened baking sheet. Place a spoonful of filling in the centre of each circle. Damp round the edge of each circle with a pastry brush and cover with the remaining larger circles. Seal the edges firmly, glaze with beaten egg or milk and make a small slit in the top of each puff. Decorate with pastry leaves made from the trimmings and glaze again. Bake in a fairly hot oven (400°F., 200°C., Gas Mark 6) for 20 minutes until puffed up, crisp and golden brown. Serve at once; a tomato sauce (see page 131) is good with these.
Serves 4
Note These make a delicious suppertime snack.
Freezing note Freeze the unbaked puffs and pack in a rigid polythene container.

Stuffings & Accompaniments

The first and foremost task of a stuffing or forcemeat mixture, which is served as an accompaniment, is to create a harmonious blend of taste and contrast to the meat, poultry or fish. A little care must be given to choosing a stuffing, as a highly seasoned mixture will ruin the delicate flavour of a bland meat, in the same way that a bland stuffing with a spicy meat or game, such as hare or venison, would be useless.

The main ingredients for stuffings are breadcrumbs, onions, rice, apples, chestnuts, minced pork, veal or ham. These ingredients can be varied to suit the dish and mixed with egg and various chopped herbs. Do not pack stuffing too tightly in poultry and game as it tends to swell and come out; allow roughly 2 oz. (50 g.) stuffing per 1 lb. (450 g.) of bird. If the meat has no cavity, cook the stuffing (forcemeat) separately in a greased baking dish.

Sausage meat stuffing

IMPERIAL/METRIC
2 oz./50 g. Stork margarine
1 onion, finely chopped
1 lb./450 g. pork sausage meat
1 oz./25 g. fresh white
   breadcrumbs
1 teaspoon powdered thyme
1 teaspoon dried mixed herbs
2 teaspoons chopped parsley
salt and pepper
1 beaten egg or milk to bind

Melt the margarine and sauté the onion and sausage meat for 2–3 minutes. Turn into a bowl and mix in the remaining dry ingredients. Adjust the seasoning if necessary and bind with the beaten egg or milk. This stuffing is traditionally used with turkey and veal.

Parsley and thyme stuffing

IMPERIAL/METRIC
4 oz./100 g. fresh white breadcrumbs
2 oz./50 g. Stork margarine, chilled
   and coarsely grated
1 Onion Oxo cube, crumbled
1 tablespoon finely chopped parsley
1 teaspoon powdered thyme
grated rind of ½ lemon
salt and pepper
little beaten egg or milk to bind

Stuffed roast turkey with gravy, roast potatoes, cranberry sauce and bread sauce (page 130)

Mix all the ingredients, except the egg, together with a fork. Moisten with the egg or milk, making sure the stuffing is not too wet. Press the mixture together with the finger-tips until it forms a ball. This stuffing is excellent with beef, veal, chicken and turkey.

Chestnut stuffing

IMPERIAL/METRIC
2 oz./50 g. Stork margarine
1 large onion, finely chopped
8 oz./225 g. pork sausage meat
8 oz./225 g. chestnut purée (see
   note)
1 tablespoon chopped parsley
1–2 oz./25–50 g. fresh breadcrumbs
salt and pepper

Melt the margarine and sauté the onion for 5 minutes until soft. Cool. Add the sausage meat, chestnut purée and parsley. Mix with enough breadcrumbs to bind and season to taste. This stuffing is traditionally used to stuff a turkey.
Note Canned unsweetened chestnut purée may be used or canned whole chestnuts drained and lightly mashed. If making fresh chestnut purée, use 1 lb. (450 g.) chestnuts. Score and cook the chestnuts in boiling water for 10–15 minutes; or melt ½ oz. (15 g.) Stork margarine and cook the skinned chestnuts gently for 4–5 minutes. Remove the skins where necessary then peel and mince.

Variation
Fry 4 oz. (100 g.) chopped bacon with the onion.

Walnut and onion stuffing

IMPERIAL/METRIC
1½ oz./40 g. Stork margarine
1 small onion, chopped
4 oz./100 g. walnuts, coarsely
    chopped
4 oz./100 g. fresh white
    breadcrumbs
grated rind of 1 lemon
2 tablespoons chopped fresh herbs
    and parsley, mixed
½ teaspoon cinnamon
1 beaten egg or milk to bind
salt and pepper

Melt ½ oz. (15 g.) margarine and
sauté the onion gently for 5 minutes
until soft. Add the remaining margarine and fry the walnuts for 3–4
minutes. Turn into a bowl and add
the breadcrumbs, lemon rind, herbs
and cinnamon. Bind with the egg or
milk and season to taste. Mix well.
This stuffing is ideal for chicken,
turkey, game and beef.

Anchovy and sausage meat stuffing

IMPERIAL/METRIC
1 oz./25 g. Stork margarine
1 onion, chopped
8 oz./225 g. pork sausage meat
8 anchovy fillets, chopped
1 tablespoon chopped parsley
2–3 oz./50–75 g. fresh white
    breadcrumbs
salt and pepper
1 beaten egg or milk to bind

Melt the margarine and sauté the
onion for 5 minutes until soft. Add
the sausage meat, anchovy fillets,
parsley and breadcrumbs. Season
to taste and bind with the egg or
milk. This is a good stuffing for
lamb, beef and veal.

Variation
A few chopped capers, gherkins
or black olives may be added
before binding.

Apricot and mint stuffing

IMPERIAL/METRIC
1½ oz./40 g. Stork margarine
1 small onion, chopped
4 oz./100 g. fresh breadcrumbs
2 teaspoons chopped parsley
1 teaspoon chopped mint
3 oz./75 g. dried apricots, chopped
1 Chicken Oxo cube, crumbled
    and dissolved in ¼ pint/150 ml. hot
    water
salt and pepper

Melt the margarine and sauté the
onion for 2 minutes. Add the breadcrumbs, parsley and mint and mix
well. Remove from the heat and add
the apricots and enough chicken
stock to make a fairly stiff consistency. Season. This stuffing is good
with lamb.

Sage and onion stuffing

IMPERIAL/METRIC
4 onions, parboiled and finely
    chopped
4 oz./100 g. fresh white bread-
    crumbs
2 teaspoons powdered sage
1½ oz./40 g. Stork margarine,
    melted
½ teaspoon salt
¼ teaspoon pepper
little beaten egg or milk to bind

Mix all the ingredients, except the
egg, together with a fork and check
the seasoning. Moisten with the
egg or milk, making sure the stuffing is not too moist. Use to stuff
meat or bake in a well greased
shallow tin in a moderate oven
(350°F., 180°C., Gas Mark 4) until
firm and golden brown. Cut into
squares to serve. This stuffing is
best with pork, duck and goose.

Variation
Fruity sage stuffing A cooking apple,
peeled, cored and diced, may be
added to the mixture with the rind
and juice of ½ lemon.

Orange and celery stuffing

IMPERIAL/METRIC
1 oz./25 g. Stork margarine
1 onion, finely chopped
1 Onion Oxo cube, crumbled
4 oz./100 g. fresh breadcrumbs
grated rind of 1 orange
pinch thyme
2 tablespoons chopped parsley
1 stick celery, finely chopped
salt and pepper
1 beaten egg to bind

Melt the margarine and sauté the
onion for 5 minutes until soft. Mix
in the remaining ingredients thoroughly and season to taste. Bind
with the egg. This stuffing is delicious served with lamb or pork.
Illustrated opposite

Egg and anchovy stuffing

IMPERIAL/METRIC
2 oz./50 g. Stork margarine
1 onion, finely chopped
2 hard-boiled eggs, chopped
4 oz./100 g. fresh white
    breadcrumbs
1 tablespoon chopped parsley
2 teaspoons mixed herbs (or
    mixture of powdered fennel,
    thyme and marjoram)
grated rind and juice of 1 lemon
3 anchovy fillets, chopped
1 teaspoon tomato purée
1 beaten egg to bind
salt and pepper

Melt the margarine and sauté the onion for 5 minutes until soft. Add the remaining ingredients, except the egg, and mix thoroughly. Bind with the egg to make a fairly firm consistency. Season to taste and use to stuff or accompany fish.

Cranberry stuffing

IMPERIAL/METRIC
1 oz./25 g. Stork margarine
1 onion, chopped
8 oz./225 g. fresh or frozen
    cranberries, minced or chopped
8 oz./225 g. pork sausage meat
4 oz./100 g. fresh white
    breadcrumbs
1 tablespoon chopped parsley
grated rind and juice of 1 orange
pinch ginger
salt and pepper
pinch sugar
1 beaten egg or milk to bind

Melt the margarine and sauté the onion for 5 minutes until soft. Add the cranberries and fry quickly until lightly cooked. Mix in the pork or sausage meat and then combine with the breadcrumbs, parsley, orange rind and juice. Season with the ginger, salt and pepper and sugar. Bind with the egg or milk and use this tangy stuffing for chicken, game, pork or lamb.

Tuna and rice stuffing

IMPERIAL/METRIC
1½ oz./40 g. Stork margarine
1 onion, chopped
3 oz./75 g. long-grain rice
2 oz./50 g. mushrooms, sliced
1 Chicken Oxo cube, crumbled and
    dissolved in ½ pint/275 ml. hot
    water
3½-oz./100-g. can tuna, drained
½ teaspoon tomato purée
½ teaspoon anchovy essence
1 tablespoon chopped parsley
grated rind and juice of ½ lemon
salt and pepper

Melt the margarine and sauté the onion for 5 minutes until soft. Stir in the rice and fry for 3–4 minutes. Add the mushrooms and chicken stock and simmer until the liquid is absorbed and rice cooked – about 15–20 minutes. Mix in the flaked tuna, tomato purée, anchovy essence, parsley and lemon rind and juice. Season to taste. This is a delicious stuffing for fish and chicken.

To freeze stuffings
Certain stuffings may be frozen, or the dry ingredients can be mixed and frozen with the liquid added just before using. Alternatively, freeze the breadcrumbs separately. *Storage time* for stuffings – 4 weeks, for breadcrumbs – 3 months.
   Do not freeze made-up stuffings which contain hard-boiled egg or uncooked fresh fruit; do not freeze poultry stuffed.

Crown roast (page 182) with orange and celery stuffing (page 90)

Spinach and mushroom stuffing

IMPERIAL/METRIC
1½ oz./40 g. Stork margarine
8 oz./225 g. spinach, cooked, drained and chopped
1 onion, finely chopped
4 oz./100 g. mushrooms, diced
3–4 oz./75–100 g. fresh white breadcrumbs
1 Chicken Oxo cube, crumbled
pinch nutmeg
grated rind of ½ lemon
salt and pepper
1 beaten egg to bind

Melt ½ oz. (15 g.) margarine and sauté the spinach. Melt the remaining margarine in another pan and sauté the onion for 5 minutes until soft, add the mushrooms and fry for a further 2-3 minutes. Mix with the spinach, breadcrumbs, chicken cube, nutmeg and rind. Season to taste and mix in sufficient beaten egg to bind. This is a good stuffing for fish, chicken and veal.

Mussel stuffing

IMPERIAL/METRIC
1½ oz./40 g. Stork margarine
1 onion, chopped
1 pint/575 ml. mussels, scrubbed and beards removed
1 Onion Oxo cube, crumbled and dissolved in ¼ pint/150 ml. hot water
1 clove garlic, crushed
3 oz./75 g. fresh white breadcrumbs
1 tablespoon chopped parsley
1 teaspoon chopped lemon thyme or savory
grated rind and juice of ½ lemon
1 beaten egg to bind
salt and pepper

Melt the margarine and sauté the onion for a few minutes. Place the mussels in a pan with the garlic and onion stock. Cook until the shells open, then remove the mussels and reserve the stock. Discard the mussel shells. Mix the onion, garlic, mussels, breadcrumbs, herbs and lemon rind and juice together, bind with the egg and enough of the reserved stock to make a fairly stiff consistency. Season to taste. This unusual stuffing complements fish or chicken.

Celery, apple and sweetcorn stuffing

IMPERIAL/METRIC
1½ oz./40 g. Stork margarine
1 onion, chopped
4 oz./100 g. fresh white breadcrumbs
3 sticks celery, chopped
1 dessert apple, peeled, cored and diced
7-oz./198-g. can sweetcorn
1 tablespoon chopped parsley
1 Chicken Oxo cube, crumbled
salt and pepper
little lemon juice
2–3 tablespoons cream or top of the milk

Melt the margarine and sauté the onion for 5 minutes until soft. Mix with the remaining dry ingredients. Season to taste and bind with a little lemon juice and the cream or milk. This stuffing goes well with chicken and turkey.

Variation
A bunch of finely chopped watercress may be used instead of the sweetcorn. This stuffing is very good with lamb or chicken.

Devilled rice stuffing

IMPERIAL/METRIC
1½ oz./40 g. Stork margarine
1 onion, chopped
1 clove garlic, crushed
2 oz./50 g. bacon, derinded and chopped
3 oz./75 g. long-grain rice
1 small red pepper, deseeded and chopped
3 oz./75 g. button mushrooms, sliced
1 Curry Oxo cube, crumbled and dissolved in ½ pint/275 ml. hot water
1 tablespoon chopped parsley
few snipped chives
grated rind of ½ lemon
salt and pepper

Melt the margarine and sauté the onion and garlic for 5 minutes until soft. Add the bacon and rice and fry for 3–4 minutes. Add the pepper and mushrooms and continue cooking a few minutes before adding the curry stock. Cook gently for 15–20 minutes until the rice is cooked and all the liquid is absorbed. Add the

parsley, chives and lemon rind. Season to taste. This rice stuffing goes well with chicken, lamb and beef.
Note If using to stuff a chicken, the chopped giblets may be added and fried with the onion.

Variation
Omit the mushrooms and bacon and add 2 oz. (50 g.) raisins, 1 oz. (25 g.) chopped dried apricots and 1 oz. (25 g.) chopped blanched split almonds.

Mushroom, bacon and cheese stuffing

IMPERIAL/METRIC
1½ oz./40 g. Stork margarine
2 oz./50 g. bacon, chopped
1 onion, chopped
8 oz./225 g. mushrooms, chopped
3–4 oz./75–100 g. fresh white breadcrumbs
1 Onion Oxo cube, crumbled
1 oz./25 g. Parmesan cheese, grated
cayenne pepper
dry mustard
1 tablespoon chopped parsley
salt and pepper
1 beaten egg or milk to bind

Melt the margarine and sauté the bacon and onion for 5 minutes until soft. Add the mushrooms and cook for 2–3 minutes. Mix in the remaining dry ingredients, parsley and season. Bind with the egg or milk.

Meat, poultry and game accompaniments chart

Meat, poultry or game	Type of gravy	Accompaniments	Special points
Roast beef (top side, foreribs, sirloin, fillet, aitch bone, wing rib – round)	Thin gravy, do not add too much flour	Yorkshire pudding (see page 111) Horseradish sauce (see page 130)	Roast beef should be served red or slightly pink in the middle.
Roast veal (leg, loin, boned shoulder, breast)	Thick gravy	Parsley and thyme stuffing (see page 89) Glazed onions	Veal should be served thoroughly cooked. A purée of spinach, and forcemeat stuffing flavoured with lemon thyme are also good.
Roast lamb (saddle, leg, shoulder, best end of neck)	Thicker than beef but never glutinous	Mint sauce (see page 131) Mint jelly Redcurrant jelly	Can be roasted with rosemary or garlic added. Lamb can be served very slightly pink.
Roast mutton (same joints as lamb)	As lamb	Redcurrant jelly Onion purée	
Roast pork (leg, shoulder, fillet, loin, spare ribs)	Thick gravy	Apple sauce (see page 130) Sage and onion stuffing (see page 90)	Serve meat thoroughly cooked *not* pink. Other fruits are excellent with pork, e.g. apricots, prunes, pineapple and peaches.
Baked or boiled ham		Cider sauce Horseradish sauce (see page 130)	Can be served with fruit, e.g. pineapple or peaches.
Roast chicken	Slightly thickened gravy made from giblets and stock	Crisp bacon rolls Bread sauce (see page 130) Savoury stuffing Chipolatas	Poultry should be thoroughly cooked so that joints are *not* pink.
Roast turkey	Thick gravy made from giblets and stock with a little wine if possible	Cranberry sauce Chestnut or sausage meat stuffing (see page 89) Bacon rolls, small sausages Bread sauce (see page 130)	Protect large turkeys from burning by covering with foil after several hours cooking.
Roast duck	Slightly thickened gravy made from giblets and stock with a little red wine added	Apple sauce (see page 130) Sage and onion stuffing (see page 90)	Orange salad is a good accompaniment. Cherries also make an excellent garnish.
Roast grouse	Slightly thickened gravy	Fried breadcrumbs Bread sauce (see page 130) Game chips	Watercress and apple and celery salads are particularly good.
Roast partridge	Thin gravy	Fried breadcrumbs Game chips	Apple and celery salad is good.
Roast pheasant	Thin gravy	Fried breadcrumbs Game chips Bread sauce (see page 130)	Tail feathers can be served on the bird on the table for special occasions. Hang game by the neck until you can easily pull out a tuft of feathers above the tail.
Roast pigeon	Slightly thickened gravy	As for duck	Fruit is excellent with pigeon.
Roast rabbit	Thick gravy	Stuffings as for chicken Redcurrant jelly Bread sauce (see page 130)	Try a prune stuffing for a change.
Roast hare (saddle, back and legs)	Rich, thick gravy	Herb, chestnut or sausage stuffing, or forcemeat balls served separately Redcurrant jelly	Hare should really be marinated for at least 24 hours before roasting to help flavour and tenderise.
Roast venison (loin and haunch)	Thick gravy with wine. Sour cream is a welcome addition	Redcurrant jelly	Marinate as described under hare. Good served with a purée of chestnuts.

Poultry and Game

Due to modern methods of producing poultry we now have a good selection available throughout the year of fresh and frozen chicken, turkey and duck. Chicken and turkey are excellent value for money and when used properly nothing is wasted, as even the carcass can be used to produce a delicious pot of soup.

Free range or fresh farm chickens will usually have a better flavour than a frozen battery bird. The frozen ones are, however, usually less expensive and can be made interesting by the addition of spicy sauces. For grilling, frying and roasting choose a young, tender, plump bird. A more mature bird of about one year old can be used for boiling and casseroling. They will require cooking for 2½–3 hours but are relatively inexpensive and as a bonus produce excellent stock for soup.

Allow 10 oz. (275 g.) oven-ready chicken per head, or you will need 2½–3 lb. (1¼–1½ kg.) for four people. Chicken joints are first-class stand-bys and are widely used in most homes. Chicken is now sold halved, quartered or in drumsticks and these joints are suitable for casseroling, frying or grilling. You may find it cheaper to joint a whole chicken yourself if time permits. Small turkeys are a good buy for larger families, and these are widely available all the year round.

Do make sure poultry is thoroughly thawed before cooking. Unlike meat it is not safe to cook straight from the frozen state as in the centre of the bird the frozen flesh will only warm up slowly allowing more time for bacteria to multiply.

Duck is widely available frozen but do remember that it has a lot of bone so you need to allow 12 oz.–

Poultry roasting chart

To roast	Temperature	Cooking time	Cooking time in foil (see note)
			Roast all foil-wrapped poultry in a hot oven (425°F., 220°C., Gas Mark 7).
Chicken	400°F., 200°C., Gas Mark 6	20 minutes per lb. (450 g.) and 20 minutes over	*up to 4 lb. (1¾ kg.) 30–35 minutes per lb. (450 g.)* *over 4 lb. (1¾ kg.) and up to 8 lb. (3½ kg.)* 25 minutes per lb. (450 g.)
Turkey	425°F., 220°C., Gas Mark 7 for 15 minutes, reducing to 350°F., 180°C., Gas Mark 4.	*up to 12 lb. (5½ kg.)* 15 minutes per lb. (450 g.) and 15 minutes over *over 12 lb. (5½ kg.)* 10 minutes per lb. (450 g.) and 10 minutes over	*over 8 lb. (3½ kg).* 25 minutes per lb. (450 g.)
Duck	400°F., 200°C., Gas Mark 6	20 minutes per lb. (450 g.) and 20 minutes over	30–35 minutes per lb. (450 g.)
Goose	425°F., 220°C., Gas Mark 7 for 15 minutes, reducing to 350°F., 180°C., Gas Mark 4.	15 minutes per lb. (450 g.) and 15 minutes over	25–30 minutes per lb. (450 g.)

Note When roasting poultry in foil, fold back the foil for the last 15–20 minutes of cooking time to allow the bird to brown.

Roasting stuffed poultry and game

When roasting stuffed poultry or game, weigh the bird and calculate the cooking time *after* it has been stuffed.

1 lb. (350–450 g.) dressed weight per person. Game birds can be roasted when young and used in a casserole if they are older. Most people in towns will buy them ready hung, plucked and dressed. Ask the butcher about the age of the bird to help you decide on a method of cooking.

To stuff poultry
Poultry and game can be stuffed at the neck and/or the tail end. Remember stuffed poultry or game need a longer cooking time (see chart on page 94).

To stuff the neck end, lay the prepared bird on its back, draw back the neck flap and spoon the stuffing into the cavity, pressing in firmly. Replace the flap and secure with a skewer or sew the flap back in place.

To stuff the tail end, spoon the stuffing into the body through the vent at the rear of the bird. Skewer or sew the cavity closed to keep the stuffing from falling out when cooking.

Jointing a chicken

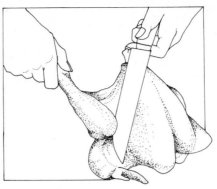

1. *Inserting a knife between the leg and body and cutting down to separate the leg from the bird, pulling the leg away with the free hand.*

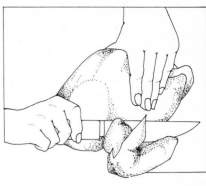

2. *Removing the wing joints carefully with a knife.*

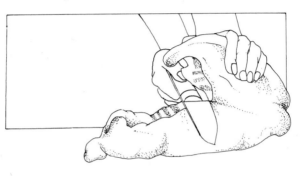

3. *Separating the breast from the lower carcass by cutting along the rib cage. The breast is then divided into two or four pieces.*

Game roasting chart

Game and season	Temperature	Cooking time	Cooking time in foil (see note)
Grouse (whole bird) 12 Aug.–10 Dec.	400°F., 200°C., Gas Mark 6	30–40 minutes per bird	50–60 minutes per bird
Partridge (whole bird) 1 Sept.–31 Jan.	400°F., 200°C., Gas Mark 6	30–45 minutes per bird	50–60 minutes per bird
Pheasant 1 Oct.–31 Jan.	400°F., 200°C., Gas Mark 6 for 15 minutes, reducing to 350°F., 180°C., Gas Mark 4	40–50 minutes for small young birds. 1–1½ hours for larger older birds.	50 minutes–1 hour for small young birds. 1¼–1¾ hours for larger older birds.
Pigeon (whole bird) all year round, best Aug.–Oct.	400°F., 200°C., Gas Mark 6	30–45 minutes per bird	50–60 minutes per bird
Rabbit all year round, best 1 Sept.–28 Feb.	400°F., 200°C., Gas Mark 6	15 minutes per lb. (450 g.) and 15 minutes over	20–25 minutes per lb. (450 g.) and 20 minutes over
Hare (marinate back or saddle to tenderise) Aug.–March	400°F., 200°C., Gas Mark 6	1½–2 hours	2–2½ hours
Venison (marinate to tenderise) late June–Jan.	400°F., 200°C., Gas Mark 6	20 minutes per lb. (450 g.) and 20 minutes over	25–30 minutes per lb. (450 g.) and 25 minutes over

Note When roasting game in foil, fold back the foil for the last 15–20 minutes of cooking time to allow the bird to brown.
Cooking times These are approximate and will vary according to the time that the game has been hung or marinated.

Poultry

Cucumbered chicken

IMPERIAL/METRIC
1 oz./25 g. Stork margarine
4 chicken portions
1 onion, finely sliced
2 tablespoons flour
2 Chicken Oxo cubes, crumbled and dissolved in ⅔ pint/400 ml. hot water
½ medium-sized cucumber, diced
salt and pepper
good squeeze lemon juice
4 tablespoons double cream

Melt the margarine and sauté the chicken portions slowly until browned. Drain well and place in a shallow ovenproof dish. Sauté the onion in the same fat for 5–10 minutes until soft but not coloured then stir in the flour. Cook for 1 minute then gradually add the chicken stock and bring to the boil. Add the cucumber, seasoning and lemon juice and pour over the chicken. Cover and cook in the middle of a moderate oven (350°F., 180°C., Gas Mark 4) for about an hour, until tender. Stir in the cream, adjust the seasoning and reheat.
Serves 4

Roast garlic chicken

IMPERIAL/METRIC
1 onion, finely chopped
salt and pepper
2 oz./50 g. fresh white breadcrumbs
2 tablespoons chopped parsley
½ teaspoon dried thyme
grated rind of ½ lemon
2 oz./50 g. garlic sausage, finely chopped
1 egg, beaten
3½-lb./1½-kg. oven-ready chicken
1½ oz./40 g. Stork margarine
2 tablespoons flour
2 Chicken Oxo cubes, crumbled and dissolved in ⅔ pint/400 ml. hot water
2 tablespoons lemon juice
Garnish
sprigs parsley

Combine the onion, seasoning, breadcrumbs, parsley, thyme, lemon rind and garlic sausage and bind together with the egg. Use to stuff the neck end of the chicken (see page 95). Secure and truss the bird then weigh it. Place in a roasting tin, season lightly and dot the margarine all over the skin. Roast in the middle of a fairly hot oven (400°F., 200°C., Gas Mark 6) for 1½–1¾ hours, allowing 15–20 minutes per lb. (450 g.) plus 20 minutes over, until tender, basting several times. Remove the bird to a serving dish and keep warm. Stir the flour into 2 tablespoons of the pan juices then slowly add the chicken stock and the lemon juice. Bring to the boil, season to taste and simmer for 2–3 minutes before serving with the chicken. Garnish with parsley and rolls of garlic sausage if liked.
Serves 6

Coq-au-vin

IMPERIAL/METRIC
1 oz./25 g. Stork margarine
4 chicken joints
4 oz./100 g. streaky bacon, diced
12 button onions, whole
1 clove garlic, crushed
2 tablespoons tomato purée
⅓ pint/200 ml. chicken stock
8 fl. oz./225 ml. red wine
pinch thyme
1 bay leaf
salt and black pepper
4 oz./100 g. button mushrooms
2 teaspoons cornflour, blended with 1 tablespoon cold water

Melt the margarine and sauté the chicken joints until golden brown; place in a casserole. Sauté the bacon, onions and garlic until golden brown. Add to the chicken. Blend the tomato purée with the chicken stock and pour over the chicken with the red wine. Add the thyme, bay leaf, seasoning and mushrooms and cover. Bake in the middle of a moderate oven (350°F., 180°C., Gas Mark 4) for 1½ hours.

Remove from the oven, skim off the excess fat and stir the cornflour and water paste into the remaining mixture. Return to the oven for 15–20 minutes. Before serving remove the bay leaf. Serve with rice and a green vegetable.
Serves 4

Roast garlic chicken

Coq-au-vin

Curried chicken mayonnaise

IMPERIAL/METRIC
3 oz./75 g. long-grain rice
1 Chicken Oxo cube, crumbled and dissolved in ⅓ pint/200 ml. hot water
3 oz./75 g. raisins
½ green pepper, diced
salt and pepper
12 oz./350 g. leftover cooked chicken, cut into small pieces, or 4 cooked chicken joints
6 tablespoons mayonnaise (see page 132)
1 Curry Oxo cube, crumbled
Garnish
½ green pepper, cut in rings
stuffed olives, sliced

Bring the rice to the boil in the chicken stock, reduce the heat to a simmer, and cook the rice until all the stock is absorbed and the rice is tender – about 15 minutes. Allow to cool. Add the raisins, diced green pepper and seasoning to taste.

Arrange the rice in a border round the edge of a dish. If using leftover cooked chicken, blend the mayonnaise with the crumbled curry cube, and fold in the chicken pieces. Pile into the centre of the dish and garnish with the rings of green pepper and the sliced stuffed olives. If using whole joints, arrange the chicken in the centre of the dish and coat with the curry flavoured mayonnaise; garnish with the pepper and olives. Serve with salad.

Serves 4

Mild chicken curry ❄

IMPERIAL/METRIC
1 lb./450 g. cooked chicken, cut into bite-sized pieces
Sauce
2 oz./50 g. Stork margarine
1 onion, finely chopped
1 apple, finely chopped
1 oz./25 g. flour
3 Curry Oxo cubes, crumbled and dissolved in 1½ pints/850 ml. hot water
salt and pepper
2 tablespoons sultanas
1 tablespoon chutney
few drops lemon juice
1 tablespoon black treacle
1 teaspoon sugar
1 tablespoon Worcestershire sauce

Melt the margarine and sauté the onion and apple until soft. Stir in the flour and cook for 2–3 minutes. Stir in the curry stock and bring to the boil. Add the remaining ingredients for the sauce and simmer for 30 minutes. Stir in the cooked chicken and simmer for a further 15–20 minutes.

Serve the curry with rice and bowls of desiccated coconut, chopped apple, chutney, cucumber, sliced banana, poppadums and a green salad.

Serves 4

Freezing note It is worthwhile making up large quantities of the curry sauce and freezing it in small portions in polythene containers or foil bags.

Variations
Substitute another cooked meat for the chicken.
Fish curry Substitute 1–1½ lb. (450–675 g.) raw chopped fish for the chicken, and simmer for 25–30 minutes in the sauce. If adding cooked fish or shellfish only cook for 5 minutes in the sauce.
For a hotter curry Add ¼ teaspoon chilli powder, ¼ teaspoon ginger, a pinch of turmeric and a pinch of cayenne pepper.

Curried chicken mayonnaise

Chicken and mushroom loaf ❄

IMPERIAL/METRIC
1 oz./25 g. Stork margarine
12 oz./350 g. chicken or turkey,
  boned and cubed
4 oz./100 g. onion, chopped
4 oz./100 g. streaky bacon, chopped
4 oz./100 g. mushrooms, chopped
4 oz./100 g. pork sausage meat
1 egg, lightly beaten
2 oz./50 g. fresh white breadcrumbs
salt and black pepper
¼ teaspoon ground nutmeg

Melt the margarine and sauté the chicken, onion and bacon for 10 minutes, adding the mushrooms for the last 5 minutes. Drain off excess liquid. Mix into the sausage meat and add the egg, breadcrumbs, seasoning and nutmeg.

Line the base of an oiled 1-lb. (450-g.) loaf tin with greaseproof paper and fill with the mixture. Bake in the middle of a moderate oven (350°F., 180°C., Gas Mark 4) for 1 hour. Serve hot or cold.

Serves 4–6
Freezing note This loaf freezes well. Cool in the tin, then turn out and wrap in cling wrap or foil.

Turkey hash

IMPERIAL/METRIC
12 oz.–1 lb./350–450 g. cooked
  turkey
10-oz./284-g. can condensed
  mushroom soup
⅓ pint/200 ml. stock
4 oz./100 g. button mushrooms,
  sliced
4 oz./100 g. sweetcorn, cooked
2 oz./50 g. cooked pasta shapes
  (optional)
Garnish
1 oz./25 g. Stork margarine
4 slices white bread, crusts
  removed, each slice cut into four
  triangles
2 tablespoons finely chopped
  parsley

Place the cooked turkey and un-diluted contents of the can of soup in a saucepan and heat slowly. Gradually blend in the stock, then add the mushrooms and simmer until they are cooked – about 10 minutes. Add the sweetcorn and

pasta shapes, if used. Heat for another 2–3 minutes.

Melt the margarine and sauté the bread until golden brown. While still hot, dip one point of each triangle in the parsley and arrange round the turkey hash in a serving dish. Sprinkle with chopped parsley.
Serves 4

Duck with cherries

IMPERIAL/METRIC
4½–5-lb./2–2¼-kg. duck
salt and pepper
15-oz./425-g. can black or red
  cherries
⅓ pint/200 ml. chicken stock
1–2 tablespoons lemon juice
1 tablespoon cornflour
Garnish
1 lemon, sliced
watercress

Place the duck in a roasting tin and prick the skin all over with a fork.

Duck with cherries

Sprinkle lightly with salt and roast in the middle of a hot oven (425°F., 220°C., Gas Mark 7) for 1¼–1½ hours. Carefully drain all the fat from the pan. Mix the cherry juice with the chicken stock and lemon juice, bring to the boil and pour over the duck. Cook for a further 20–30 minutes until tender, basting several times. Place the duck on a serving dish and keep warm. Thicken the juices with the cornflour blended in a little cold water, add the cherries, adjust the seasoning and simmer for 3–4 minutes. Pour over the duck and serve garnished with the lemon and watercress.
Serves 4

Variation
Substitute four large chicken portions for the duck. Roast the chicken in a baking tin with 1 oz. (25 g.) Stork margarine in a fairly hot oven (400°F., 200°C., Gas Mark 6) for 35–45 minutes. Continue as for duck.

Chicken Louisa

IMPERIAL/METRIC
4 large leg portions chicken
4 thin slices ham
3 tablespoons seasoned flour
1 oz./25 g. Stork margarine
1 onion, peeled and sliced
1 clove garlic, crushed
⅓ pint/200 ml. chicken stock
¼ pint/150 ml. red wine
8-oz./227-g. can tomatoes
1 red pepper, deseeded and
    sliced (optional)
salt and pepper

Carefully remove the bones from the chicken joints using a sharp knife. Roll up the ham and use to stuff the bone cavities. Secure with wooden cocktail sticks. Dip the joints in seasoned flour. Melt the margarine and sauté the joints until browned. Place in a casserole dish. Fry the onion and garlic in the same pan over a moderate heat then add 1½ tablespoons of the remaining seasoned flour, chicken stock and red wine. Bring to the boil, whisking continuously. Cook for 2–3 minutes, still whisking, until thickened. Add the tomatoes, red pepper (if used) and seasoning and pour over the chicken. Cover the casserole and cook in the middle of a moderate oven (350°F., 180°C., Gas Mark 4) for about an hour until tender. Remove the cocktail sticks before serving. **Serves 4**

Chicken Louisa

Chicken and cheese pie ❄

IMPERIAL/METRIC
1 oz./25 g. Stork margarine
1 onion, peeled and chopped
1 oz./25 g. flour
1 Chicken Oxo cube, crumbled and
    dissolved in ⅓ pint/200 ml. hot
    water
5 tablespoons milk
salt and pepper
¼ teaspoon dry mustard
2 oz./50 g. Cheddar cheese, grated
6–8 oz./175–225 g. cooked chicken
    meat, diced
1 tablespoon chopped parsley
6 oz./175 g. shortcrust pastry
    (see pages 12–13)
beaten egg or milk for glazing

Melt the margarine and sauté the onion for 5 minutes until soft but not coloured. Add the flour, chicken stock and milk to the saucepan over moderate heat. Bring to the boil, whisking continuously. Cook for 2–3 minutes, still whisking, until thickened, smooth and glossy. Season well, add the mustard and simmer for 2 minutes. Add the cheese and stir until melted then add the chicken and parsley and leave to cool. Roll out two-thirds of the pastry and use to line an 8½-inch (21-cm.) shallow tin or deep pie plate. Fill with the chicken mixture. Roll out the remaining pastry to make a lid. Damp the pastry edges and cover with the pastry. Press the edges well together and mark with a fork. Make a slit in the centre and decorate with pastry leaves made from the trimmings. Glaze with egg or milk and bake on the second shelf from the top of a hot oven (425°F., 220°C., Gas Mark 7) for 20 minutes. Reduce the heat to 350°F., 180°C., Gas Mark 4, and continue for 20–25 minutes until golden brown. Serve hot or cold. **Serves 4**

Freezing note Freeze the prepared pie before baking. Open freeze and pack in a polythene bag.

Chicken and sweetcorn pie ❄

IMPERIAL/METRIC
2 oz./50 g. Stork margarine
3½-lb./1½-kg. chicken, skinned and
    cut off the bone in 1½-inch (3-cm.)
    pieces
1 onion, chopped
1 clove garlic, crushed
1 large red pepper, sliced
1 oz./25 g. flour
½ pint/275 ml. chicken stock
pinch powdered saffron or saffron
    threads soaked for 30 minutes in
    2 tablespoons boiling water
¼ pint/150 ml. single cream
7-oz./198-g. can sweetcorn
1 tablespoon chopped parsley
salt and pepper
6 oz./175 g. flaky or rough puff
    pastry (see page 15)
beaten egg or milk for glazing

Melt the margarine and sauté the chicken pieces slowly until browned. Add the onion, garlic and red pepper and cook until soft. Add the flour, chicken stock and soaked saffron with the water to the saucepan over moderate heat. Bring to the boil, whisking continuously. Cook for 2–3 minutes, still whisking, until thickened, smooth and glossy. Add the single cream, sweetcorn and parsley and season to taste. Cool.

Place the filling in a round 2-pint (1-litre) pie dish. Roll out the chilled pastry on a lightly floured worktop to a round 1 inch (2½ cm.) larger all round than the pie dish. Cut off narrow strips round the edge of the pastry. Damp the rim and line with the pastry strips. Damp the strips and cover the filling with the remaining pastry, pressing down gently to seal. Trim, flake and flute the edges. Make a slit in the centre and decorate the top with swirls made with the back of a knife. Glaze with beaten egg or milk. Bake on the second shelf from the top of a hot oven (425°F., 220°C., Gas Mark 7) for 30 minutes, then turn the oven down to 350°F., 180°C., Gas Mark 4 and continue cooking for a further 15 minutes, when the pastry should be crisp and golden brown and the chicken filling cooked.
Serves 4–6

Freezing note Freeze the prepared pie before cooking.

Chicken pie romanoff ❄

IMPERIAL/METRIC
1½ oz./40 g. Stork margarine
4 oz./100 g. mushrooms, quartered
1 oz./25 g. flour
2 Chicken Oxo cubes, crumbled
    and dissolved in ½ pint/275 ml.
    hot water
¼ pint/150 ml. single cream
3½-lb./1½-kg. roasting chicken,
    cooked and boned
2 green peppers, sliced
salt and pepper
lemon juice
6 oz./175 g. flaky or rough puff
    pastry, well chilled (see page 15)
beaten egg or milk for glazing

Melt ½ oz. (15 g.) margarine and
sauté the mushrooms. Remove.
Place the remaining 1 oz. (25 g.)
margarine, flour and chicken stock
in a saucepan over moderate heat.
Bring to the boil, whisking continuously. Cook for 2–3 minutes,
still whisking, until thickened,
smooth and glossy. Add the cream,
cubed chicken, mushrooms and
peppers, which have been blanched
for 2 minutes in boiling water.
Season to taste and add lemon
juice. Pour into a 2-pint (1-litre)
round pie dish and leave to cool.

Roll out the chilled pastry on a
lightly floured worktop to a round
1-inch (2½ cm.) larger all round than
the pie dish. Cut off narrow strips
round the edge of the pastry. Damp
the rim and line with the pastry
strips. Damp the strips and cover
the filling with the remaining pastry,
pressing down gently to seal. Trim,
flake and flute the edges. Mark the
top of the pie in a diamond pattern
with the point of a knife. Make a
hole in the centre and decorate with
pastry leaves made from the trimmings. Glaze with beaten egg or
milk. Bake on the second shelf from
the top of a hot oven (425°F., 220°C.,
Gas Mark 7) for 30–40 minutes until
risen, crisp and browned.
Serves 4–6
Freezing note Freeze the filling
and pastry separately. Place the
pastry in a polythene bag and the
filling in a foil or polythene container. Assemble the pie and cook
when required.

Cheesy chicken and tomato pie ❄

IMPERIAL/METRIC
1 oz./25 g. Stork margarine
2 onions, sliced
1 oz./25 g. flour
1 Chicken Oxo cube, crumbled and
    dissolved in ½ pint/275 ml. hot
    water
3-lb./1¼-kg. chicken, cooked,
    boned and cut into pieces
1 teaspoon chopped fresh mixed
    herbs
1 tablespoon chopped parsley
salt and pepper
1 lb./450 g. tomatoes, skinned and
    sliced
1 teaspoon basil
2 oz./50 g. Cheddar or Parmesan
    cheese, grated
¼ pint/150 ml. cheese choux pastry
    (see page 17)
Garnish
chopped parsley

Melt the margarine and sauté the
onions for 2–3 minutes until soft.
Add the flour and chicken stock to
the saucepan over moderate heat.
Bring to the boil, whisking continuously. Cook for 2–3 minutes,
still whisking, until thickened,
smooth and glossy. Add the chicken
pieces, herbs and parsley and
season to taste. Place half the
mixture in a round 8-inch (20-cm.)
pie dish. Place on top a layer of
half the prepared tomatoes. Sprinkle
with basil. Repeat the layers.
Sprinkle with grated cheese.

Pipe the choux pastry, using a
¼-inch (½-cm.) plain pipe, in a
lattice across the top of the pie,
leaving about 1 inch (2½ cm.) between the lines. Pipe a circle round
the edge of the dish. Bake on the
second shelf from the top of a fairly
hot oven (400°F., 200°C., Gas Mark
6) for 30–40 minutes until well
puffed and golden. Sprinkle with
parsley and serve immediately.
Serves 4
Freezing note Freeze the baked
pie and wrap in foil.

Variation
Use turkey in place of chicken.

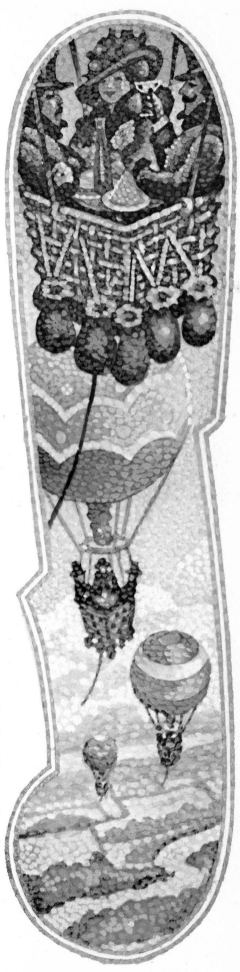

Pickled chicken puff

Pickled chicken puff ❄

IMPERIAL/METRIC
1½ oz./40 g. Stork margarine
1 onion, chopped
1 oz./25 g. flour
1 Chicken Oxo cube, crumbled and
   dissolved in ⅓ pint/200 ml. hot
   water
5 tablespoons milk
salt and pepper
10 oz./275 g. cooked chicken or
   turkey meat, diced
4 pickled walnuts, chopped, or
   2 tablespoons capers or 12 stuffed
   olives, chopped
8 oz./225 g. flaky or rough puff
   pastry (see page 15)
beaten egg or milk for glazing
Garnish
lettuce leaves
cress
tomato slices

Melt the margarine and sauté the onion for 5 minutes until soft but not coloured. Add the flour, chicken stock and milk to the saucepan over moderate heat. Bring to the boil, whisking continuously. Cook for 2–3 minutes, still whisking, until thickened, smooth and glossy. Season well, add the chicken and walnuts (or capers or olives) and simmer gently for 4–5 minutes. Leave to cool.

Roll out the pastry on a lightly floured worktop to a 12-inch (30-cm.) square and cut in half. Place one piece on a damp baking sheet and spoon the chicken mixture on top, leaving a 1-inch (2½-cm.) margin all round. Roll the other piece of pastry out to an oblong 12 inches by 7 inches (30 by 18 cm.) then carefully fold in half lengthways. Leaving a 2-inch (5-cm.) margin at each end and a 1-inch (2½-cm.) margin at the cut side, make horizontal cuts into the fold at 1-inch (2½-cm.) inter-

vals. Carefully unfold. Brush the pastry base margin with water, then place the top gently over the filling. Press the edges well together, flake and flute. Brush with beaten egg or milk and bake on the second shelf from the top of a hot oven (425°F., 220°C., Gas Mark 7) for 20 minutes. Reduce the heat to 375°F., 190°C., Gas Mark 5 for a further 15–20 minutes until golden brown. Garnish with lettuce, cress and tomato. Serve hot or cold.
Serves 4–5

Game

Jugged hare

IMPERIAL/METRIC
1 small hare, jointed (collect blood
   in a bowl while jointing)
1 tablespoon vinegar
2 oz./50 g. Stork margarine
1 onion, chopped
2 carrots, chopped
2 oz./50 g. flour
3 Chicken Oxo cubes, crumbled
   and dissolved in 1 pint/575 ml.
   hot water
¼ pint/150 ml. port
2 tablespoons cranberry or
   redcurrant jelly
bouquet garni
salt and pepper
3–4 tablespoons single cream
walnut and onion stuffing (see page
   90)

Soak the hare in enough cold water to cover, add the vinegar. Melt the margarine in a large saucepan and sauté the onion and carrot for 5 minutes. Stir in the flour and blend in the chicken stock. Bring to the boil, then simmer for 2–3 minutes until thickened. Add the port and cranberry or redcurrant jelly, bouquet garni and season to taste. Place the joints of hare in the sauce and simmer gently for 2–3 hours. Remove the bouquet garni. Mix the hare's blood with the cream and stir into the sauce. Allow to thicken but do not boil.

Make up the walnut and onion stuffing and roll into balls. Bake in a moderate oven (350°F., 180°C., Gas Mark 4) for 25 minutes. Serve the jugged hare with the walnut and onion balls.
Serves 4

Rabbit and orange casserole ❄

IMPERIAL/METRIC
1–1½ lb./450–675 g. rabbit joints
1 oz./25 g. flour
1 oz./25 g. Stork margarine
1 large onion, chopped
¼ pint/150 ml. concentrated orange juice
½ pint/275 ml. water
1 Chicken Oxo cube, crumbled and dissolved in ⅓ pint/200 ml. hot water
salt and pepper
4 oz./100 g. mushrooms, roughly chopped

Coat the rabbit joints in flour. Melt the margarine and sauté the rabbit for 10–15 minutes until golden brown. Place in a casserole. Fry the onion for 5 minutes in the remaining fat. Stir in any flour remaining after the rabbit has been coated and allow to brown. Blend in the orange juice, water, chicken stock and seasoning to taste. Pour over the rabbit in the casserole and add the mushrooms. Cover the dish and bake in a moderate oven (350°F., 180°C., Gas Mark 4) for 1–1½ hours.
Serves 4
Freezing note This casserole freezes well. Pack in a rigid polythene container or foil bag. Reduce the cooking time by 30 minutes if it is to be frozen.

Pigeon, celery and walnut casserole ❄

IMPERIAL/METRIC
4 pigeons, skinned, boned and chopped
1½ oz./40 g. seasoned flour
2 oz./50 g. Stork margarine
4 oz./100 g. streaky bacon, cut in strips
1 onion, chopped
1 small head celery, washed and sliced
2 oz./50 g. broken walnuts
2 Chicken Oxo cubes, crumbled and dissolved in 1 pint/575 ml. water
2 bay leaves
1 tablespoon chopped parsley
salt and pepper
¼ pint/150 ml. double cream
Garnish
chopped parsley

Toss the pigeon pieces in seasoned flour. Melt the margarine and sauté the bacon for 5 minutes. Add the pigeon and fry gently for 10–15 minutes until brown. Remove. Add the onion, celery and walnuts to the pan and fry for 5–7 minutes until the onion is softened. Return the pigeon mixture to the pan, add the chicken stock, bay leaves and parsley and season to taste. Cook in a covered casserole in a moderate oven (350°F., 180°C., Gas Mark 4) for 1–1½ hours. Stir in the double cream just before serving. Sprinkle with chopped parsley.
Serves 4–6
Freezing note This casserole freezes well without the cream.

Roast hare

IMPERIAL/METRIC
1 young hare, prepared
salt and pepper
¼ teaspoon ground ginger
2 tablespoons wine vinegar
¼ pint/150 ml. red wine
6 whole cloves
6 rashers streaky bacon, derinded
1½ oz./40 g. Stork margarine
1 Red Oxo cube, crumbled and dissolved in ½ pint/275 ml. hot water
grated rind and juice of 1 orange

Rub the hare with the seasoning and ginger and place in a large bowl. Pour over the vinegar and wine mixed together, add the cloves and leave to marinate for 12–24 hours in a cool place, turning the hare several times. Drain the hare, reserving the marinade, and place on a rack in a roasting tin. Cover the back of

the hare with the bacon and rub all over with margarine. Roast in a hot oven (425°F., 220°C., Gas Mark 7) for 20 minutes then reduce the heat to 350°F., 180°C., Gas Mark 4 and pour the marinade over the hare. Continue to roast for 1–1¼ hours or until the hare is tender, basting several times. Remove from the tin and keep warm. Spoon off the excess fat from the pan juices, then add the beef stock, orange rind and juice and simmer for 5 minutes. Adjust seasoning and serve the gravy separately.
Serves 5–6

Pigeon pie ❄

IMPERIAL/METRIC
2 prepared pigeons, halved
4 oz./100 g. stewing steak, finely diced
little seasoned flour
1 tablespoon dripping or cooking fat
½ teaspoon dried thyme
1 tablespoon freshly chopped parsley
salt and pepper
1 Red Oxo cube, crumbled and dissolved in ⅓ pint/200 ml. hot water
6 oz./175 g. flaky or rough puff pastry (see page 15)
beaten egg or milk for glazing

Toss the pigeons and steak in seasoned flour. Melt the dripping or cooking fat and sauté the meat for a few minutes until browned. Place in a pie dish. Sprinkle with thyme, parsley and seasoning and add the beef stock. Roll out the chilled pastry on a lightly floured worktop to 1 inch (2½ cm.) larger all round than the pie dish. Cut off narrow strips round the edge of the pastry. Damp the rim and line with the pastry strips. Damp the strips and cover the filling with the remaining pastry, pressing down gently to seal. Trim, flake and flute edges. Make a hole in the centre and decorate with pastry leaves made from the trimmings. Glaze with beaten egg or milk. Bake in a hot oven (425°F., 220°C., Gas Mark 7) for 20 minutes then reduce the heat to 350°F., 180°C., Gas Mark 4 and continue for 1–1¼ hours until the meat is tender. Cover the pastry with foil to prevent over-browning.
Serves 4

Pigeon and cranberry pie ❄️

IMPERIAL/METRIC
4 pigeons, skinned, boned and chopped
1 oz./25 g. seasoned flour
2 oz./50 g. Stork margarine
2 onions, chopped
½ oz./15 g. flour
1 Chicken Oxo cube, crumbled and dissolved in ½ pint/275 ml. hot water
8 oz./225 g. fresh or frozen cranberries
1 oz./25 g. sugar
juice and grated rind of 1 orange
pinch thyme
salt and pepper
¼ pint/150 ml. double cream
8 oz./225 g. flaky pastry (see page 15)
beaten egg or milk for glazing

Toss the pigeon pieces in seasoned flour. Melt the margarine and sauté the pieces for 10–15 minutes until browned. Remove. Add the onion to pan and cook until soft. Add the flour and cook for a few minutes before adding the chicken stock, cranberries, sugar, orange juice and rind and thyme. Return the pigeon meat to the pan and mix well. Season to taste. Cook in a casserole in a moderate oven (350°F., 180°C., Gas Mark 4) for 1 hour. Mix in the double cream and turn into a 2-pint (1-litre) pie dish to cool.

Turn the oven up to 425°F., 220°C., Gas Mark 7. Roll out the chilled pastry on a lightly floured worktop to 1 inch (2½ cm.) larger all round than the pie dish. Cut off narrow strips round the edge of the pastry. Damp the rim and line with the pastry strips. Damp the strips and cover the filling with the remaining pastry, pressing down gently to seal. Trim, flake and flute edges. Make a hole in the centre and decorate with pastry leaves made from the trimmings. Glaze with beaten egg or milk. Return the pie to the oven and cook for 35–45 minutes until the pastry is well risen and golden brown.
Serves 4–6
Note This pigeon pie makes a delightful new addition to your recipe repertoire.
Freezing note Freeze the baked pie, wrap in foil.

Variations
If fresh or frozen cranberries are unobtainable use cranberries in syrup or coarse cranberry jelly and omit the sugar.

A glass of red wine may be added; use only ⅓ pint (200 ml.) stock.

Rabbit and juniper pie ❄️

IMPERIAL/METRIC
2 oz./50 g. Stork margarine
2 lb./900 g. rabbit meat, cut into 2-inch/5-cm. pieces
1 onion, chopped
1 clove garlic, crushed
1 oz./25 g. flour
1 Chicken Oxo cube, crumbled and dissolved in ½ pint/275 ml. hot water
¼ pint/150 ml. red wine
1 tablespoon tomato purée
1 teaspoon made mustard
12 juniper berries, slightly crushed (see note)
1 bay leaf
1 tablespoon chopped parsley
salt and pepper
6 oz./175 g. streaky bacon rashers, derinded
8 oz./225 g. flaky pastry (see page 15)
beaten egg or milk for glazing

Melt the margarine and sauté the rabbit pieces for 10–15 minutes until golden brown. Add the onion and garlic and fry for 7–10 minutes until soft. Add the flour and cook for a few minutes before adding the chicken stock, wine, tomato purée and mustard. Bring to the boil, then add the juniper berries, bay leaf and parsley. Season to taste and simmer for 30 minutes on top of the cooker or in a casserole in a moderate oven (350°F., 180°C., Gas Mark 4).

Meanwhile stretch the bacon rashers with the back of a knife and cut each into two pieces. Make into small rolls and grill lightly. Place the rabbit mixture in a 2-pint (1-litre) pie dish, removing the bay leaf. Mix in the cooked bacon rolls and allow to cool.

Roll out the chilled pastry on a lightly floured worktop to 1 inch (2½ cm.) larger all round than the pie dish. Cut off narrow strips round the edge of the pastry. Damp the rim and line with the pastry strips. Damp the strips and cover the filling with the remaining pastry, pressing down gently to seal. Trim, flake and flute the edges. Cut three slits in the centre and decorate with pastry leaves made from the trimmings. Glaze with beaten egg or milk. Bake in a hot oven (425°F., 220°C., Gas Mark 7) for 45 minutes until well risen and golden brown.
Serves 4–6
Note Juniper berries grow on bushes which are found in woods and mountain gullies. The berries have a pungent flavour and are often used in marinades and for seasoning various foods, as well as in the distillation of gin.

This is an unusual pie which is suitable when entertaining.
Freezing note Open freeze the baked pie, then wrap in foil.

Hare pie ❄

IMPERIAL/METRIC
8 oz./225 g. flaky pastry, well
    chilled (see page 15)
beaten egg or milk for glazing
Marinade
½ pint/275 ml. red wine
1 onion, chopped
1 tablespoon chopped parsley
1 teaspoon mixed herbs
salt and pepper
Filling
1½ lb./675 g. hare meat (1 medium-
    sized hare), cut in 1½-inch/3-cm.
    pieces
2 oz./50 g. seasoned flour
2 oz./50 g. Stork margarine
4 oz./100 g. lean bacon, derinded
    and cut in strips
1 onion, sliced
1 clove garlic, crushed
6 oz./175 g. whole button
    mushrooms
½ pint/275 ml. chicken stock
salt and pepper

Combine the marinade ingredients
and pour over the hare pieces in a
bowl. Leave to marinate overnight.
Drain thoroughly and reserve the
marinade. Toss the hare in seasoned
flour. Melt the margarine and sauté
the hare pieces for 10–15 minutes
until browned. Remove. Add the
bacon, onion, garlic and whole
mushrooms and fry for 5–7 minutes.
Add the chicken stock and reserved
marinade. Cook for a few minutes
before mixing with the hare ; season
to taste. Place in a pie dish.

Roll out the chilled pastry on a
lightly floured worktop to 1 inch
(2½ cm.) larger all round than the
pie dish. Cut off narrow strips
round the edge of the pastry. Damp
the rim and line with the pastry
strips. Damp the strips and cover
the filling with the remaining pastry,
pressing down gently to seal. Trim,
flake and flute the edges. Cut three
slits in the centre and decorate with
pastry leaves made from the trimmings. Glaze with beaten egg or
milk. Bake in a hot oven (425°F.,
220°C., Gas Mark 7) for 30 minutes,
then reduce the temperature to
350°F., 180°C., Gas Mark 4 and continue cooking for a further 50–60
minutes, until the meat is cooked. If
the pastry browns too rapidly, cover
the pie with greaseproof paper.
Serves 4–6
Freezing note Freeze the baked
pie, wrapped in foil.

Rabbit in beer

Rabbit in beer ❄

IMPERIAL/METRIC
1¾-lb./800-g. rabbit (head
    removed), jointed
1 tablespoon seasoned flour
1 oz./25 g. Stork margarine
4 oz./100 g. streaky bacon rashers,
    derinded and chopped
1 onion, sliced
½ pint/275 ml. light ale
1 Red Oxo cube, crumbled and
    dissolved in ½ pint/275 ml. hot
    water
1 teaspoon sugar
1 tablespoon vinegar
1 bay leaf
1–2 teaspoons French mustard
12 soaked prunes (optional)
1 tablespoon cornflour, blended
    with a little cold water (optional)

Coat the rabbit joints in seasoned
flour. Melt the margarine and sauté
the rabbit gently for 10–15 minutes
until golden brown. Remove. Fry
the bacon and onion in the same fat
until browned, then pour off excess
fat. Add the ale, beef stock, sugar,
vinegar, bay leaf, mustard and the
rabbit joints. Bring to the boil, cover
and simmer for about 45 minutes
until almost tender. Add the prunes,
season to taste and continue cooking for 20–25 minutes until tender.
If you prefer a thick sauce, add the
blended cornflour during the last
10 minutes of cooking. Serve with
jacket or creamed potatoes and
green beans.
Serves 4
Note Redcurrant jelly is a good
accompaniment to all rabbit dishes.

Variation
Substitute 4 oz. (100 g.) button
mushrooms for the prunes. Add the
mushrooms 15 minutes before the
end of the cooking time.

Cheese soufflé (page 109)

106

Savoury Eggs and Cheese

Eggs and cheese are perhaps the most versatile fresh foods we have in our daily diet. They are nutritious too, for they contain ample supplies of body-building protein and health-giving vitamins and minerals. Because they are so flexible they can easily be included in our daily meals. Whenever you want a light meal or a quick snack, eggs and cheese are ideal.

Eggs

Remember there is exactly the same food value in a white egg as there is in a brown one! Vary your menu by preparing eggs in different ways. Scramble them with left-over pieces of bacon, tomato or vegetables for a delicious and unusual breakfast. A quiche lorraine (see page 111) makes an economical and tasty hot or cold midday meal or supper dish and you will impress your guests with pancakes or a fluffy soufflé omelette at dinner.

Storage Eggs should be stored in a very cool larder if they are used fairly quickly, but most people have small kitchens these days and keep them in the refrigerator. Store them pointed end down at the bottom of the fridge or in the egg storage compartment. To use for meringues or similar mixtures allow the eggs to come to room temperature. This also applies to yolks for mayonnaise.

Cracked and broken eggs can be a problem. Store whole eggs out of the shell in a small dish covered with a little water to prevent a skin forming. Add spare egg yolks to scrambled egg, omelettes, custards, sauces, mashed potatoes or use as a glaze for pastry. Make the whites into meringues.

To freeze eggs see the freezing section on page 189.

Grading Since February 1973 eggs have been labelled according to the EEC regulations. At present the size is graded as large, standard, medium and small and the quality as class A, class B and class C. The third quality is only suitable for the manufacture of foodstuffs and is not on sale in shops.

The label also carries either the date of packing or the EEC week number, which is calculated from the first Sunday in January, the week running from Sunday to Saturday. All UK packing station numbers begin with the figure 9.

Cheese

There are scores of different British and continental cheeses and most supermarkets have a very good selection.

Use firm-textured Cheddar for your basic cooking needs in sauces and omelettes. Lancashire is the traditional cheese for toasting. Parmesan, a very hard Italian cheese, is used in this country grated on such dishes as spaghetti bolognese and minestrone soup. Try the more unusual continental cheeses such as Camembert, Brie, Bel Paese and Gorgonzola and see which ones the family favours.

Storage Store cheese under a ventilated cover in a cool place, or in a refrigerator, well away from the freezing unit, wrapped in foil, cling film or polythene. Remember to remove from the refrigerator at least one hour before serving.

Cheese freezes extremely well; wrap in foil in family-sized pieces and remember to thaw out in the refrigerator overnight. Firm cheese grates well straight from the freezer. Any small pieces of hard cheese can be grated for topping dishes and kept in a polythene bag in the freezer or screw-top jar in the refrigerator.

Ham and cheese soufflé

Savoury cheese and tomato rarebit

IMPERIAL/METRIC
1 oz./25 g. Stork margarine
1 oz./25 g. flour
1 Onion Oxo cube, crumbled
¼ pint/150 ml. milk
1 teaspoon French mustard
1 tablespoon tomato sauce or purée
salt and pepper
8 oz./225 g. cheese, grated
4 large slices toast spread with
   Stork margarine
Garnish
tomato slices
chopped parsley

Place the margarine, flour, onion cube, milk, mustard, tomato purée and seasoning in a saucepan over moderate heat. Bring to the boil, whisking continuously, and simmer for 2–3 minutes until smooth and thick. Stir in most of the cheese and allow to melt slowly. Pour over the slices of toast, sprinkle the remaining cheese on top, garnish with slices of tomato and brown under a hot grill for a few minutes. Sprinkle with parsley and serve.
Serves 4

Ham and celery au gratin

IMPERIAL/METRIC
4 slices cooked ham
1 lb. 2½-oz./524-g. can celery
   hearts
½ pint/275 ml. cheese sauce, with
   1 crumbled Onion Oxo cube
   added (see page 130)
½ oz./15 g. breadcrumbs, dried
   golden brown
2 oz./50 g. cheese, grated.

Wrap a slice of ham round each celery heart and place in an ovenproof dish. Pour over the sauce and sprinkle with the breadcrumbs and then the grated cheese. Bake in a fairly hot oven (400°F., 200°C., Gas Mark 6) for 20–30 minutes.
Serves 4

Variation
Use four cooked leeks in place of the celery hearts. Garnish with chopped chives.

Ham and cheese soufflé ❄

IMPERIAL/METRIC
3 large eggs, separated
½ pint/275 ml. coating sauce (see
   page 130), slightly cooled
½ oz./15 g. gelatine
4 tablespoons water
8 oz./225 g. cooked ham, chopped
2 oz./50 g. Cheddar cheese, grated
2 tablespoons chopped parsley
   (optional)
salt and pepper
¼ pint/150 ml. single cream
Garnish
cucumber, sliced
radish, sliced
sprig parsley

Beat the egg yolks into the sauce. Dissolve the gelatine in the water and add to the sauce; leave until beginning to set. Stir in the ham, cheese, parsley, seasoning and cream. Whisk the egg whites until stiff, then fold into the ham mixture. Tie a double band of greaseproof paper around a 1-pint (½-litre) soufflé dish, so that it stands 3 inches (7 cm.) above the rim. Pour the mixture in and leave in a cool place to set.

   Remove the greaseproof paper carefully using the blade of a knife to ease it away. Garnish with cucumber, radish and parsley.
Serves 4
Freezing note Open freeze then wrap in a polythene bag. Add the garnish on thawing.

1. *Whisking the margarine, flour, milk and seasonings in a saucepan over moderate heat.*

2. *Continuously whisking the thickened sauce while on the boil.*

3. *Adding the egg yolks to the cooled sauce and beating them in thoroughly.*

4. *Folding the grated cheese into the mixture with a metal spoon.*

5. *Mixing the whisked egg whites thoroughly into the mixture with the metal spoon.*

6. *Pouring the cheese soufflé mixture into a greased 7-inch (18-cm.) soufflé dish.*

Cheese soufflé

IMPERIAL/METRIC
2 oz./50 g. Stork margarine
2 oz./50 g. plain flour
½ pint/275 ml. milk
salt and pepper
¼ teaspoon cayenne pepper
pinch dry mustard
3 large eggs, separated
4 oz./100 g. Cheddar or Cheshire
　cheese, grated

Place the margarine, flour, milk and seasonings in a saucepan over a moderate heat and bring to the boil, whisking continuously (see steps 1 and 2). Cook for 1–2 minutes then allow to cool.

　Beat the egg yolks into the sauce (step 3). Fold in the grated cheese (step 4). Whisk the egg whites and fold into the mixture with a metal spoon (step 5).

　Pour into a greased 7-inch (18-cm.) soufflé dish (step 6). Place on a baking sheet. Bake in the middle of a moderately hot oven (375°F., 190°C., Gas Mark 5) for 40–45 minutes. Serve immediately.
Serves 4

Variations
Use 4 oz. (100 g.) chopped ham, shrimps or tuna instead of cheese. *Illustrated on page 106*

Soufflé omelette

IMPERIAL/METRIC
2 large eggs, separated
2 tablespoons hot water
salt and pepper
½ oz./15 g. Stork margarine

Whisk the egg yolks with the water until pale yellow. Whisk the egg white until stiff and fold into the yolks. Season. Melt the margarine in a 6-inch (15-cm.) omelette pan ensuring that the whole surface of the pan is coated. Pour in the egg mixture and cook gently until fluffy and golden brown on the underside. Place under a hot grill for a few minutes to allow the surface to cook. Cover with any filling to be used, fold in half and slide out of the pan on to a hot plate, and serve.
Serves 1–2

Savoury fillings
Allow 2 rashers crisp fried bacon, crumbled, per person.

　Add 1–2 teaspoons chopped fresh herbs.

　Allow 2 oz. (50 g.) cooked smoked haddock per person.

　Crumble ¼ Curry Oxo cube into the centre of each omelette.

　Mix ¼ Onion Oxo cube with a little natural yogurt and 1 tablespoon chopped cucumber and pour over the folded omelette.

Sweet fillings
Omit the pepper and salt from the mixture. Allow 2 tablespoons sweetened apple purée, 1 tablespoon heated jam, or ½ banana, mashed with a little lemon juice, per serving. Spoon the filling on to the omelette, fold and sprinkle with icing sugar.

Pancakes with tuna and pepper filling

Basic pancake batter ❄

IMPERIAL/METRIC
1 large egg, separated
salt
¼ teaspoon finely grated lemon rind
4 oz./125 g. plain flour
½ pint/275 ml. milk
1 oz./25 g. Stork margarine, melted
Stork margarine or oil for frying

Beat the egg yolk, ¼ teaspoon salt and the lemon rind together. Sieve the flour with a pinch of salt into a mixing bowl, then gradually add the milk, beating until smooth, to form a mixture the consistency of thick cream. Beat in the egg yolk mixture and strain through a fine sieve. Add the melted margarine. Beat the egg white stiffly and fold in.

Heat a 6-inch (15-cm.) frying pan, brush with margarine, and pour in enough batter to cover the surface of the pan thinly. Cook over a high to moderate heat until lightly browned and puffed. Turn and cook for 1 minute. Turn out on to grease-proof paper sprinkled with castor sugar and sprinkle with castor

sugar and lemon juice. Roll up, place on a plate and keep hot in the oven. Alternatively keep warm on a plate and fill with any of the suggested fillings.

Makes 8 pancakes

Freezing note Freeze pancakes in a rigid polythene container with cling film or greaseproof dividers.

Variations

Savoury pancakes Omit the lemon rind and add 1 Red, Curry or Chicken Oxo cube if liked, crumbled into the flour. Fill with any of the savoury fillings below.

Savoury fillings

Tuna and pepper Blanch 1 green pepper, chopped and deseeded, in boiling water for 1–2 minutes. Melt 1 oz. (25 g.) Stork margarine, blend in 1 oz. (25 g.) flour and cook for a few moments. Add 3 tablespoons top of the milk, 1 small carton yogurt, the pepper, 1 7-oz. (198-g.) can tuna fish and salt and pepper. Fill the pancakes, roll up and place in an ovenproof dish, cover and reheat in a moderate oven (350°F., 180°C., Gas Mark 4) for 15–20 minutes.

Chicken and cheese Make a coating sauce (see page 130) using half milk and half chicken stock made by crumbling 1 Chicken Oxo cube into ¼ pint (150 ml.) hot water. Stir in 8 oz. (225 g.) chopped cooked chicken, 2 oz. (50 g.) grated cheese and seasoning to taste. Fill the pancakes. Roll up and sprinkle with 2 oz. (50 g.) grated cheese mixed with 1 oz. (25 g.) dried breadcrumbs and ½ crumbled Onion Oxo cube if liked. Reheat at 400°F., 200°C., Gas Mark 6 for 15–20 minutes.

Sweet fillings

Banana with chopped nuts Peel and slice 2 bananas and sauté in a pan in 2 oz. (50 g.) Stork margarine until lightly cooked. Add 1 oz. (25 g.) chopped nuts. Use to fill pancakes. *Pear and almond* Cream together 4 oz. (100 g.) Stork margarine and 2 oz. (50 g.) icing sugar until light and fluffy. Stir in 2 oz. (50 g.) ground almonds, ¼ teaspoon almond essence, the grated rind of 1 lemon and a 15-oz. (425-g.) can diced pears. Use to fill pancakes.

Bacon and smoked cheese pies ❄

IMPERIAL/METRIC
8 oz./225 g. shortcrust pastry (see pages 12–13)
1 oz./25 g. Stork margarine
4 oz./100 g. streaky bacon, chopped
1 onion, chopped
3 oz./75 g. smoked cheese, grated
2 eggs
¼ pint/150 ml. milk
1 Onion Oxo cube, crumbled
½ teaspoon dry mustard
salt and black pepper
beaten egg or milk for glazing

Prepare the pastry and roll out thinly on a floured worktop. Use half to line four individual pie or flan dishes about 4 inches (10 cm.) in diameter.

Melt the margarine and sauté the bacon and onion for 5–10 minutes then drain off excess fat and divide the bacon and onion between the pastry cases. Sprinkle over the grated cheese. Whisk together the eggs, milk, onion cube, mustard and seasoning, and pour into the pastry cases.

Roll out the remaining pastry, damp the rims of the bases and cover the pies, sealing the edges well. Make a hole in the centre of each and decorate with pastry leaves. Brush with beaten egg or milk. Bake in a fairly hot oven (400°F., 200°C., Gas Mark 6) for 30–35 minutes. Serve hot or cold – these are excellent for a picnic.

Serves 4

Freezing note Freeze the baked pies in a rigid polythene container.

Macaroni cheese with crunchy topping

IMPERIAL/METRIC
8 oz./225 g. macaroni
1 oz./25 g. Stork margarine
1 small onion, chopped
2 oz./50 g. streaky bacon, chopped
Sauce
1 pint/575 ml. coating sauce (see page 130)
1 teaspoon dry mustard
1 Onion Oxo cube, crumbled
8 oz./225 g. Cheddar cheese, grated
6 black olives (optional)
Topping
1 small packet Twiglets

Cook the macaroni in boiling salted water for 15–20 minutes or according to the instructions on the packet, then drain and rinse well in hot water. Meanwhile melt the margarine and sauté the onion and bacon. Make the sauce, adding mustard and onion cube. Add the macaroni, bacon, onion and three-quarters of the cheese. Stir in the chopped black olives if used. Pour into an ovenproof dish and sprinkle with the remaining grated cheese. Bake in a fairly hot oven (400°F., 200°C., Gas Mark 6) for 20–30 minutes or until the cheese is golden brown. Arrange the Twiglets on top in a pattern and return to the oven for 5–10 minutes. Sprinkle with parsley.

Serves 4

Yorkshire pudding

IMPERIAL/METRIC
4 oz./125 g. plain flour
salt and pepper
2 eggs
½ pint/275 ml. milk
1 oz./25 g. cooking fat

Place the flour and seasoning in a mixing bowl and make a well in the centre. Add the eggs and mix well. Stir in the milk gradually and beat with a wooden spoon for 4–5 minutes. Allow to stand for 30 minutes before using.

Melt the cooking fat in a 7- by 11-inch (18- by 28-cm.) baking tin or in a tray of 15 patty tins in the oven until really hot. Pour in the batter. Bake near the top of a hot oven (425°F., 220°C., Gas Mark 7) for 40–45 minutes for the large tin and 20–25 minutes for the individual tins.

Serves 4–6

Illustrated on page 56

Quiche lorraine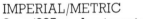

IMPERIAL/METRIC
8 oz./225 g. shortcrust pastry (see pages 12–13)
3 oz./75 g. bacon rashers, chopped
3 oz./75 g. Gruyère or Cheddar cheese, grated
2 large eggs
¼ pint/150 ml. milk or cream
salt and pepper
2 tablespoons chopped chives

Make up the pastry. Roll it out on a lightly floured worktop and line an 8-inch (20-cm.) flan ring on a baking sheet. Chill for about 20 minutes. Sprinkle the bacon and cheese on the base of the flan. Whisk the eggs, milk or cream, seasoning and chives together and pour into the flan case. Bake on the second shelf from the top of a fairly hot oven (400°F., 200°C., Gas Mark 6) for 15 minutes. Reduce the heat to 350°F., 180°C., Gas Mark 4 and bake for a further 10–15 minutes.

Serves 4

Freezing note Wrap in foil or a polythene bag.

Variations
Asparagus quiche Substitute 1 10-oz. (283-g.) can drained asparagus tips for the bacon. Place the asparagus in a wheel design (see below).
Tomato and onion quiche Substitute 3 skinned and sliced tomatoes and 1 onion, finely chopped and sautéed in ½ oz. (15 g.) Stork margarine, for the bacon and cheese.

Asparagus quiche

Vegetables & Salads

In this country we have not enjoyed a good reputation for serving vegetables and salads, although this is gradually improving. The main fault in cooking vegetables is prolonged boiling which gives a soggy and unappetising appearance and spoils the nutrient value. Cook green vegetables in a small amount of boiling salted water until *just* tender, using the vegetable cooking water for soup or gravy.

Vegetables

It is helpful to know the many ways of making full use of vegetables as they are now so costly for most of the year. A vegetable with a tasty sauce and some eggs, cheese or left-over chopped cooked meat makes a dish which is a meal in itself. Remember to make soup with the outer leaves and stalks of vegetables such as cauliflower, also left-over salad ingredients such as watercress and the outside leaves of lettuce. Tomatoes, peppers, aubergines and cabbage leaves can be stuffed with rice mixed with minced beef or chicken, and served with a sauce this makes a nutritious, filling yet economical meal.

Sprinkle some herbs on your vegetables to give extra flavour – savory with broad beans, tarragon and basil with tomatoes, chervil with carrots, and parsley, mint, basil, tarragon or chives may be snipped over salads.

Green vegetables keep well in the refrigerator if they are washed and put in a plastic box. Do be careful about storing vegetables in polythene bags as they tend to become soft and unpleasant – root vegetables in particular do not like to be closed up. Prepacked, pre-washed vegetables should be used promptly as they do not keep as well as 'straight from the garden' vegetables.

Use the chart on the next page to help you cook your vegetables to perfection.

Salads

The types of salads which can be served are endless. The salad recipes in this chapter give many new ideas for rice and potato salads, coleslaws and salads including fruits – proving that there is much more to a salad than lettuce, tomatoes and cucumber. Remember to add a little chopped celery, green or red pepper, onions or a few nuts to a basic salad to give variation in colour and textures. Do remember that salads can also bring variety to winter meals and hard white cabbage, carrots, chicory, celery, cauliflower and beetroot all make excellent winter salads.

As salad vegetables are particularly expensive these days, it is more economical to serve the salad cream or French dressing separately so that the left-over salad vegetables can be stored in polythene containers in the refrigerator, to be used at another meal.

A selection of fresh vegetables and salad ingredients

Vegetables preparation and cooking chart

Vegetable	Method of preparation and cooking	Time	Quantities for four (uncooked)
Artichokes (Jerusalem)	Peel and place immediately in cold water with a little lemon juice added. Cook in boiling salted water with lemon. Drain and serve with a white sauce or with a little melted margarine.	15–20 minutes	1½ lb./675 g.
Asparagus	Trim the stems removing any woody parts and tie in one or individual bundles. Place upright in boiling salted water, keeping the green heads above water (a round grater stood in the saucepan is often useful for this). Drain and serve hot with melted margarine or Hollandaise sauce (see page 130) or cold with French dressing (see page 131) or mayonnaise (see page 132).	10–15 minutes	6–8 stems per person
Beans (Broad)	Pod and cook in boiling salted water. Drain and serve with parsley sauce (see page 130).	10–15 minutes	2 lb./900 g.
Beans (Runner and French)	Top and tail and remove any stringy pieces. Slice thinly into 2-inch (5-cm.) pieces or leave French beans whole. Cook in boiling salted water. Drain and toss in melted margarine.	10–15 minutes	1–1½ lb./450–675 g.
Broccoli (Dark green and purple-flowering)	Trim, removing any coarse stems or outer leaves. Cook in boiling salted water. Drain and serve hot with melted margarine or Hollandaise sauce (see page 130).	10–15 minutes	1½–2 lb./675–900 g.
Brussels sprouts	Trim outer leaves and cut a cross in the stalk. Cook in the minimum of boiling salted water.	10–15 minutes	1½ lb./675 g.
Cabbage	Trim, quarter and remove core. Cook either in wedges or shredded, in boiling salted water. Drain well.	wedges 10–15 minutes; shredded 5–8 minutes	1 lb./450 g.
Carrots	Peel or scrape. Cook whole or sliced in boiling salted water with a pinch of sugar. Drain and toss in melted margarine and chopped parsley.	10–20 minutes	1–1½ lb./450–675 g.
Cauliflower	Remove damaged leaves. If cooking whole cut a cross in the base of the stem; or divide into florets. Cook in boiling salted water (with a little lemon juice added to keep it white). Drain and serve with a white, cheese or parsley sauce (see page 130).	10–20 minutes	1 large
Celery	Remove the green tops and any damaged outer stalks. Separate the sticks and scrub clean. Cut into even lengths and cook in boiling salted water. Serve with a white, cheese or parsley sauce (see page 130).	15–20 minutes	2 heads
Corn	Remove husks and any silky threads. Cook in unsalted boiling water with a good pinch of sugar. Serve with plenty of melted margarine and black pepper.	10–20 minutes	1 cob per person
Courgettes	Trim the ends, do not peel. Leave whole or slice. Cook in boiling salted water. Drain and toss in melted margarine.	5–10 minutes	1 lb./450 g.
Leeks	Cut off the roots and green tops. Slice lengthways, open out and clean. Cook in boiling salted water. Drain and serve with a white or cheese sauce (see page 130).	whole 15–20 minutes; sliced 10 minutes	1½ lb./675 g.
Marrow	Peel and remove inner seeds. Cut into thick rings or cubes. Cook in boiling salted water. Drain and serve with a white sauce (see page 130).	10 minutes	1½ lb./675 g.
Onions	Peel and slice or leave whole. Cook in boiling salted water. Alternatively, slice and sauté in hot fat; or slice, dip in milk, then toss in flour and deep-fry.	sliced 10 minutes; whole 20–30 minutes 3 minutes	1–1½ lb./450–675 g.
Parsnips	Peel and cut into quarters. Cook in boiling salted water. Drain and toss in melted margarine or mash with melted margarine and a little black pepper. Alternatively, parboil for 5 minutes and roast around a joint of meat.	30–40 minutes 1 hour	1½ lb./675 g.
Peas	Pod and cook in boiling salted water with mint and a pinch of sugar.	15–20 minutes	1 lb./450 g.
Potatoes	Scrape new or peel old potatoes. Place old ones in cold salted water and bring to the boil. Place new ones in boiling salted water with a sprig of mint. Old potatoes of even medium size can be scrubbed and baked in their skins. Prick or cut a cross in each one and bake in a fairly hot oven (400°F., 200°C., Gas Mark 6).	20–30 minutes; 15–20 minutes 1–1¾ hours	1½–2 lb./675–900 g. 1 per person
Spinach	Wash well in several changes of water. Do not dry. Place in a saucepan without any extra water and cook covered, with a little salt. Drain and chop. Toss in margarine.	5–10 minutes	2 lb./900 g.
Swedes	Peel thickly to remove inner coarse layer and slice or cut into cubes. Cook in boiling salted water. Drain and mash with freshly ground black pepper and margarine.	15–20 minutes	1½ lb./675 g.
Turnips	Peel and slice or if young leave whole. Cook in boiling salted water. Drain and serve with a white sauce (see page 130).	15–20 minutes	1½ lb./675 g.

French beans with bacon ❄

IMPERIAL/METRIC
1 lb./450 g. small French beans,
    topped and tailed
1 oz./25 g. Stork margarine
6 oz./175 g. streaky bacon,
    derinded and diced
1 onion, chopped
1 clove garlic, crushed
1 Chicken Oxo cube, crumbled and
    dissolved in ¼ pint/150 ml. hot
    water
1 tablespoon tomato purée
salt and pepper
chopped parsley

Blanch the beans in boiling salted
water for 2–3 minutes. If using large
beans break in half. Drain. Melt the
margarine and sauté the bacon,
onion and garlic for about 5 minutes
until soft; add the chicken stock and
tomato purée and season to taste.
Simmer for 10 minutes, then add the
beans and cook for a further 10
minutes until the beans are tender
and the liquid is reduced. Turn into
a serving dish and sprinkle with
parsley.
Serves 4

Cauliflower indienne

IMPERIAL/METRIC
1 large cauliflower, broken into
    sprigs
1 oz./25 g. Stork margarine
1 onion, finely chopped
½ oz./15 g. flour
1 Curry Oxo cube, crumbled and
    dissolved in ½ pint/275 ml. hot
    water
salt and pepper
¼ pint/150 ml. yogurt or double
    cream
salted cashew nuts, chopped
paprika pepper

Blanch the cauliflower sprigs in
boiling salted water for 10 minutes.
Drain. Melt the margarine and sauté
the onion for 5 minutes until soft.
Add the flour and curry stock and
cook for 2–3 minutes until smooth
and thickened. Season to taste. Add
the cauliflower and simmer for
7–10 minutes until tender. Stir in the
yogurt or cream carefully and turn
into a serving dish. Top with nuts
and sprinkle with paprika.
Serves 4

Aubergines au gratin

Aubergines au gratin ❄

IMPERIAL/METRIC
2 medium-sized aubergines, cut into
    ½-inch (1-cm.) cubes
salt and pepper
2¾ oz./70 g. Stork margarine
1 onion, sliced
¾ oz./20 g. flour
½ pint/275 ml. milk
2 oz./50 g. cheese, grated
cayenne pepper
12 oz./350 g. tomatoes, skinned
    and sliced
little grated Parmesan cheese
anchovy fillets
extra Stork margarine

Sprinkle the aubergines with salt.
Leave for 30 minutes. Rinse and dry
the aubergine. Melt 2 oz. (50 g.) of
the margarine and sauté the onion
and aubergine for about 5 minutes
until soft. Place the remaining margarine, flour and milk in a saucepan
over a moderate heat. Bring to the
boil, whisking continuously. Cook
for 2–3 minutes, still whisking, until
smooth. Add the grated cheese and
season to taste.

Layer half of the aubergines,
tomatoes and sauce in a greased
ovenproof dish. Repeat the layers
and sprinkle with Parmesan cheese.
Cut the anchovy fillets in half
lengthways and arrange in a lattice
pattern on top. Dot with a little extra
margarine. Bake in a moderately
hot oven (375°F., 190°C., Gas Mark
5) for 30 minutes.
Serves 4
Freezing note Prepare and bake
the aubergines in a moulded foil
container.

Sweet and sour red cabbage

Butter beans with gammon

IMPERIAL/METRIC
12 oz./350 g. butter beans or 8 oz./
   225 g. small haricot beans, soaked
   overnight
1 oz./25 g. Stork margarine
2 large onions, chopped
1 clove garlic, crushed
6 oz./175 g. lean gammon, diced
1 Chicken Oxo cube, crumbled and
   dissolved in 1 pint/575 ml. hot
   water
salt and pepper
8 oz./225 g. tomatoes, skinned,
   deseeded and coarsely chopped
¼ pint/150 ml. single cream
pinch basil
3 teaspoons chopped parsley or
   chives

Drain the beans thoroughly. Melt
the margarine and sauté the onion,
garlic and gammon for about 5
minutes until lightly browned. Add
the beans and chicken stock. Season
to taste and simmer for 1–1½ hours
until the beans are tender and the
liquid is reduced. Add tomatoes,
cream, pinch basil and 2 teaspoons
parsley or chives. Cook for 5
minutes. Check seasoning and
spoon into a serving dish. Sprinkle
with remaining parsley or chives.
Serves 4
Freezing note Add the cream and
herbs on reheating.

Sweet and sour red cabbage ❄

IMPERIAL/METRIC
2 oz./50 g. Stork margarine
2 medium-sized onions, chopped
1 clove garlic, crushed
4 oz./100 g. bacon, diced
1 medium-sized red cabbage,
   washed, cored and finely
   shredded
1 Red Oxo cube, crumbled and
   dissolved in ⅓ pint/200 ml. hot
   water
3 tablespoons red wine vinegar
3 tablespoons honey or brown sugar
grated rind and juice of ½ orange
pinch powdered cloves
salt and pepper
2 cooking apples, peeled, cored
   and chopped

Melt the margarine and sauté the
onion, garlic and bacon for 5
minutes until beginning to brown.
Add the cabbage, beef stock, vinegar, honey or sugar, orange rind
and juice, cloves and seasoning.
Cover and simmer for 30 minutes,
stirring occasionally. Add the apples
and cook for a further 15–20 minutes until tender. Raise the temperature to reduce the liquid if necessary
before serving.
Serves 4
Freezing note Red cabbage freezes
well. Reheat gently.

Variation
Layer the onion mixture, cabbage
and apple in a casserole and cook
in a moderate oven (350°F., 180°C.,
Gas Mark 4) for 1½ hours. Use red
wine instead of stock.

Braised celery with walnuts

IMPERIAL/METRIC
1 head celery, washed, trimmed
   and cut in ½-inch (1-cm.) strips
1 oz./25 g. Stork margarine
1 onion, finely chopped
¼ pint/150 ml. stock
salt and pepper
2 oz./50 g. broken walnuts
chopped parsley

Blanch the celery in boiling salted
water, then drain and dry. Melt the
margarine and sauté the onion and
celery for 5–7 minutes until soft.
Add the stock and seasoning and
simmer until just tender, about 10
minutes. Add the walnuts, toss carefully and heat through. Turn into a
dish and sprinkle with parsley.
Serves 4

Carrots and onions in a creamy sauce

IMPERIAL/METRIC
1 oz./25 g. Stork margarine
8 oz./225 g. button onions, skinned
1 lb./450 g. new carrots, scraped
    and quartered
1 Chicken Oxo cube, crumbled and
    dissolved in ½ pint/275 ml. hot
    water
½ oz./15 g. sugar
salt and pepper
¼ pint/150 ml. double cream
½ tablespoon chopped parsley
2 oz./50 g. cheese, grated

Melt the margarine in a deep pan and sauté the onions and carrots for 5–10 minutes until beginning to brown. Add the chicken stock and sugar. Season and cook for 20–25 minutes until the vegetables are tender and the liquid is reduced to a syrupy consistency. Adjust the seasoning. Add the cream and parsley and spoon into an ovenproof serving dish. Sprinkle with grated cheese and brown under a hot grill.
Serves 4

Variation
Large spring onions may be used if button onions are not available. Trim off the top ½ inch (1 cm.) of the green part, chop the remaining tops finely and mix in. If using large carrots, peel and cut into 2-inch (5-cm.) long matchsticks.

Leeks and bacon

IMPERIAL/METRIC
1 lb./450 g. leeks, trimmed, washed
    and cut in 1½-inch (4-cm.) lengths
1 oz./25 g. Stork margarine
6 oz./175 g. streaky bacon, cut into
    strips
salt and pepper
Garnish
chopped parsley

Cook the leeks in boiling salted water for 10 minutes, then drain thoroughly. Melt the margarine and sauté the bacon for 5 minutes until browned. Remove. Add the leeks and sauté for 5–7 minutes until cooked. Return the bacon to the pan. Mix well, season to taste and garnish with parsley.
Serves 4

Stuffed onions

IMPERIAL/METRIC
4 large Spanish onions, peeled
1 oz./25 g. Stork margarine
1 clove garlic, crushed
1 Curry Oxo cube mixed with 2
    tablespoons boiling water
3–4 oz./75–100 g. cooked ham,
    chopped
pinch sage
1 teaspoon chopped parsley
salt and pepper
browned breadcrumbs
1 oz./25 g. Stork margarine, melted

Boil the onions whole in water for 20 minutes. Drain well. Remove the centre of the onions using a sharp knife. Place the hollowed-out onions in an ovenproof dish. Chop the centres from the onions. Melt the margarine and sauté the garlic and chopped onion for 5 minutes until soft. Add the curry stock, ham, sage and parsley. Season to taste. Fill the onions with the mixture. Top with breadcrumbs and spoon over the melted margarine. Cover with foil. Cook in a moderate oven (350°F., 180°C., Gas Mark 4) for 30 minutes until browned.
Serves 4

Variation
Diced leftover chicken or flaked tuna fish may be used instead of ham. Omit the breadcrumb topping and pour over ½ pint (275 ml.) curried béchamel sauce (see page 130). Cook in an ovenproof dish covered with foil as before. Sprinkle over a little Parmesan cheese and return to the oven or place under a preheated grill to brown.

Danish cauliflower gratin ❄

IMPERIAL/METRIC
1 large cauliflower, broken into
    sprigs
1 oz./25 g. Stork margarine
6 oz./175 g. lean bacon, cut into
    pieces
¾ oz./20 g. flour
1 Onion Oxo cube, crumbled and
    dissolved in ⅓ pint/200 ml. hot
    water
2–3 tablespoons cream
salt and pepper
2 oz./50 g. cheese, grated

Cook the cauliflower in boiling salted water for 10–15 minutes until almost cooked. Drain. Melt the margarine and sauté the bacon for 5 minutes until browned. Remove. Add the flour and onion stock to the remaining margarine and bacon fat, bring to the boil over a moderate heat, whisking continuously. Cook for 2–3 minutes, still whisking, until smooth. Add the cream and season to taste. Combine the cauliflower and bacon and place in an ovenproof serving dish. Pour over the sauce. Sprinkle with grated cheese and place under a preheated hot grill for 5 minutes until browned.
Serves 4
Freezing note Put the cauliflower, bacon and sauce in a moulded foil pie dish and sprinkle on the cheese. Freeze. Reheat from frozen in a moderately hot oven (375°F., 190°C., Gas Mark 5) for 30 minutes. Brown under the grill if necessary.

Courgette and tomato casserole

IMPERIAL/METRIC
2 oz./50 g. margarine
1 onion, chopped
1 lb./450 g. courgettes, cut
    diagonally in ¼-inch (½-cm.)
    slices
1 lb./450 g. tomatoes, skinned and
    sliced
2 teaspoons fresh chopped mint
salt and pepper
¼ pint/150 ml. stock
2 oz./50 g. fresh white
    breadcrumbs
Garnish
chopped parsley

Melt 1 oz. (25 g.) margarine and sauté the onion for 5 minutes until soft. Add the courgettes and fry for 5–7 minutes until beginning to brown. Layer in an ovenproof dish with the tomato, mint and seasoning. Pour over the stock.
Fry the breadcrumbs in the remaining margarine until crisp and golden. Spoon over the courgette mixture. Bake in a moderate oven (350°F., 180°C., Gas Mark 4) for 30 minutes. Garnish with parsley.
Serves 4
Note This dish is delicious with a grilled steak or roasted joint of any other meat.

Stuffed peppers ❄

IMPERIAL/METRIC
4 green or red peppers
2 oz./50 g. Stork margarine
4 oz./100 g. long-grain rice
**1 Chicken Oxo cube, crumbled and
dissolved in ½ pint/275 ml. hot
water**
1 onion, finely chopped
2 oz./50 g. mushrooms, sliced
**3 hard-boiled eggs, chopped
parsley**
2 tablespoons cream (optional)
salt and pepper
**1 Red Oxo cube, crumbled and
dissolved in ⅓ pint/200 ml. hot
water**
2 tablespoons tomato purée

Remove the tops from the peppers
and reserve. Scoop out the pith and
seeds. Blanch the peppers for 5
minutes in boiling water, drain well.
    Melt 1 oz. (25 g.) of the margarine
and sauté the rice for a few minutes
until beginning to colour, then add
the chicken stock. Bring to the boil
and simmer until the rice is cooked
and the liquid is absorbed – about
20–30 minutes. Meanwhile melt the
remaining margarine and sauté the
onion for 2–3 minutes until soft. Add
the mushrooms and cook for a few
minutes. Add to the cooked rice
with the hard-boiled egg, parsley
and cream, if used. Season to taste
and spoon the mixture into the
peppers. Return the tops and place
in a shallow ovenproof dish. Pour
the beef stock and tomato purée
over the peppers. Cook in a moderate oven (350°F., 180°C., Gas Mark
4) for 35–45 minutes until tender,
basting occasionally.
Serves 4
Note Stuffed peppers can be served
as a vegetable or as a lunch or
suppertime dish.
Freezing note Freeze the peppers
in the sauce in a rigid polythene
container. Omit the hard-boiled
eggs when freezing.

Variation
Use 4 oz. (100 g.) peeled prawns,
cooked flaked fish, tuna fish or
minced leftover cooked meat instead of the eggs. Cook in ½ pint
(275 ml.) tomato sauce (see page
131).

Stuffed peppers, Mexican potatoes and peas bonne femme

Peas bonne femme

IMPERIAL/METRIC
1 oz./25 g. Stork margarine
4 oz./100 g. bacon, cut into strips
1 small bunch spring onions, sliced
2 teaspoons flour
**1 Chicken Oxo cube, crumbled and
dissolved in ⅓ pint/200 ml. hot
water**
**1 small Cos or Webb's Wonderful
lettuce, trimmed, washed and
shredded**
1 lb./450 g. shelled peas
1 teaspoon chopped mint
salt and pepper

Melt the margarine and sauté the
bacon and spring onions for 5
minutes until lightly browned. Add
the flour, chicken stock, lettuce,
peas and mint and simmer in a
covered pan for 10–15 minutes until
the peas are tender and the liquid is
reduced. Season. Boil rapidly to
reduce if necessary. Serve at once,
piling the peas on the bed of cooked
lettuce.
Serves 4

Mexican potatoes

IMPERIAL/METRIC
**1–1½ lb./450–675 g. potatoes, peeled
and thinly sliced**
1 onion, coarsely grated
7-oz./198-g. can sweetcorn
salt and pepper
**1 Chicken Oxo cube, crumbled and
dissolved in ½ pint/275 ml. hot
water**
½ oz./15 g. Stork margarine
2 oz./50 g. bacon, diced
2–3 tablespoons cream

Layer the potatoes, onion and sweetcorn in a greased ovenproof dish,
seasoning well between the layers.
Finish with a layer of potato. Pour
over the chicken stock and bake in
a moderately hot oven (375°F.,
190°C., Gas Mark 5) for 45 minutes.
Meanwhile melt the margarine and
sauté the bacon for 5 minutes until
soft. Mix in the cream and spoon
in the centre of the potato. Bake for
a further 15 minutes until brown and
heated through.
Serves 4

Leeks in soured cream

IMPERIAL/METRIC
8 thin leeks, trimmed, cut in half
  lengthways and thoroughly
  washed
1 Chicken Oxo cube, crumbled and
  dissolved in ⅓ pint/200 ml. hot
  water
grated rind and juice of ½ lemon
¾ oz./20 g. Stork margarine
¾ oz./20 g. flour
¼ pint/150 ml. soured cream
salt and pepper
Garnish
chopped parsley

Blanch the leeks in boiling salted water for 5 minutes, then drain thoroughly. Place in a shallow oven-proof dish. Mix the hot chicken stock with the lemon rind and juice and pour over the leeks. Cover with greased paper or foil. Bake in a moderate oven (350°F., 180°C., Gas Mark 4) for 20–30 minutes until tender. Strain off the liquid and reserve ¼ pint (150 ml.). Melt the margarine in a saucepan, add the flour and reserved leek stock and, over a moderate heat, bring to the boil whisking continuously. Cook for 2–3 minutes, still whisking, until smooth. Add the soured cream and beat well. Season to taste, and pour over the leeks. Garnish with chopped parsley.
Serves 4

Spinach soufflé

IMPERIAL/METRIC
little grated Parmesan cheese
1½ oz./40 g. Stork margarine
8-oz./227-g. packet frozen
  spinach or 1 lb./450 g. fresh
  spinach, cooked, well drained
  and finely chopped
1 oz./25 g. flour
⅓ pint/200 ml. creamy milk
salt and pepper
pinch grated nutmeg
pinch mace
4 large eggs, separated
1 extra egg white

Grease a 6-inch (15-cm.) soufflé dish and dust with grated Parmesan cheese.
  Melt ½ oz. (15 g.) margarine and sauté the spinach to remove excess liquid. Remove. Place the remaining margarine, flour and milk in a saucepan over moderate heat. Bring to the boil, whisking continuously. Cook for 2–3 minutes, still whisking, until thickened, smooth and glossy. Add the spinach and season with salt, pepper, nutmeg and mace. Beat in the egg yolks one at a time. Whisk the whites until stiff and stir 1 tablespoon of egg white into the spinach mixture to soften it. Fold in the remaining egg white. Turn into the prepared soufflé dish, sprinkle with a little Parmesan cheese and bake in the middle of a moderately hot oven (375°F., 190°C., Gas Mark 5) for 25 minutes until well risen and firm to the touch. Serve immediately.
Serves 4
Note This mixture may be spooned into six individual soufflé dishes, cooked for 15–20 minutes and served as a starter for six.

Stuffed tomatoes duchesse

IMPERIAL/METRIC
4 large even-sized tomatoes,
  halved and carefully deseeded
  with a teaspoon
salt and pepper
1 oz./25 g. Stork margarine, melted
1 Onion Oxo cube, finely
  crumbled
8 oz./225 g. potatoes, cooked and
  sieved
1 teaspoon snipped chives
1 teaspoon chopped parsley
1 tablespoon cream (optional)
little melted margarine
Garnish
chopped parsley

Season the tomatoes and drain up-side down. Beat the margarine and crumbled onion cube into the potato. Season, then add the herbs and cream, if used. Spoon into a piping bag fitted with a large star nozzle. Place the tomatoes in a greased shallow ovenproof dish and pipe in the potato mixture. Sprinkle with melted margarine and bake in the top of a fairly hot oven (400°F., 200°C., Gas Mark 6) for 10 minutes until browned, or brown under the grill. Sprinkle with parsley to serve.
Serves 4

Parsnip casserole

IMPERIAL/METRIC
2 oz./50 g. Stork margarine
8 oz./225 g. bacon, cut in shreds
1 onion, chopped
1½ lb./675 g. parsnips, peeled and
  thinly sliced
1 oz./25 g. sugar
salt and pepper
1 Red Oxo cube, crumbled and
  dissolved in ¼ pint/150 ml. hot
  water
¼ pint/150 ml. cream
1 oz./25 g. cheese, grated
little extra margarine

Melt the margarine and fry the bacon for 5 minutes until browned. Remove. Add the onion to the pan and sauté for 5 minutes until soft. Add the parsnip. Toss for 5 minutes. Place a layer of bacon in an oven-proof dish. Cover with a layer of onion and parsnip mixture, then sprinkle with sugar and seasoning. Repeat the layers. Pour over the beef stock and cream. Sprinkle with grated cheese and dot with a little extra margarine. Bake in a moderate oven (350°F., 180°C., Gas Mark 4) for 35–40 minutes until well browned and the parsnips are soft.
Serves 4

Baked new potatoes

IMPERIAL/METRIC
1½ oz./40 g. Stork margarine
1 clove garlic, crushed
½ Red Oxo cube, crumbled
salt and pepper
1 lb./450 g. small new potatoes,
  washed and scrubbed
Garnish
chopped mint
chopped parsley

Melt the margarine with the garlic, crumbled beef cube and seasoning and toss the potatoes. Turn into a shallow ovenproof dish. Bake in a moderately hot oven (375–400°F., 190–200°C., Gas Mark 5–6) for 30–45 minutes depending on the size of the potatoes. Turn occasionally during cooking. When crisp and browned sprinkle with mint and parsley and serve at once.
Serves 4

Sweetcorn au gratin

IMPERIAL/METRIC
1½ oz./40 g. Stork margarine
2 onions, chopped
2 small green peppers, deseeded
  and finely chopped
2 sticks celery, washed and finely
  chopped
7-oz./198-g. can sweetcorn
8 oz./225 g. tomatoes, skinned,
  deseeded and sliced
½ oz./15 g. flour
salt and pepper
paprika
½ teaspoon made mustard
1 Chicken Oxo cube, crumbled
  and dissolved in ¼ pint/150 ml.
  hot water
2 egg yolks
2 tablespoons double cream
browned breadcrumbs

Melt 1 oz. (25 g.) margarine and
sauté the onion for 5 minutes until
soft. Add the peppers and celery
and cook for a further 5 minutes
before adding the sweetcorn. Mix
in the tomatoes, flour, seasonings
and chicken stock. Place in a
casserole and bake in a moderate
oven (350°F., 180°C., Gas Mark 4)
for 30 minutes. Remove from the
oven. Mix the egg yolks and cream
together in a basin. Add to the
casserole and bake for a further
5 minutes to thicken. Adjust the
seasoning and spoon into a gratin
dish. Sprinkle with browned
crumbs and the remaining margarine, melted, and brown under a hot
grill. Serve at once.
Serves 4

Ratatouille

Ratatouille

IMPERIAL/METRIC
1 large aubergine, sliced
2 courgettes, sliced
salt and pepper
1½ oz./40 g. Stork margarine
1 onion, sliced
2 cloves garlic, crushed
1 green pepper, halved, deseeded
  and sliced
1 tablespoon tomato purée
12 oz./350 g. tomatoes, skinned
  and thickly sliced
pinch basil
pinch oregano or marjoram
Garnish
chopped parsley

Sprinkle the aubergine and courgettes with salt. Leave for 30
minutes, then drain well and pat
dry. Melt the margarine and sauté
the onion and garlic for 5 minutes
until soft. Add the green pepper

and sauté for 2–3 minutes before
adding the aubergine, courgettes
and tomato purée. Cook for 5
minutes. Put half the mixture into a
deep casserole. Cover with half
the tomatoes. Sprinkle with herbs
and season. Spoon over the remaining mixture and top with the
rest of the tomatoes. Add 2 tablespoons water and cook in a moderate oven (350°F., 180°C., Gas Mark
4) for 35–40 minutes. Sprinkle with
chopped parsley to serve.
Serves 4
Freezing note Freeze the ratatouille
in a foil-lined casserole. When
frozen, remove the casserole and
overwrap the block of ratatouille.

Variation
This may be served cold as an
hors-d'œuvre, sprinkled with a little
grated Parmesan cheese. Serve
with delicious hot garlic bread (see
page 174).

Herbs and their uses

Naturally herbs are at their best when fresh. Not everyone has a herb garden and dried herbs are almost as good and are always at hand when needed. It is important though to use them up as soon as possible after purchase as the flavour and colour deteriorate during storage. The choice of herbs is often entirely personal, but there are some that are especially good with particular foods. If you grow your own herbs, it is possible to freeze them for use throughout the year. Parsley, mint, chives and rosemary freeze particularly well.

Basil
One of the most delicate herbs. Suitable for tomato dishes, pasta, oily fish, chicken and duck.

Bay leaf
This is the leaf of the sweet bay tree. Ideal for flavouring stock, soups, casseroles and pâtés. Commonly used in a bouquet garni. Use sparingly.

Chervil
A fan-like herb resembling parsley, but with an aniseed flavour. Suitable for use in salads, soups, sauces, with delicate fish dishes and as garnishes.

Dill
This herb can be used in leaf or seed form. It is at its best in lamb casseroles, fish soups and salad dressings.

Garlic
This pungent member of the onion family is used as a flavouring rather than as a vegetable on its own. A little goes a long way, but despite its distinctive flavour it is very versatile and is used in many savoury dishes, e.g. casseroles, dressings and shellfish dishes.

Horseradish
This is a very peppery root, used in horseradish sauce as an accompaniment to roast beef or smoked trout.

Marjoram
A very aromatic herb of the mint family. Used to flavour stuffings for white meat and poultry. Also used with oily fish and duck.

Mint
There are many varieties of mint, the most useful being spearmint and peppermint. Traditionally used to make mint sauce, and to flavour new potatoes, peas, carrots and vinegars.

Oregano
Stronger and more pungent flavour than marjoram. Use the leaves with pasta dishes especially spaghetti bolognese, meat, rabbit and stuffings.

Parsley
This is the most popular and widely used herb and the easiest to grow. Use to flavour and to garnish savoury dishes, in savoury butters and in a bouquet garni.

Rosemary
This herb is another member of the mint family and has a pungent aroma. It blends well with rich or fatty foods; use with oily fish, roast lamb, pork and duck; try it in sauces, soups and vinegars.

Sage
The strong aroma of this herb blends very well with pork dishes. Mainly used in stuffings for pork, duck and chicken.

Tarragon
This herb has a smell and flavour reminiscent of aniseed. Use to flavour white wine vinegar, salad dressings and mayonnaise. Excellent with oily fish, chicken and in omelettes.

Thyme
Also a member of the mint family. Can be bought either ground or as whole leaves. Use to flavour oily fish, roast pork and poultry.

Pepper salad

Salads

Pepper salad

IMPERIAL/METRIC
2 red peppers
2 green peppers
lettuce
12 oz./350 g. tomatoes, skinned and
    sliced
6–8 tablespoons French dressing,
    with basil added (see page 131)
1 can anchovy fillets
2 oz./50 g. black olives, stoned

Place the peppers under a hot grill
until charred all over. Rinse under
cold running water to remove the
skins. Halve the peppers, remove
the seeds and slice. Line a salad
bowl with lettuce leaves and arrange layers of pepper and tomato,
finishing with a tomato layer. Pour
over the French dressing. Arrange
the anchovy fillets in a lattice
pattern over the salad and place
the olives on top of the salad. Leave
to chill for at least 30 minutes before
serving.
Serves 4–6

Curried potato salad

IMPERIAL/METRIC
2 lb./1 kg. new potatoes, scrubbed
1 tablespoon vinegar
1 clove garlic, crushed
salt and pepper
1 green pepper, chopped
2 oz./50 g. cooked bacon, chopped
¼ pint/150 ml. mayonnaise (see
    page 132)
1 Curry Oxo cube, crumbled
juice of ½ lemon
¼ pint/150 ml. natural yogurt or
    single cream

Boil the potatoes for 10–15 minutes
until just cooked. Skin and dice
them. Add the vinegar, garlic and
seasoning while still warm. Leave
to cool. Add the pepper and bacon.
When making the mayonnaise, add
the crumbled curry cube with the
seasonings and beat well with the
egg yolks. Mix the curry mayonnaise with the lemon juice and
yogurt and stir into the salad. Combine well and serve.
Serves 4–6

Hot potato salad

IMPERIAL/METRIC
1 oz./25 g. Stork margarine
1 Onion Oxo cube, crumbled
6 oz./175 g. streaky bacon, chopped
1 onion, chopped
1½ lb./675 g. hot cooked potatoes,
    sliced
salt and pepper
Dressing
8 tablespoons oil
3 tablespoons wine vinegar
½ tablespoon made mustard
1 tablespoon chopped parsley
1 tablespoon snipped chives
Garnish
chopped parsley or snipped chives

Melt the margarine. Add the onion
cube and bacon and sauté quickly
for 2–3 minutes. Add the onion and
sauté until soft. Stir into the potatoes.
Mix together the dressing ingredients in a bowl. Carefully stir this
into the potato mixture and season
to taste. Spoon into a warmed
serving dish and sprinkle with
parsley or chives. Serve hot.
Serves 4–6

Variation
Add sliced salami (4 oz./100 g.), cut
into shreds, to the mixture.

Red cabbage and beetroot salad

IMPERIAL/METRIC
1 small red cabbage, finely
    shredded
8 oz./225 g. cooked beetroot,
    peeled and diced
1 onion, finely chopped
2 dessert apples, peeled, cored and
    chopped
¼ pint/150 ml. French dressing,
    using red wine vinegar (see page
    131)
2 teaspoons soft brown sugar
salt and pepper

Mix together the red cabbage,
beetroot, onion and apple. Stir in
the French dressing and sugar.
Combine thoroughly, adjust the
seasoning and serve.
Serves 4–6

Variation
Add a few walnuts and the grated
rind of ½ orange.

Italian salad

IMPERIAL/METRIC
8 oz./225 g. pasta shells
1 Chicken Oxo cube, crumbled
1 tablespoon oil
4 oz./100 g. cooked ham, cut in
    ¼-inch (1-cm.) slices and diced
2 oz./50 g. black or green olives,
    stoned
½ teaspoon French mustard
juice of 1 lemon
¼ pint/150 ml. mayonnaise (see page
    132)
2–3 tablespoons cream
salt and pepper
Garnish
paprika pepper

Cook the pasta in boiling, salted
water, with the chicken cube and
oil added, for 10–12 minutes until
cooked just firm to bite – al dente.
Strain, rinse in cold water and drain
well. Mix with the ham and olives.
Stir the mustard and lemon juice
into the mayonnaise and thin down
with the cream. Pour on to the pasta
mixture, stir in gently and season to
taste. Spoon into a serving dish and
sprinkle with paprika pepper.
Serves 4–6

Celery, apple, cheese and nut salad

IMPERIAL/METRIC
2 dessert apples, cored and diced
juice of ½ lemon
1 small head celery, diced
4 oz./100 g. Cheddar or Edam
    cheese, diced
2 oz./50 g. raisins
2 oz./50 g. broken walnuts or salted
    peanuts
¼ pint/150 ml. mayonnaise (see
    page 132)
¼ pint/150 ml. soured cream
Garnish
½ apple, sliced and mixed with a
    little lemon juice
chopped nuts

Mix the apple with the lemon juice
to prevent discoloration. Add the
celery, cheese, raisins and nuts.
Stir the mayonnaise and soured
cream into the salad. Turn into a
serving dish and garnish the edge
with apple slices, sprinkling the
chopped nuts on top.
Serves 4–6

Savoury rice ring

Mushroom and tomato salad

IMPERIAL/METRIC
4 tablespoons oil
¼ pint/150 ml. water
1 Onion Oxo cube, crumbled
1 bay leaf
pinch thyme
1 clove garlic, crushed
1 lb./450 g. button mushrooms, trimmed
8 oz./225 g. tomatoes, skinned, quartered and deseeded
salt and pepper
chopped parsley
Garnish
snipped chives

Place the oil, water, onion cube, bay leaf, thyme and garlic in a saucepan. Bring to the boil and cook for 3 minutes before adding the mushrooms. Simmer for 5 minutes then remove from the heat. Add the tomatoes. Remove the bay leaf. Strain the mixture and place the vegetables in a serving dish. Return the liquid to the pan and reduce by half. Season to taste and add a little chopped parsley. Spoon over the salad and chill. Sprinkle with chives before serving.
Serves 4

Savoury rice ring

IMPERIAL/METRIC
8 oz./225 g. long-grain rice
1 Onion Oxo cube, crumbled and dissolved in ¾ pint/425 ml. hot water
½ cucumber, peeled and diced
½ onion, finely chopped
8 oz./225 g. tomatoes, skinned, seeded and chopped
7-oz./198-g. can sweetcorn
½ green pepper, seeded and chopped
1 clove garlic, crushed
5–6 tablespoons French dressing (see page 131)
salt and pepper
Garnish
cress

Simmer the rice in the onion stock for 15–20 minutes until cooked and the stock is absorbed. (Or cook the rice according to the packet instructions.) Cool. Add the cucumber, onion, tomatoes, sweetcorn and green pepper.

Add the crushed garlic to the French dressing and use to moisten the rice mixture. Season to taste. Pack into an 8–9-inch (20–23-cm.) oiled ring mould, smooth over the top and leave in the refrigerator for at least 1 hour until firm. Turn out on to a serving dish. The rice ring may be filled with prawns, leftover chicken or tuna fish mixed with mayonnaise (see page 132). Garnish with cress.
Serves 4–6

Variation

Spicy rice ring Add 2 Curry cubes to the rice cooking water. Omit the tomato and cucumber and add 2 oz. (50 g.) raisins, 1 dessert apple, peeled, chopped and mixed with a little lemon juice, and 2 oz. (50 g.) chopped browned almonds or cashew nuts.

Scalloped crab salad

IMPERIAL/METRIC
6 oz./175 g. long-grain rice
1 Onion Oxo cube, crumbled and dissolved in 12 fl. oz./350 ml. hot water
6 oz./175 g. fresh or canned crabmeat
1 green or red pepper, sliced
4 oz./100 g. button mushrooms, sliced and blanched for 2 minutes in boiling water
1 oz./25 g. walnuts, coarsely chopped
4–5 tablespoons French dressing, with lemon juice (see page 131)
salt and pepper
Garnish
watercress
lemon slices

Cook the rice in the onion stock for about 15 minutes until tender and stock absorbed. (Or cook rice according to the packet instructions.) Mix the rice with the drained crabmeat, pepper, mushrooms and walnuts. Add enough French dressing to moisten. Mix well and season to taste. Pile into individual scallop shells and garnish.
Serves 4–6

Curried bean salad

IMPERIAL/METRIC
1 oz./25 g. Stork margarine
1 onion, finely chopped
6 oz./175 g. haricot beans, soaked
    overnight in water to cover
1 Curry Oxo cube, crumbled and
    dissolved in ½ pint/275 ml. hot
    water
2 dessert apples, peeled, cored and
    chopped
juice of ½ lemon
1 oz./25 g. sultanas
1 oz./25 g. almonds, blanched and
    shredded
French dressing (see page 131)
salt and pepper
Garnish
lettuce leaves
1 hard-boiled egg, sliced
2 oz./50 g. cooked ham, in strips
chopped parsley

Curried bean salad

Melt the margarine and sauté the onion for 5 minutes until soft. Drain the beans and add to the onion with the curry stock. Cook for 45 minutes until tender. Cool. Add the apple mixed with lemon juice, sultanas and almonds. Moisten with French dressing and season to taste.

Spoon into a serving dish lined with the lettuce. Place egg slices down the centre of the beans and make a lattice pattern with the ham strips. Sprinkle with parsley.
Serves 4–6

Pineapple coleslaw

IMPERIAL/METRIC
½ white cabbage, shredded
1 small pineapple, cored and
    shredded, or 13-oz./369-g. can
    crushed pineapple, drained
5–6 tablespoons French dressing,
    with lemon juice (see page 131)
2 oz./50 g. raisins
2 oz./50 g. broken walnuts or
    chopped browned hazelnuts
salt and pepper

Mix the cabbage and pineapple together. Stir in the French dressing and leave in the refrigerator for 1 hour before adding the raisins and nuts. Adjust the seasoning, adding more lemon juice if necessary.
Serves 4–6

Celery and mint salad

IMPERIAL/METRIC
2 dessert apples, cored and sliced
juice of ½ lemon
1 small head celery, thinly sliced
    diagonally
½ cucumber, quartered and sliced
½ pint/275 ml. natural yogurt
1 tablespoon chopped mint
salt and pepper
Garnish
mint leaves

Mix the apple with the lemon juice to prevent discoloration. Add the celery, cucumber and stir in the yogurt and mint. Mix thoroughly and season to taste. Place in a serving dish and garnish with mint leaves.
Serves 4–6

Rice and pineapple salad, beetroot and orange salad and pepper salad (page 123)

Pepper slaw

IMPERIAL/METRIC
½ white cabbage, finely shredded
1 green pepper, thinly sliced
1 red pepper, thinly sliced
½ bunch spring onions, trimmed
and sliced
1 bunch radishes, sliced
2–3 tablespoons French dressing
(see page 131)
6–8 tablespoons mayonnaise (see
page 132)
1 teaspoon horseradish sauce
salt and pepper
Garnish
chopped parsley

Mix together the cabbage, peppers, spring onion and radishes. Moisten with the French dressing and leave for 30 minutes to marinate.

Mix the mayonnaise and horse-radish sauce and stir into the salad mixture. Season to taste and turn into a serving dish. Garnish with parsley
Serves 4–6

Beetroot and orange salad

IMPERIAL/METRIC
3 large oranges
1 lb./450 g. cooked beetroot, peeled
and diced
Dressing
2 tablespoons orange juice
1 tablespoon red wine vinegar
1 tablespoon clear honey
4 tablespoons oil
salt and pepper
coarsely grated rind of 1 orange
pinch cinnamon

Grate the rind of one orange and reserve. Remove the skin and pith from all the oranges. To remove the segments, cut down between the membranes with a sharp knife to divide the orange flesh, keeping any juice. Mix the orange with the beetroot.

Put all the dressing ingredients and the reserved rind and juice into a screw-topped jar and shake together. Pour over the salad and chill for at least 30 minutes before serving. Sprinkle with grated rind.
Serves 4

Tomato, orange and mint salad

IMPERIAL/METRIC
3 oranges
1 lb./450 g. tomatoes, skinned and
sliced
Dressing
2 tablespoons orange juice
1 tablespoon cider vinegar
4 tablespoons oil
1 teaspoon sugar
salt and pepper
2 teaspoons chopped mint
1 teaspoon chopped parsley

Pare the rind of one orange with a potato peeler. Cut into fine shreds and blanch in boiling water for 10 minutes. Remove the skin from all the oranges with a sharp knife and slice the oranges thinly.

Arrange alternate slices of orange and tomato in a serving dish. Shake together the ingredients for the dressing in a screw-topped jar, including any juice from preparing the oranges. Spoon over the salad and sprinkle the drained, blanched orange rind on top.
Serves 4

Chicory and orange salad

IMPERIAL/METRIC
12 oz./350 g. chicory, cut diagonally
in ½-inch (1-cm.) slices
juice of ½ lemon
3 oranges, pith removed
7-oz./198-g. can sweetcorn
Dressing
2 tablespoons orange juice
juice of ½ lemon
3 tablespoons oil
pinch sugar
2 tablespoons cream
salt and pepper
Garnish
chopped parsley

Mix the chicory with the lemon juice to prevent discoloration. Cut the oranges in ½-inch (1-cm.) slices and add with the sweetcorn. Shake the dressing ingredients together in a screw-top jar with any orange juice from preparing the oranges. Pour over the salad in a salad bowl and sprinkle with chopped parsley.
Serves 4

Rice and pineapple salad

IMPERIAL/METRIC
6 oz./175 g. long-grain rice
1 Chicken Oxo cube, crumbled and
dissolved in 12 fl. oz./350 ml. hot
water
3 tablespoons French dressing (see
page 131)
8-oz./226-g. can pineapple rings,
drained and chopped
1 green pepper, deseeded and
diced
2 spring onions, trimmed and
shredded
2 oz./50 g. sultanas
salt and pepper

Simmer the rice in the chicken stock for 15–20 minutes until cooked and the stock is absorbed. (Or cook the rice according to the packet instructions.) Add the French dressing to the hot rice. Leave to cool. Add the remaining ingredients, mix well and season to taste.
Serves 4

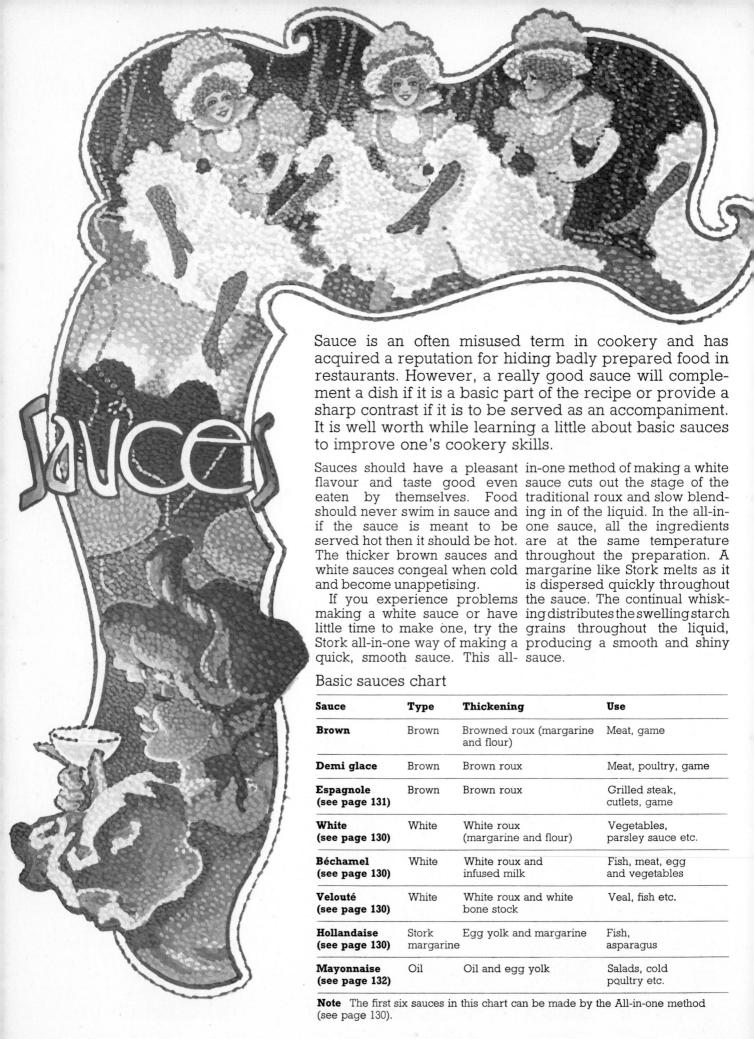

Sauce is an often misused term in cookery and has acquired a reputation for hiding badly prepared food in restaurants. However, a really good sauce will complement a dish if it is a basic part of the recipe or provide a sharp contrast if it is to be served as an accompaniment. It is well worth while learning a little about basic sauces to improve one's cookery skills.

Sauces should have a pleasant flavour and taste good even eaten by themselves. Food should never swim in sauce and if the sauce is meant to be served hot then it should be hot. The thicker brown sauces and white sauces congeal when cold and become unappetising.

If you experience problems making a white sauce or have little time to make one, try the Stork all-in-one way of making a quick, smooth sauce. This all-in-one method of making a white sauce cuts out the stage of the traditional roux and slow blending in of the liquid. In the all-in-one sauce, all the ingredients are at the same temperature throughout the preparation. A margarine like Stork melts as it is dispersed quickly throughout the sauce. The continual whisking distributes the swelling starch grains throughout the liquid, producing a smooth and shiny sauce.

Basic sauces chart

Sauce	Type	Thickening	Use
Brown	Brown	Browned roux (margarine and flour)	Meat, game
Demi glace	Brown	Brown roux	Meat, poultry, game
Espagnole (see page 131)	Brown	Brown roux	Grilled steak, cutlets, game
White (see page 130)	White	White roux (margarine and flour)	Vegetables, parsley sauce etc.
Béchamel (see page 130)	White	White roux and infused milk	Fish, meat, egg and vegetables
Velouté (see page 130)	White	White roux and white bone stock	Veal, fish etc.
Hollandaise (see page 130)	Stork margarine	Egg yolk and margarine	Fish, asparagus
Mayonnaise (see page 132)	Oil	Oil and egg yolk	Salads, cold poultry etc.

Note The first six sauces in this chart can be made by the All-in-one method (see page 130).

Cauliflower with cheese sauce (page 130)

Savoury sauces

Basic white sauce

IMPERIAL/ METRIC	POURING	COATING	PANADA (BINDING)
Stork margarine	½ oz./15 g.	1 oz./25 g.	2 oz./50 g.
plain flour	½ oz./15 g.	1 oz./25 g.	2 oz./50 g.
milk	½ pint/275 ml.	½ pint/275 ml.	½ pint/275 ml.

All-in-one method Place all the ingredients in a saucepan over a moderate heat. Bring to the boil, whisking continuously. Cook for 2–3 minutes, still whisking, until thickened, smooth and glossy.
Traditional roux method Melt the margarine in a saucepan over a moderate heat. Remove from the heat and stir in the flour. Return to the heat and cook for 1–2 minutes, stirring. Remove from the heat and gradually stir in the milk. Heat gently and bring to the boil, stirring continuously; cook for 2–3 minutes.
Makes ½ pint (275 ml.)
Freezing note White sauces can be frozen, but tend to become thinner in consistency when thawed, therefore use a little less liquid when making the sauce. When reheating after thawing, whisk well to prevent any lumps appearing.

Variations
Béchamel sauce Place the milk in a saucepan and add 1 carrot, 1 onion, a bay leaf, a few peppercorns and a pinch of nutmeg. Bring to the boil, remove and infuse for 30 minutes. Strain and use in place of milk in the basic white sauce recipe.
Caper sauce Add 1–2 tablespoons capers and a few drops of vinegar to the basic sauce.
Cheese sauce Stir 2 oz. (50 g.) grated cheese and a pinch of mustard into the sauce. Do not allow the sauce to boil after adding the cheese.
Egg sauce Stir in 1 finely chopped hard-boiled egg and 1 tablespoon chopped parsley.
Mushroom sauce Stir in 2 oz. (50 g.) chopped mushrooms sautéed in ½ oz. (15 g.) margarine.
Onion sauce Stir in 2 chopped and boiled onions.
Parsley sauce Stir in 2 tablespoons chopped parsley.
Savoury sauces Use one Red, Chicken, Onion or Curry Oxo cube to ½ pint (275 ml.) milk. Add, crumbled, with the flour and proceed as for white or béchamel sauce.

Apple sauce

IMPERIAL/METRIC
1 lb./450 g. cooking apples, peeled, cored and sliced
3 tablespoons water
½ teaspoon sugar
salt and pepper
½ oz./15 g. Stork margarine

Simmer the apples in the water until soft. Add the sugar, seasoning and margarine. Sieve and reheat.
Makes ½ pint (275 ml.)

Bread sauce

IMPERIAL/METRIC
1 onion, peeled
4–6 cloves
½ pint/275 ml. milk
2 oz./50 g. fresh breadcrumbs
1 oz./25 g. Stork margarine
salt and pepper

Stud the onion with the cloves. Simmer in the milk for 10 minutes. Stir in the breadcrumbs and infuse for 30 minutes. Remove the onion and cloves from the sauce, reheat it gently, then stir in the margarine and season to taste. If you prefer a stronger onion flavour remove the cloves from the onion and liquidise the sauce and onion.
Makes ½ pint (275 ml.)

Horseradish sauce

IMPERIAL/METRIC
4 tablespoons fresh, peeled and grated horseradish
1 teaspoon sugar
salt and pepper
4–5 tablespoons milk or cream
little vinegar to taste

Mix all the ingredients together, adding the vinegar to taste. Store in the refrigerator in a screw-top jar for up to a week.

Hollandaise sauce

IMPERIAL/METRIC
2 tablespoons wine vinegar
6 peppercorns
4 tablespoons water
3 egg yolks
6 oz./175 g. Stork margarine, cut into small pieces
salt and pepper
lemon juice

Place the vinegar, peppercorns and water in a saucepan and bring to the boil. Allow to boil rapidly until reduced by a third. Strain into a basin and place over a saucepan of hot water. Stir in the egg yolks and cook for 20–30 minutes until the mixture thickens. Add the margarine, a piece at a time, and beat or whisk into the sauce. Season and add a few drops of lemon juice.
Makes about ½ pint (275 ml.)

Velouté sauce

IMPERIAL/METRIC
¾ oz./20 g. Stork margarine
¾ oz./20 g. flour
1 Chicken Oxo cube, crumbled and dissolved in ⅔ pint/400 ml. hot water
2 tablespoons single cream or top of the milk
few drops lemon juice
salt and pepper

Place the margarine, flour and chicken stock in a saucepan over moderate heat. Bring to the boil, whisking continuously. Cook for 2–3 minutes, still whisking, until thickened, smooth and glossy. Remove from the heat and add the cream or milk, lemon juice and seasoning to taste.
Makes ¾ pint (425 ml.)
Freezing note Freeze without the addition of the cream and lemon juice.

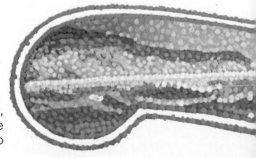

Espagnole sauce

IMPERIAL/METRIC
2 oz./50 g. Stork margarine
2 oz./50 g. bacon, chopped
1 onion, sliced
1 carrot, sliced
2 oz./50 g. plain flour
4 oz./100 g. mushrooms, chopped
2 Red Oxo cubes, crumbled and
    dissolved in 1 pint/575 ml. hot
    water
2 bay leaves
salt and pepper
2 tablespoons tomato purée
1 tablespoon sherry (optional)

Melt the margarine and sauté the bacon, onion and carrot for 5–10 minutes. Stir in the flour and cook for 1 minute. Add the remaining ingredients except the sherry and bring to the boil, then simmer for 1–1½ hours. Strain and adjust the seasoning. Add the sherry if used.
Makes 1 pint (575 ml.)

Tomato sauce

IMPERIAL/METRIC
½ oz./15 g. Stork margarine
1 onion, finely chopped
1 tablespoon flour
14-oz./397-g. can tomatoes
1 Onion Oxo cube, crumbled
½ teaspoon Worcestershire sauce
½ teaspoon basil
salt and pepper

Melt the margarine and sauté the onion until golden brown – about 5 minutes. Stir in the flour and cook for 1 minute. Stir in the remaining ingredients, bring to the boil, stirring continuously, and simmer for 5–10 minutes. Liquidise or strain. Serve with fish, meat or vegetable dishes.
Serves 4
Freezing note Freeze in a rigid polythene container or foil bag.

Lemon sauce

IMPERIAL/METRIC
1 oz./25 g. Stork margarine
¾ oz./20 g. flour
1 Chicken Oxo cube, crumbled and
    dissolved in ½ pint/275 ml. water
thinly pared rind of ½ lemon
3 tablespoons lemon juice
2 egg yolks
2 tablespoons single cream or top
    of the milk
chopped parsley
salt and pepper

Place the margarine, flour, chicken stock and lemon rind in a saucepan over moderate heat. Bring to the boil, whisking continuously. Cook for 2–3 minutes, still whisking, until thickened, smooth and glossy. Mix the lemon juice and egg yolks in a basin, pour on the hot sauce and stir well. Remove the lemon rind and return the mixture to the pan. Heat very gently to just below boiling point, stirring continuously, *but do not allow to boil*. Add the cream or top of the milk and parsley. Season to taste and serve.
Makes ½ pint (275 ml.)
Illustrated on page 35

Mint sauce

IMPERIAL/METRIC
4 tablespoons washed and dried
    chopped mint
1–2 teaspoons sugar
4 tablespoons boiling water
½ pint/275 ml. vinegar

Sprinkle the mint with sugar and pour on the boiling water. When cooled add the vinegar. Store in a screw-top jar. Mint sauce will keep for a few weeks.
Makes ½ pint (275 ml.)

French dressing

IMPERIAL/METRIC
pinch salt and pepper
½ teaspoon dry mustard
½ teaspoon sugar
2 tablespoons vinegar or lemon
    juice
4–5 tablespoons oil

Place all the ingredients in a small screw-top jar and shake well for 1–2 minutes, until emulsified. The oil and vinegar will separate on standing, so shake well before using.
    You can make up a larger quantity of this dressing and store in a bottle.
Makes scant ¼ pint (125 ml.)

Variations
Substitute wine, tarragon or other herb vinegars for the vinegar or lemon juice.

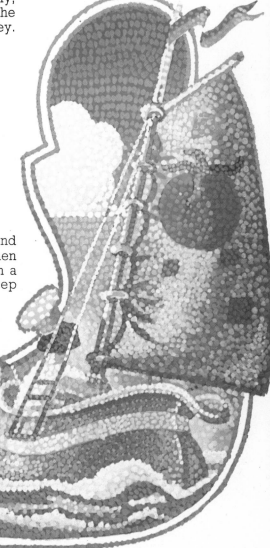

1. *Lightly whisking the egg yolks, mustard, seasoning and sugar until blended.*

2. *Slowly pouring in the oil, drop by drop, whisking continuously.*

3. *The thickened mayonnaise, with lemon juice or vinegar added to thin it to the desired consistency.*

Mayonnaise

IMPERIAL/METRIC
2 egg yolks
pinch dry mustard
salt and pepper
¼ teaspoon sugar
½ pint/275 ml. oil
1–2 tablespoons lemon juice or vinegar

Lightly whisk the egg yolks, mustard, seasoning and sugar (see step 1) until blended. Slowly pour in the oil drop by drop, whisking continuously (step 2). When thickened (step 3) add the lemon juice or vinegar to thin the mayonnaise down. Add any remaining oil and adjust the seasoning to taste. Keep in an airtight container in the refrigerator.

Makes ½ pint (275 ml.)
Note If your ingredients are not at room temperature or if you add the oil too quickly the mayonnaise can curdle. If this happens, just start again with a clean dry bowl and whisk, and a third egg yolk. Whisk the egg lightly, add a little oil and whisk until it emulsifies, then finally add the curdled mixture very slowly as if it were the remaining oil.

Variations

To the basic mayonnaise add 2 teaspoons chopped onion; or 2 teaspoons chopped parsley and 1 teaspoon tomato purée.

Tartare sauce To the basic mayonnaise add 2 teaspoons chopped chives, 2 teaspoons capers, 3 teaspoons chopped gherkins, 3 teaspoons chopped parsley and 1–2 tablespoons lemon juice.
Curry mayonnaise Add a crumbled Curry Oxo cube with the seasonings and beat well with the egg yolks.
Blender mayonnaise Use a whole egg instead of the 2 egg yolks. Put the egg, seasonings and half the vinegar or lemon juice in the blender goblet and switch on at minimum speed. Pour the oil in slowly through the hole in the cap. Stop the motor, add the remaining vinegar or lemon juice, then switch on at maximum speed and add the remaining oil.

Mayonnaise for coating hard-boiled eggs, to make egg mayonnaise

Sweet sauces

Coffee sauce

IMPERIAL/METRIC
1 oz./25 g. Stork margarine
½ oz./15 g. cornflour
½ pint/275 ml. strong black coffee
1 oz./25 g. sugar
2–3 drops vanilla essence
1 egg yolk

Place the margarine, cornflour and coffee in a saucepan over moderate heat. Bring to the boil, whisking continuously. Cook for 2–3 minutes, still whisking, until thickened, smooth and glossy. Add the sugar and vanilla essence. Stir in the egg yolk and heat gently to thicken.
Makes ½ pint (275 ml.)

Custard sauce

IMPERIAL/METRIC
1½ tablespoons custard powder
2 tablespoons sugar
½ pint/275 ml. milk

Blend the custard powder with the sugar and a little of the milk. Bring the rest of the milk to the boil and stir on to the blended custard powder. Return to the saucepan and reheat until smooth and thickened, stirring continuously. Serve hot.
Makes ½ pint (275 ml.)

Fudge sauce

IMPERIAL/METRIC
½ pint/275 ml. milk
1 vanilla pod or 2–3 drops vanilla
    essence
2 oz./50 g. Stork margarine
3 oz./75 g. soft light brown sugar
1 tablespoon golden syrup
2 teaspoons arrowroot blended with
    1 tablespoon water

Warm the milk in a saucepan with the vanilla pod or essence and margarine. Remove the vanilla pod if used. Place the sugar and syrup in another saucepan and heat gently until beginning to caramelise. Add the flavoured milk and beat until smooth. Add the blended arrowroot and, stirring continuously, cook until thickened.
Makes ½ pint (275 ml.)

Walnut sauce

IMPERIAL/METRIC
2 tablespoons golden syrup
2 tablespoons soft brown sugar
1 oz./25 g. Stork margarine
½ pint/275 ml. water
1 teaspoon custard powder blended
    with 2 teaspoons water
juice of ½ lemon
2 tablespoons broken walnuts,
    toasted

Place the syrup, sugar and margarine in a saucepan and cook until toffee brown in colour. Add the water and pour on to the blended custard powder. Return to the pan and bring to the boil. Add the lemon juice and walnuts.
Makes ½ pint (275 ml.)

Chocolate sauce

IMPERIAL/METRIC
2 oz./50 g. plain chocolate
4 tablespoons golden syrup
½ oz./15 g. Stork margarine

Put all the ingredients in a bowl placed over a saucepan of hot water. When melted, beat until smooth and glossy.
Serves 4

Melba sauce

IMPERIAL/METRIC
1 teaspoon arrowroot blended with
    2 tablespoons water
4–6 oz./100–175 g. fresh or frozen
    raspberries
sugar to taste
2 tablespoons redcurrant jelly

Place all the ingredients together in a saucepan and, stirring continuously, heat gently until clear. Rub through a sieve and serve.
Serves 4

Jam sauce

IMPERIAL/METRIC
3 tablespoons jam
¼ pint/150 ml. water
2 teaspoons arrowroot blended
    with 2 tablespoons cold water
few drops lemon juice

Heat the jam and water in a saucepan and simmer for 5 minutes. Add the blended arrowroot, stirring continuously. Cook until the sauce thickens and clears. Add the lemon juice and sieve before serving.
Makes ¼ pint (150 ml.)

Beignets (page 142) with cherry sauce

Cherry sauce

IMPERIAL/METRIC
2 oz./50 g. sugar
⅓ pint/200 ml. water
thinly pared rind of ½ lemon
juice of ½ lemon
½ cinnamon stick
8 oz./225 g. black cherries, stoned
1 teaspoon arrowroot mixed with a
　little cold water

Dissolve the sugar in the water in a saucepan and bring to the boil with the lemon rind, lemon juice and cinnamon. Add the stoned cherries with any juice and simmer for 5–7 minutes. Remove the lemon rind and cinnamon stick, then add the blended arrowroot and cook, stirring continuously, until thickened.
Makes ½ pint (275 ml.)

Lemon sauce

IMPERIAL/METRIC
1 oz./25 g. Stork margarine
½ oz./15 g. flour or cornflour
½ pint/275 ml. water
1–2 tablespoons sugar
grated rind and juice of 1 lemon
1–2 egg yolks

Bring the margarine, flour and water to the boil in a saucepan, whisking continuously. Cook for 2–3 minutes, then add the sugar and lemon rind and juice and bring back to the boil. Remove from the heat, beat in the egg yolks and cook for 1 minute.
Makes ½ pint (275 ml.)

Variation
Orange sauce Use orange rind and juice instead of lemon.

Hard sauce

IMPERIAL/METRIC
3 oz./75 g. Stork margarine
3 oz./75 g. soft brown sugar
2–3 tablespoons brandy
finely grated rind of ½ orange
　(optional)

Cream the margarine and sugar together until well mixed. Beat in the brandy a little at a time, together with the orange rind, if used. Chill and allow to harden before serving.
Serves 4

Caramel sauce

IMPERIAL/METRIC
3 oz./75 g. Stork margarine
3 oz./75 g. soft brown sugar
3 tablespoons syrup
few drops lemon juice

Gently heat the margarine, sugar and syrup until melted. Bring to the boil and simmer for 1 minute. Add the lemon juice and serve immediately.
Serves 4

Egg custard

IMPERIAL/METRIC
½ pint/275 ml. milk
few drops vanilla essence
2 large egg yolks, beaten
2 teaspoons castor sugar

Heat the milk and vanilla essence until lukewarm. Pour over the beaten egg yolks. Strain into a double saucepan, or into a basin over a saucepan of gently simmering water, and add the sugar. Cook over a gentle heat, stirring, until thickened (do not boil).
Makes ½ pint (275 ml.)

Brandy sauce

IMPERIAL/METRIC
1 tablespoon cornflour
1 tablespoon sugar
½ pint/275 ml. milk
small knob Stork margarine
1–2 tablespoons brandy

Blend the cornflour, sugar and a little of the milk together in a basin. Bring the remaining milk to the boil and pour over the cornflour mixture. Return to the pan and cook, stirring continuously, until thickened. Stir in margarine and brandy.
Makes ½ pint (275 ml.)

Christmas pudding (page 141) with hard sauce

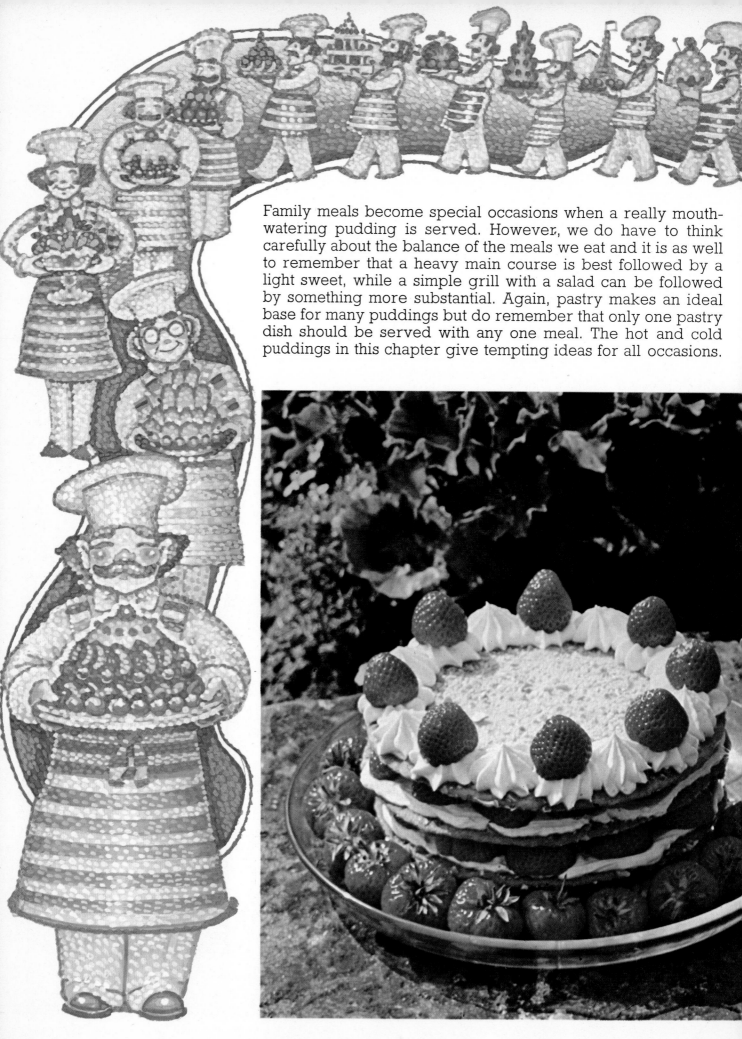

Family meals become special occasions when a really mouth-watering pudding is served. However, we do have to think carefully about the balance of the meals we eat and it is as well to remember that a heavy main course is best followed by a light sweet, while a simple grill with a salad can be followed by something more substantial. Again, pastry makes an ideal base for many puddings but do remember that only one pastry dish should be served with any one meal. The hot and cold puddings in this chapter give tempting ideas for all occasions.

Puddings

Eggs add nourishment to an economy meal. Make an egg custard (see page 135) and use the egg whites as a meringue topping for a pudding the next day.

Make the most of the summer fruits when they are in season by serving them fresh with sugar and cream and for a really special occasion try the strawberry box or walnut and raspberry roll on page 148. If you have a freezer you can freeze surplus summer and autumn fruits and use these in winter for making hot and cold soufflés as well as fruit pies and crumbles. Supermarkets now stock a good variety of frozen fruits so everyone can enjoy fruit puddings out of season. For anyone who is on a diet but loves puddings, fruit can be sweetened with artificial sweetener.

Danish hazelnut and strawberry galette (page 149) and strawberry chocolate box (page 147)

Blackberry and cherry charlotte

Hot puddings

Blackberry and cherry charlotte

IMPERIAL/METRIC
12 oz./350 g. fresh or frozen
   blackberries
8 oz./225 g. cherries, halved and
   stoned
1–2 oz./25–50 g. sugar
2 oz./50 g. Stork margarine
2 oz./50 g. demerara sugar
4 oz./100 g. digestive biscuits,
   crushed
grated rind of ½ lemon
½ teaspoon cinnamon

Reserve a little uncooked fruit for
decoration. Barely cover the bottom
of a large pan with water, then add
the fruit and sugar and simmer until
nearly cooked.

Melt the margarine in a frying pan
and add the demerara sugar, biscuits, lemon rind and cinnamon.
Cook gently for 3–5 minutes.

Place the fruit and biscuit mixture
in alternate layers in a deep 6-inch
(15-cm.) ovenproof dish. On top of
the final layer of fruit arrange a few
blackberries and cherries round
the edge of the dish and sprinkle
some of the biscuit mixture into the
centre. Bake in a moderate oven
(350°F., 180°C., Gas Mark 4) for
20–30 minutes until the surface is

crisp. Decorate with the reserved,
uncooked fruit.
Serves 4

Variations
Apple and ginger charlotte Use 1¼
lb. (575 g.) apples and 1 oz. (25 g.)
chopped crystallised ginger, and
ginger biscuits instead of digestives.
Blackberry and apple charlotte Replace the cherries with apple.
Rhubarb and orange charlotte Use
1¼ lb. (575 g.) rhubarb and add the
juice and grated rind of 1 orange.
Omit the lemon rind.
Apricot and almond charlotte Use
1¼ lb. (575 g.) apricots, and add 2 oz.
(50 g.) chopped almonds to the
biscuit mixture.

Apricot soufflé

IMPERIAL/METRIC
2 oz./50 g. dried apricots
1 pint/575 ml. water
1 oz./25 g. Stork margarine
1 oz./25 g. flour
¼ pint/150 ml. milk
2 oz./50 g. sugar
grated rind and juice of ½ lemon
3 large eggs, separated
Decoration
icing sugar, sieved

Simmer the apricots in the water for about 30 minutes, then liquidise or sieve them with the water they were cooked in. Place the margarine, flour and milk in a saucepan over moderate heat and bring to the boil, whisking continuously. Cook for 2–3 minutes until smooth and thick. Add the apricot purée, sugar, lemon rind and juice and return to the boil. Remove from the heat and cool slightly, then add the egg yolks. Beat in well. Whisk the egg whites until stiff and fold into the mixture with a metal spoon. Pour into a greased 2-pint (1-litre) soufflé dish. Bake in a moderate oven (350°F., 180°C., Gas Mark 4) for 45 minutes. Serve immediately, dusted with icing sugar.
Serves 4

Hot orange soufflé

IMPERIAL/METRIC
¼ pint/150 ml. milk
3 oz./75 g. sugar
pared rind and juice of 1 orange
1 oz./25 g. Stork margarine
1 oz./25 g. plain flour, sieved
4 large egg yolks
5 large egg whites
icing sugar

Bring the milk with the sugar and orange rind to just below boiling point, then allow to cool. Strain through a fine sieve. Place the margarine, flour and milk in a saucepan over moderate heat and bring to the boil, whisking continuously. Cook for 2–3 minutes until smooth, then remove from the heat, add the egg yolks one at a time and beat into the mixture thoroughly with the orange juice. Whisk the egg whites until stiff. Stir in a spoonful of the egg white then fold in the remainder with a metal spoon and turn into a 2-pint (1-litre) soufflé

dish. Sieve a little icing sugar on top and bake in a moderately hot oven (375°F., 190°C., Gas Mark 5) for 35–40 minutes until well risen and firm. Serve immediately. Serve with Melba sauce (see page 133).
Serves 4

Variation
Grand Marnier soufflé Use 4 tablespoons Grand Marnier instead of orange juice.

Apple and ginger pudding

IMPERIAL/METRIC
Filling
1 oz./25 g. Stork margarine
1 lb./450 g. cooking apples, peeled, cored and sliced
grated rind of ½ lemon
sugar to taste
Sponge
4 oz./125 g. Stork margarine
4 oz./125 g. sugar
1 egg, beaten
4 oz./125 g. treacle
6 oz./175 g. plain flour, sieved with 1 teaspoon ginger, ¼ teaspoon allspice and 1 teaspoon cinnamon
1 teaspoon bicarbonate of soda
7½ fluid oz./225 ml. soured milk
Decoration
1 oz./25 g. crystallised ginger, chopped

Melt the margarine and cook the apples with the lemon rind to a thick pulp. Sweeten with sugar. To make the sponge, cream the margarine and sugar together until light and fluffy ; beat in the egg gradually. Add the treacle alternately with the flour and spices. Dissolve the bicarbonate of soda in the soured milk and stir into the mixture. Turn into a greased 8-inch (20-cm.) ring mould and bake in a moderate oven (350°F., 180°C., Gas Mark 4) for 1 hour until firm. Turn out and fill with the warm apple. Sprinkle the ginger on top and serve hot with cream.
Serves 4–6

Rhubarb and ginger crumble

IMPERIAL/METRIC
1½ lb./675 g. rhubarb, cut in 1-inch/2½-cm. lengths
sugar to taste
1 oz./25 g. stem or crystallised ginger, chopped (optional)
3 oz./75 g. Stork margarine
6 oz./175 g. plain flour, sieved with 1 teaspoon ground ginger
3 oz./75 g. demerara sugar

Place the fruit in a deep 6- to 7-inch (15- to 18-cm.) ovenproof dish. Add sugar to taste and 2 tablespoons water. Sprinkle on the ginger, if used. Rub the margarine into the flour, ginger and sugar until the mixture resembles fine breadcrumbs. Spoon over the fruit and bake on the second shelf from the top of a fairly hot oven (400°F., 200°C., Gas Mark 6) for 45–60 minutes.
Serves 4

Grapefruit meringue pie

Grapefruit meringue pie

IMPERIAL/METRIC
4 oz./100 g. shortcrust pastry (see
  pages 12–13)
Filling
3 tablespoons cornflour
¼ pint/150 ml. water
grated rind and juice of 1 grapefruit
1–2 oz./25–50 g. granulated sugar
2 large egg yolks
½ oz./15 g. Stork margarine
Meringue
2 large egg whites
2 oz./50 g. granulated sugar
2 oz./50 g. castor sugar

Roll out the pastry on a lightly
floured worktop and line a 7½- to
8-inch (19- to 20-cm.) shallow pie tin
or flan case. Line the inside with
greaseproof paper and baking
beans and bake blind in a fairly hot
oven (400°F., 200°C., Gas Mark 6)
for 15–20 minutes. Allow to cool.

Blend the cornflour, water, grapefruit rind and juice, made up to
¼ pint (150 ml.) with water if necessary, in a saucepan and bring
slowly to the boil, stirring continuously. Stir in the sugar according to
taste, and remove from the heat.
Beat in the egg yolks and margarine
and pour into the pastry case.

Whisk the egg whites until stiff,
beat in the granulated sugar a little
at a time, then fold in the castor
sugar. Spread or pipe over the
filling and bake in a moderate oven
(350°F., 180°C., Gas Mark 4) for
about 10 minutes until lightly
browned.
Serves 4

Apple and almond puff ❄

IMPERIAL/METRIC
1 lb./450 g. apples, peeled, cored
  and sliced
sugar to taste
2 oz./50 g. ground almonds
2 oz./50 g. raisins
6 oz./175 g. flaky or rough puff
  pastry, well chilled (see page 15)
beaten egg or milk for glazing
few flaked almonds

Stew the apples in the minimum of
water for about 5 minutes until soft
then sweeten to taste and beat in the
almonds and raisins. Leave to cool.
Roll out half the pastry thinly on a
lightly floured worktop and cut into
an 8-inch (20-cm.) round. Place on a
dampened baking sheet. Spoon the
apple on top, leaving a 1-inch (2½-
cm.) margin all round. Brush the
margin with beaten egg or milk.
Roll out the remaining pastry to a
9-inch (23-cm.) round. Fold in half
and make horizontal cuts through
the fold to within 2 inches (5 cm.) of
the edge. Position over the apple,
pressing the edges well together to
seal. Trim, flake and flute the edges
then brush with beaten egg or milk.
Sprinkle with flaked almonds and
bake in a hot oven (425°F., 220°C.,
Gas Mark 7) for 20–25 minutes until
golden brown and well puffed.
Serves 4–6
Freezing note Freeze this pudding
in a rigid polythene container.

Stuffed peaches ❄

IMPERIAL/METRIC
1½ oz./40 g. Stork margarine
1 oz./25 g. icing sugar
3 oz./75 g. ground almonds
grated rind of ½ lemon
4 large peaches, peeled, halved
  and stoned
1 tablespoon sherry
grated rind and juice of ½ orange
castor sugar

Cream 1 oz. (25 g.) of the margarine and the icing sugar in a mixing bowl. Add the ground almonds and lemon rind and form into eight balls. Put a ball into each peach half and press the halves together in pairs so that some of the filling is visible. Pack close together in a shallow ovenproof dish. Melt the remaining margarine with the sherry, orange rind and juice and pour over. Dredge heavily with sugar. Bake in a moderately hot oven (375°F., 190°C., Gas Mark 5) for 25–35 minutes until the sugar forms a syrupy glaze and the peaches are tender. Serve hot or cold with cream.
Serves 4
Freezing note Freeze the cold peaches with their syrup in a rigid polythene container.

Christmas pudding

IMPERIAL/METRIC
8 oz./225 g. Stork margarine
8 oz./225 g. soft brown sugar
7 oz./200 g. plain flour, sieved
12 oz./350 g. currants
8 oz./225 g. raisins
6 oz./175 g. sultanas
2 oz./50 g. mixed cut peel
1 oz./25 g. blanched almonds,
  chopped
1 oz./25 g. glacé cherries, washed
  and chopped
6 oz./175 g. fresh breadcrumbs
grated rind of 1 lemon
grated rind and juice of 1 orange
1 teaspoon nutmeg
1 tablespoon black treacle
2 large eggs
3–4 tablespoons milk or beer
2 tablespoons brandy or rum

Melt the margarine and mix all the remaining ingredients in well. Place the mixture in a greased 2-pint (1-litre) pudding basin. Cover tightly with greaseproof paper and foil. Secure with string under the rim. Place in a steamer two-thirds full with boiling water or a saucepan of boiling water to come halfway up the sides of the basin. Steam for 7–8 hours, adding more boiling water to pan when necessary. Remove from the saucepan and cool. When cold cover with fresh greased greaseproof paper and store in a cool place. Steam again for 2–3 hours before serving. Serve with hard sauce (see page 135).
Serves 6
Note This pudding should be made well in advance (4–6 weeks) to allow time to mature.
Illustrated on page 135

Blackcurrant shortcake

IMPERIAL/METRIC
1 lb./450 g. blackcurrants,
  destalked
2 tablespoons water
3 oz./75 g. sugar
Shortcake
6 oz./175 g. self-raising flour sieved
  with a pinch salt and ½ teaspoon
  grated nutmeg
3 oz./75 g. Stork margarine
2 oz./50 g. sugar
Decoration
icing sugar
¼ pint/150 ml. double cream,
  whipped
few blackcurrant sprigs dipped in
  castor sugar

Simmer the blackcurrants in the water with the sugar for 5 minutes. Cool then drain. Reserve the juice.
Place the flour in a bowl and rub in the margarine until the mixture resembles fine breadcrumbs. Mix in the sugar. Line a 7-inch (18-cm.) square or round loose-bottomed shallow sandwich tin with greaseproof paper. Press half the mixture into the tin. Spoon over the drained blackcurrants. Cover with the remaining mixture and press down lightly. Bake in a moderate oven (350°F., 180°C., Gas Mark 4) for 25–30 minutes. This may be served hot or cold. If to be served cold, cool in the tin. Turn out on to a serving dish and dredge with icing sugar. Pipe rosettes of cream around the shortcake and decorate with blackcurrant sprigs. If to be served hot, turn out on to a serving plate and shake over a little icing sugar. Serve with fresh cream, and the reserved juice if liked.
Serves 4–6

Variations
Fill with gooseberries poached in syrup or halved strawberries or fresh raspberries sprinkled with 1 tablespoon sugar.

Bavarian apricot and apple roll ❄

IMPERIAL/METRIC
4 oz./125 g. Stork margarine
6 oz./175 g. plain flour, sieved
2 tablespoons castor sugar
2–3 tablespoons milk
Filling
12 oz./350 g. cooking apples,
   peeled, cored and sliced
12 oz./350 g. fresh apricots, sliced
2 tablespoons sugar
2 tablespoons fresh breadcrumbs
1 oz./25 g. flaked almonds
Glaze
milk
castor sugar

Rub the margarine into the flour.
Add the sugar and mix with the milk

to a dough. Knead on a floured worktop then place in a polythene bag and leave to rest for 30 minutes in the refrigerator.

Roll the dough out to a 10- by 8-inch (25- by 20-cm.) rectangle and place on a baking sheet. Mix the apples, apricots, sugar, bread-crumbs and almonds and spoon down the centre of the pastry. Fold the sides in gently so that the filling is still visible down the centre and trim the ends neatly. Brush with a little milk and sprinkle with castor sugar. Bake in a fairly hot oven (400°F., 200°C., Gas Mark 6) for 30–40 minutes until crisp and golden. Serve hot, cut into thick slices and dusted with more castor sugar.
Serves 4–6
Freezing note Wrap the baked roll in foil.

Beignets with cherry sauce

IMPERIAL/METRIC
oil for deep-frying
¼ pint/150 ml. choux pastry (see
   page 17)
castor sugar
pinch cinnamon

Heat the oil in a deep fat frying pan to 370°F. (188°C.). Pipe the choux pastry into the fat in 1-inch (2½-cm.) lengths, cutting off with a damp knife, or spoon in using a teaspoon. As the beignets begin to swell turn them over and cook until golden brown – about 7–10 minutes. Drain well and toss in sugar and cinna-mon. Serve with hot cherry sauce (see page 135).
Serves 4
Illustrated on page 134

Cherry and almond tart ❄

IMPERIAL/METRIC
6 oz./175 g. rich flan pastry (see
   page 13)
1 lb./450 g. fresh cherries, stoned
1 tablespoon sugar
2 oz./50 g. Stork margarine
2 oz./50 g. castor sugar
1 large egg, beaten
few drops almond essence
2 oz./50 g. ground almonds
few flaked almonds

Roll out the pastry on a lightly floured worktop and line an 8-inch (20-cm.) flan case. Line the inside with greaseproof paper and baking beans and bake blind in a fairly hot oven (400°F., 200°C., Gas Mark 6) for 10 minutes. Arrange the cherries over the pastry and sprinkle with sugar. Cream the margarine and castor sugar until soft and fluffy. Beat in the egg and almond essence and fold in the ground almonds. Spread the mixture over the fruit and sprinkle the flaked almonds on top. Return to the oven at 350°F., 180°C., Gas Mark 4 for 30–40 minutes until golden. Serve hot.
Serves 4–6

Variations
Use 3 sliced peaches, 1 lb. (450 g.) stoned halved plums or 1 lb. (450 g.) blackcurrants instead of cherries.

Cherry and almond tart

Delaware pudding

IMPERIAL/METRIC
4 oz./125 g. Stork margarine
4 oz./125 g. castor sugar
2 large eggs, beaten
6 oz./175 g. self-raising flour, sieved
2–3 tablespoons milk
8 oz./225 g. apples, peeled, cored
  and chopped
2 oz./50 g. currants
1 oz./25 g. mixed peel
2 tablespoons demerara sugar
1 teaspoon ground cinnamon

Place the margarine, sugar, eggs and flour in a mixing bowl and beat together with a wooden spoon until well mixed – 2–3 minutes. Beat in the milk to make a dropping consistency. Combine the apples, currants, peel, demerara sugar and cinnamon. Place half the fruit mixture in the bottom of a well greased 2-pint (1-litre) pudding basin. Spoon half the sponge mixture on top then cover with the rest of the fruit and finally the remaining sponge mixture. Cover the basin with greased greaseproof paper or foil and secure with string under the rim. Place in a saucepan of boiling water to come halfway up the sides of the basin and simmer gently for 1½ hours, adding more boiling water to the pan if necessary. Turn out and serve with cream or custard.
Serves 4–6

Pineapple streusel flan ❄

IMPERIAL/METRIC
4 oz./125 g. Stork margarine
6 oz./175 g. plain flour, sieved
1 oz./25 g. ground almonds
1 tablespoon castor sugar
1 egg yolk
1–2 tablespoons cold water
1 small pineapple, peeled, cored
  and thinly sliced, or 15-oz./
  425-g. can pineapple rings
Topping
4 oz./125 g. Stork margarine
3 oz./75 g. soft brown sugar
2 teaspoons cinnamon
2 tablespoons flour
1½ oz./40 g. walnuts, chopped

Rub the margarine into the flour until the mixture resembles fine breadcrumbs. Add the almonds and sugar and bind with the egg yolk and water to make a soft dough. Knead on a lightly floured worktop, place in a polythene bag, then chill in the refrigerator for 30 minutes.

Roll out and line an 8-inch (20-cm.) fluted flan ring. Fill with pineapple slices. Make up the topping by melting the margarine and adding the sugar, cinnamon, flour and walnuts. Mix well and spread over the pineapple. Bake in a fairly hot oven (400°F., 200°C., Gas Mark 6) for 35–40 minutes. Serve hot with cream.
Serves 4–6

Freezing note Wrap the baked flan in foil.

Fruit fritters

IMPERIAL/METRIC
4 oz./100 g. flour, sieved
1 egg
¼ pint/150 ml. milk
1 oz./25 g. Stork margarine, melted
4 apples
oil for deep-frying
2–3 oz./50–75 g. castor sugar
1 teaspoon cinnamon
4 bananas

Place the flour in a mixing bowl, add the egg and milk and beat thoroughly. Finally add the melted margarine and beat in well. Peel the apples and cut into rings about ¼ inch (½ cm.) thick. Remove the core from each slice with a small cutter. Coat immediately in the batter and fry in the hot oil (360°F., 185°C.) until golden brown. Drain on absorbent paper then roll in the sugar mixed with the cinnamon. Repeat with the bananas, cutting each in half lengthways and again into half if too large.
Serves 4

Caramel bread and butter pudding

IMPERIAL/METRIC
6 thin slices white bread, crusts
  removed
2 oz./50 g. Stork margarine
2 oz./50 g. currants or sultanas
1½ oz./40 g. castor sugar
1 pint/575 ml. milk, warmed
2 large eggs
Caramel
2 tablespoons cold water
5 oz./150 g. castor sugar
3 tablespoons boiling water

Spread the bread thickly with margarine. Cut into fingers or small squares. Put half the fingers or squares into a 2-pint (1-litre) greased ovenproof dish. Sprinkle with all the fruit and half the sugar. Top with the remaining bread and sprinkle with the rest of the sugar.

Prepare the caramel by pouring the cold water into a small thick-based saucepan. Stir in the sugar and place over a low heat to dissolve, stirring occasionally. When the sugar has dissolved, bring to the boil and cook without stirring until the sugar turns a dark, golden brown. Remove at once from the heat and slowly spoon in the boiling water, stirring to loosen the caramel.

Add the caramel to the warmed milk and reheat slowly until the caramel is completely dissolved. Beat the eggs and milk mixture well together. Strain into the dish over the bread. Leave to stand for 30 minutes, then bake in the middle of a very moderate oven (325°F., 160°C., Gas Mark 3) for 45–60 minutes (or until the pudding is set and the top is crisp and golden).
Serves 4

Cold puddings

Blackberry and apple crisps

IMPERIAL/METRIC
12 oz./350 g. cooking apples,
    peeled, cored and sliced
8 oz./225 g. blackberries
sugar to taste
1 oz./25 g. Stork margarine
1 tablespoon golden syrup
¾ oz./20 g. cornflakes
6 tablespoons double cream
1 tablespoon top of the milk

Stew the apples and blackberries in the minimum of water until soft – about 5 minutes. Sweeten to taste and beat until smooth or blend in an electric liquidiser for a few minutes. Cool then chill. Melt the margarine and syrup in a pan, add the cornflakes and toss carefully until well coated. Whip the cream and milk together lightly. Divide the fruit among four glasses or fruit bowls. Spoon a layer of cream over the fruit and top with a pile of coated cornflakes.
Serves 4

Rum mousse with raspberries

IMPERIAL/METRIC
2 large eggs, separated
2 oz./50 g. castor sugar
6 fluid oz./175 ml. milk, warmed
½ oz./15 g. Stork margarine
1 tablespoon rum
½ oz./15 g. gelatine
2 tablespoons water
¼ pint/150 ml. double cream
1 tablespoon top of the milk
8 oz./225 g. raspberries, fresh or
    frozen

Beat the egg yolks and sugar together then add the warmed milk and place the mixture in the top of a double saucepan or bowl over a pan of hot water. Cook over a gentle heat until the custard thickens sufficiently to coat the back of a spoon. Beat in the margarine and rum. Dissolve the gelatine in the water in a basin over hot water, add to the custard and then chill until it is about to set. Whip the cream and milk together until thick and fold into the custard. Beat the egg whites until stiff and fold in with a metal spoon.

Turn into a lightly greased 2-pint (1-litre) mould or a glass bowl with a tumbler standing upright in the centre. Chill until set. Either turn out the mousse from the mould or pour hot water carefully into the glass, twist slightly and remove. Decorate or fill the centre hole with raspberries.
Serves 4

Variations
Omit the rum for a plain mousse. Serve with other fresh fruits in season.

Orange sorbet

IMPERIAL/METRIC
3 oz./75 g. castor sugar
juice of ½ lemon made up to ½ pint/
    275 ml. with water
grated rind of 1 orange
6-oz./170-g. can concentrated
    orange juice
1 egg white

Place the sugar, lemon juice and water in a saucepan and heat slowly until the sugar has dissolved. Allow the syrup to cool.

Add the orange rind and the undiluted orange juice to the sugar syrup. Pour into a plastic container with a tight-fitting lid. Place in the freezer or freezing compartment of the refrigerator until just firm. Turn out into a mixing bowl and mash with a fork until the crystals are broken down. Whisk the egg white until stiff and fold into the mixture with a metal spoon. Return to the plastic container and place in the freezer until firm. Allow the sorbet to soften in the refrigerator for 30 minutes before serving.
Serves 4

Variations
Grapefruit sorbet Substitute concentrated grapefruit juice for the concentrated orange juice.
Party sorbet Cut the lid off four oranges and scoop out the flesh, removing the pips and pithy membrane. Return the flesh to the hollowed out oranges and pile the sorbet on top. Replace the lids. Decorate with a sprig of mint.

Mocha soufflé with brandy snaps

IMPERIAL/METRIC
3 large eggs, separated
3 oz./75 g. castor sugar
1–2 tablespoons coffee essence
½ oz./15 g. gelatine
3 tablespoons water
2 oz./50 g. plain chocolate, melted
¼ pint/150 ml. double cream
2 tablespoons top of the milk
Brandy snaps
ingredients as brandy cornets
    (see page 158)

Secure a double band of greaseproof paper, to come about 2 inches (5 cm.) above the top of, and also around the outside of a 6-inch (15-cm.) soufflé dish and brush the inside with oil. Place the egg yolks, sugar and coffee essence in a bowl over hot water and whisk until very thick. Dissolve the gelatine in the water in another bowl over hot water. Cool slightly and add the egg mixture followed by the cooled melted chocolate. Whip the cream and top of the milk until thick and fold into the mixture with a metal spoon. Finally whisk the egg whites until stiff and fold in. Turn into the prepared soufflé dish or glass bowl and chill until set.

Make up the mixture for the brandy cornets on page 158 and bake in teaspoonfuls. Mould the biscuits around well greased wooden spoon handles. When cold, arrange on top of the soufflé.
Serves 4–6

Old-fashioned trifle

IMPERIAL/METRIC
1 jam-filled plain swiss roll (see
    page 155)
15-oz./425-g. can raspberries or
    blackcurrants, drained and juice
    reserved
3–4 tablespoons sherry
½ pint/275 ml. red jelly made up
    according to the packet
    instructions
½ pint/275 ml. custard sauce (see
    page 133), cooled, or 14½-oz./
    411-g. can custard
½ pint/275 ml. double cream
Decoration
glacé cherries
angelica leaves
flaked almonds

Cut the swiss roll into ½-inch (1-cm.) slices and use to line a glass bowl. Arrange the fruit over the top and pour over the juice, sherry and jelly. Leave in a cool place and when the jelly is set pour over the cooled custard. When the custard is firm, lightly whip the cream and pour half over the surface of the trifle. Whip the remaining cream until stiff enough to pipe. Decorate the top with whirls of cream, glacé cherries, angelica leaves and almonds.
Serves 4

Chocolate and orange pots

IMPERIAL/METRIC
4 oz./100 g. plain chocolate
½ oz./15 g. Stork margarine
2 large eggs, separated
½ teaspoon coffee essence
few drops vanilla essence
grated rind of ½ orange
1 tablespoon sherry, brandy or
   rum (optional)
1 oz./25 g. walnuts, roughly
   chopped
Decoration
thinly pared rind of ½ orange, cut in
   julienne strips

Chocolate and orange pots

Melt the chocolate and margarine in a fairly large bowl over a pan of hot water. Mix in the egg yolks and remaining ingredients except the egg whites. Whisk the egg whites until stiff and fold into the chocolate mixture with a metal spoon. Pour into four individual pots or glasses and chill. Decorate with the orange rind.
Serves 4

Apricot crème caramel

IMPERIAL/METRIC
3–4 tablespoons apricot jam
Caramel
2 oz./50 g. granulated sugar
2 tablespoons water
Custard
3 large eggs
¾ pint/425 ml. milk
1 oz./25 g. castor sugar
few drops vanilla essence
Decoration
whipped cream (optional)

To make the caramel, place the sugar and water in a saucepan and heat gently until the sugar has dissolved. Quickly bring to the boil and boil steadily until the sugar turns golden brown. Pour on to an oiled baking sheet and allow to cool.

Place the jam in the base of a greased 1-pint (½-litre) soufflé dish. To make the custard lightly beat the eggs. Heat the milk and sugar together until the sugar dissolves, and then pour on to the eggs. Add the vanilla essence. Strain the mixture on to the jam. Place the soufflé dish in a baking tin filled a quarter full with water. Bake in a very slow oven (275°F., 140°C., Gas Mark 1) for 1¼–1½ hours. Allow to cool.

Break up the set caramel with a rolling pin and sprinkle on top of the custard. Decorate if liked with rosettes of whipped cream.
Serves 4–5

Variation
Use raspberry, greengage or peach jam instead of the apricot.

Summer pudding

IMPERIAL/METRIC
6 thin slices white bread, crusts
   removed
2 oz./50 g. Stork margarine
1½ lb./675 g. mixed soft fruit – any
   combination of raspberries,
   blackberries, blackcurrants,
   redcurrants or strawberries
sugar to taste
¼ pint/150 ml. double cream

Spread the bread with margarine. Line a greased 1-pint (½-litre) pudding basin with four slices bread.

Cook the fruit in a little water for a few minutes and sweeten to taste. Pour into the bread-lined pudding basin and cover with the remaining bread. Put a saucer on top and stand a heavy weight on the saucer. Leave in the refrigerator for several hours, preferably overnight.

Turn out of the basin on to a serving plate and decorate with whipped cream.
Serves 4

Orange marquise

Orange marquise

IMPERIAL/METRIC
¾ pint/425 ml. milk
grated rind and juice of 1 orange
3 large egg yolks
2½ oz./65 g. castor sugar
¾ oz./20 g. gelatine
3 oz./75 g. Stork margarine
6 oz./175 g. digestive biscuits,
    crushed
pinch each cinnamon and nutmeg
¼ pint/150 ml. double cream,
    whipped
1 egg white
Decoration
¼ pint/150 ml. double cream,
    whipped
3 oranges, peeled and divided into
    segments with the membrane
    removed
1 orange, cut into slices with the
    rind left on (optional)

Bring the milk and orange rind slowly to the boil. Beat the egg yolks and sugar well together until pale, then pour on the milk. Rinse out the pan and return the custard mixture to a gentle heat until it thickens *but do not boil*. Strain into a bowl to cool. Dissolve the gelatine in the orange juice. Meanwhile melt the margarine and mix with the digestive biscuits and spices; cool. When the custard mixture has cooled stir in the dissolved gelatine, cream and beaten egg white. When the mixture begins to set pour half into a deep 7-inch (18-cm.) oiled flan tin. Sprinkle with a layer of half the biscuit mixture, carefully spoon over the remaining custard mixture and leave to set.

Turn the mould out on to a serving dish and spread the top and sides with cream. Mark the top with a knife to form a diamond pattern. Arrange the orange segments round the top edge. Cover the sides with the reserved crumbs. Decorate the edge of the serving dish with orange slices, if liked.

Serves 6
Freezing note Freeze the mould without decoration.

Variation
Use plain chocolate-coated digestive biscuits for the crumbs and omit the spices. Sprinkle grated chocolate on top.

Florida cheesecake ❄

IMPERIAL/METRIC
4 oz./100 g. digestive biscuits,
    crushed
1 oz./25 g. Stork margarine, melted
Filling
½ pint/275 ml. milk
1 tablespoon orange juice
4 eggs
grated rind of 1 orange
grated rind of 1 lemon
3 oz./75 g. castor sugar
1 oz./25 g. flour
1 lb./450 g. cottage cheese,
    sieved
Decoration
icing sugar
orange segments

Mix the crushed biscuits and melted margarine together and press into the bottom of a greased 8-inch (20-cm.) loose-bottomed tin.

Place all the filling ingredients in a bowl and beat by hand or with an electric mixer until smooth. Pour the mixture into the tin. Bake in the middle of a very moderate oven (325°F., 160°C., Gas Mark 3) for 1–1¼ hours. Chill then carefully remove from the tin. Place on a serving dish. Dredge with icing sugar and decorate with the orange segments.

Serves 4–6
Freezing note Freeze before decorating.

Chestnut shortcakes ❄

IMPERIAL/METRIC
3 oz./75 g. plain flour, sieved
1 oz./25 g. castor sugar
2 oz./50 g. Stork margarine
1 oz./25 g. walnut halves, chopped
1 egg white
¼ pint/150 ml. double cream
1 tablespoon top of the milk
3 tablespoons sweetened chestnut
    purée
1 tablespoon sherry
few walnut halves

Place the flour, sugar and margarine in a mixing bowl and beat with a wooden spoon until well mixed – about 2–3 minutes. Add the chopped nuts and knead into a smooth dough. Roll out and cut into four 5-inch (13-cm.) fluted rounds. Place on a baking sheet, prick well and bake in a moderate oven (350°F., 180°C., Gas Mark 4) for 15–20 minutes until lightly browned. Cool slightly then remove to a wire tray to cool.

Whisk the egg white until stiff. Whip the cream and milk together until stiff. Soften the chestnut purée by adding the sherry then fold in first the cream and finally the egg white, using a metal spoon. Spoon or pipe on top of the shortcakes and decorate with walnut halves.

Serves 4
Freezing note Freeze baked shortcakes only.

Normandy gâteau ❄ Strawberry chocolate box ❄

Normandy gâteau

IMPERIAL/METRIC
3 large eggs
4½ oz./125 g. castor sugar
1 tablespoon coffee essence
3 oz./75 g. plain flour, sieved with a
 pinch salt
1½ oz./40 g. hazelnuts, skinned,
 browned and ground
½ oz./15 g. Stork margarine, melted
Filling
½ oz./15 g. Stork margarine, melted
1 lb./450 g. dessert apples, peeled,
 cored and diced
juice and grated rind of 1 lemon
sugar to taste
½ pint/275 ml. double cream,
 whipped
Decoration
sifted icing sugar
cream
whole hazelnuts, browned, or sliced
 dessert apple dipped in lemon
 juice

Whisk the eggs, sugar and coffee essence together in a bowl over a pan of hot water until thick and mousse-like. Remove the bowl from the heat and whisk until cold. Fold in the flour with a metal spoon. Add the hazelnuts and margarine and fold in carefully. Turn into two prepared 8-inch (20-cm.) sandwich tins lined with greased greaseproof paper and dusted with flour. Bake in a moderately hot oven (375°F., 190°C., Gas Mark 5) for 25 minutes until the sponges spring back when gently pressed with a finger. Turn out on to a wire tray to cool. When cold remove the greaseproof paper.

To make the filling melt the margarine and add the prepared apples and lemon juice and rind and cook gently until soft. Sweeten to taste and leave to cool. Whip the cream and reserve some for decoration. Place one cake on a serving dish and spread a layer of cream over it. Cover with the apple mixture. Place the second sponge on top and press down lightly.

Dust the cake with icing sugar. Pipe rosettes of cream on top and decorate with hazelnuts or apple.

Serves 4–6

Freezing note Freeze the filled cake before decorating. Open freeze, then wrap in film or foil.

Variation

Add a few sultanas and stem ginger slices to the apple mixture.

Strawberry chocolate box

IMPERIAL/METRIC
4 large eggs
4 oz./100 g. sugar
grated rind of ½ lemon
3 oz./75 g. plain flour, sieved with
 1 oz./25 g. cornflour
2 oz./50 g. Stork margarine, melted
Filling
2 lb./900 g. strawberries
juice of 2 oranges
2 tablespoons Grand Marnier
 (optional)
¾ pint/425 ml. double cream,
 whipped
sugar to taste
4 oz./100 g. plain chocolate

Whisk the eggs, sugar and lemon rind together in a bowl over hot water until thick and mousse-like. Remove the bowl from the heat and whisk until cold. Fold in the flour and cornflour with a metal spoon. Add the melted margarine and fold in carefully. Turn into an 8-inch (20-cm.) square tin lined with greased greaseproof paper on the bottom and sides and dusted with flour. Bake in a moderately hot oven (375°F., 190°C., Gas Mark 5) for 30–35 minutes until the cake springs back to the touch. Turn out on to a wire tray to cool. Remove the paper.

Reserve half the whole strawberries for decoration and halve the remainder. Cut the cake into three layers. Place the bottom layer on a serving dish and spoon over half the orange juice and liqueur, if used. Spread with a third of the cream, sweetened to taste, and half the halved strawberries. Place the second sponge layer on top and press down lightly. Repeat the orange juice, cream and strawberries. Place the remaining sponge layer on top. Spread the remaining cream over the top and sides of the cake and arrange the reserved whole strawberries on top.

To make the chocolate squares, melt the coarsely grated chocolate in a bowl over hot water. Spread thinly on to waxed paper and leave to set. Mark into squares. Peel away from the paper and arrange slightly overlapping round the sides of the gâteau.

Serves 6–8

Freezing note Freeze the baked sponge before filling.

Variations

Fill with raspberries or cherries.
 Use sliced peaches or apricots. These should be covered with apricot glaze on top, the sides decorated with browned flaked almonds and cream piped in a border on the top.
Illustrated on page 137

Walnut and raspberry roll

Walnut and raspberry roll

IMPERIAL/METRIC
4 large eggs
3 oz./75 g. castor sugar
1½ oz./40 g. walnuts, ground
1½ oz./40 g. plain flour, sieved with a pinch cinnamon
1 oz./25 g. Stork margarine, melted icing sugar
Filling
½ pint/275 ml. double cream, whipped until thick
sugar to taste
12 oz./350 g. raspberries
Decoration
¼ pint/150 ml. double cream, whipped

Line a 12- by 10-inch (30- by 25-cm.) baking tray or swiss roll tin with greased greaseproof paper, and dust lightly with flour.

Whisk the eggs and sugar until thick and creamy. Fold in the walnuts and the flour and cinnamon with a metal spoon. Fold in the melted margarine and spread evenly on to the prepared baking tray or tin. Bake in a moderately hot oven (375°F., 190°C., Gas Mark 5) for 20–25 minutes until the sponge springs back to the touch. Turn out on to a sheet of greaseproof paper sprinkled with icing sugar and peel off the paper. Leave to cool.

Trim away the edges of the cake. Sweeten the whipped cream to taste and spread over the sponge. Cover to within ½ inch (1 cm.) of the edge with raspberries, reserving a few for decoration. Fold over gently with the aid of the sheet of grease-proof to ensure that the filling is in the centre. Wrap in foil with the fold underneath. Chill for 30 minutes.

To serve, unwrap and place on a serving dish. Spread the roll all over with a thin layer of whipped cream, pipe rosettes down the centre with the remaining cream and decorate with the reserved raspberries.
Serves 6–8
Freezing note Fill the roll and freeze wrapped in the foil. Decorate on thawing.

Variations
Slice 12 oz. (350 g.) strawberries and sprinkle with Grand Marnier. Leave to macerate for 30 minutes before using to fill the roll.

Fill with ½ pint (275 ml.) apple purée blended with 2 oz. (50 g.) sultanas and the juice of ½ lemon.

Danish hazelnut and strawberry galette ❄

IMPERIAL/METRIC
4 oz./100 g. hazelnuts
6 oz./175 g. Stork margarine
4 oz./100 g. castor sugar
grated rind of ½ lemon
6 oz./175 g. plain flour, sieved with ¼ teaspoon cinnamon and a pinch salt
Filling
½ pint/275 ml. double cream
¼ pint/150 ml. single cream
1 tablespoon castor sugar
1½ lb./675 g. strawberries

Place the hazelnuts on a tray and warm under the grill until the skins split. Rub off the skins and chop roughly. Place the margarine, sugar and lemon rind in a mixing bowl and beat until creamy, light and fluffy. Fold in the flour sifted with the cinnamon and salt. Knead together and leave in the refrigerator for 30 minutes. Divide into three portions. Lightly grease and flour three baking sheets (see note). Mark a 7-inch (18-cm.) circle on each and press and roll a portion of pastry into each marked circle. Sprinkle with the prepared hazelnuts. Bake in a moderate oven (350°F., 180°C., Gas Mark 4) for 20–25 minutes until golden. Cool for 10 minutes on the tray before loosening with a knife and carefully transferring to a cooling tray.

Whisk the double and single creams together until thick and sweeten with the sugar. Reserve some cream for decoration. Reserve some strawberries for decoration. Slice the remainder and mix with the cream. Use to sandwich the biscuit layers together. Leave the top biscuit uncovered and pipe with rosettes of cream and decorate with whole strawberries. Leave in a cool place or the refrigerator for at least 30 minutes before serving.
Serves 6–8
Note If you cannot bake all the biscuit layers at once do it in batches.
Freezing note Biscuit pastry is suitable for freezing raw or cooked.
Illustrated on page 136

Choux puffs with chocolate ❄

IMPERIAL/METRIC
¼ pint/150 ml. choux pastry (see page 17)
little beaten egg or milk for glazing
1 oz./25 g. almonds, blanched and finely chopped
castor sugar
Filling
3 oz./75 g. sugar
4 tablespoons water
2 egg yolks
4 oz./100 g. Stork margarine
3 oz./75 g. plain chocolate
2 teaspoons instant coffee powder
¼ pint/150 ml. extra thick double cream
Decoration
icing sugar

Pipe the choux pastry into small balls on a lightly greased baking sheet, using a ½-inch (1-cm.) plain éclair pipe. Brush with beaten egg or milk. Sprinkle with almonds and sugar and bake in a fairly hot oven (400°F., 200°C., Gas Mark 6) until crisp and brown – about 25 minutes. Cool on a wire tray. Make a small hole in the base of each puff with a sharp pointed knife or slit across in half to fill.

To make the filling dissolve the sugar in the water in a saucepan over gentle heat and then boil until the syrup forms a thread between the finger and thumb. Pour on to the lightly beaten egg yolks in a steady stream, whisking continuously until thick and mousse-like. Cream the margarine and add the whisked mixture gradually. Melt the chocolate with the coffee over a pan of hot water and allow to cool. Add to the mixture. Stir in the cream and pipe or spoon into the puffs. Dust with a little icing sugar. Serve with chocolate sauce (see page 133).
Serves 4–6
Freezing note Baked choux pastry freezes well.

Raspberry flan ❄

IMPERIAL/METRIC
6 oz./175 g. all-in-one shortcrust pastry (see page 12)
12 oz./350 g. fresh raspberries
Confectioners' custard
1 oz./25 g. Stork margarine
1 oz./25 g. plain flour
¼ pint/150 ml. milk
1 oz./25 g. castor sugar
1 standard egg yolk
1 tablespoon cream
1 tablespoon Kirsch or sherry
Glaze
¼ pint/150 ml. diluted fruit juice
2 teaspoons arrowroot
1 oz./25 g. sugar
1 tablespoon lemon juice

Roll out the pastry on a lightly floured worktop and line an 8-inch (20-cm.) flan ring. Line the inside with greaseproof paper and baking beans. Bake blind in a fairly hot oven (400°F., 200°C., Gas Mark 6) for 15 minutes. Remove the greaseproof paper and beans and bake for a further 10–15 minutes. Cool on a wire tray.

For the custard, place the margarine, flour and milk in a saucepan. Bring to the boil whisking continuously over a moderate heat and cook for 2–3 minutes, then cool. Whisk in the remaining ingredients and spread the custard over the base of the flan case.

Wash the raspberries and dry well. Arrange them over the top of the custard.

Mix a little fruit juice with the arrowroot until blended. Heat the remainder of the fruit juice with the sugar and lemon juice then pour on to the blended arrowroot. Return to the heat for 1–2 minutes and cook until clear, stirring all the time. Spread over the raspberries and allow to cool.
Serves 6–8
Freezing note Freeze the cooked pastry case.
Illustrated on page 10

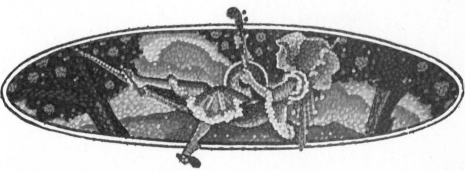

Tea-time is treated differently throughout the country, being usually a cooked meal in the North and Scotland and sandwiches and cakes in the South. However, all households with children have a meal at tea-time and this is where home baking comes into its own. Although it is no longer cheap to bake, it gives much pleasure and satisfaction to make cakes, bread and biscuits at home.

If you find cake making difficult try the Stork all-in-one method. This is a really quick and foolproof way to make cakes. The all-in-one method works because the soft blend of oils in Stork margarine promotes the quick mixing of all the ingredients. The additional raising agent (baking powder) compensates for the fact that less air is incorporated during the initial mixing than with the creaming method. During baking, the raising agent reacts with the liquid from the eggs to produce carbon dioxide and steam, which make the cake rise. The texture of the all-in-one cake is more open, due to the size of the increased air cells.

Yeast cookery

An aroma of freshly baked bread or buns will make you very popular with the family.

Points to note

Yeast Fresh or dried yeast should be used; brewers yeast is not for baking. 1 oz. (25 g.) fresh yeast equals ½ oz. (15 g.) dried yeast. Fresh yeast will keep up to 4 weeks in a refrigerator and up to a year in the freezer if it is tightly wrapped. To use from the freezer, grate the yeast; for dried yeast follow the manufacturer's directions carefully.
Temperature Cold retards the growth of yeast and extreme heat will destroy the yeast altogether, so when putting the dough to prove leave it at room temperature.

Flour Strong flour is best for yeast recipes as it absorbs the liquid easily and develops into a firm, elastic dough when kneaded.
Liquid You will need slightly less than ½ pint (275 ml.) to 1 lb. (450 g.) flour to make a bread dough and the temperature of the liquid should always be blood heat or hand warm.
Kneading The success of the bread depends on the kneading. It is necessary to work and pummel the dough for at least 10 minutes until it is firm and springy to the touch. Alternatively, this stage can be carried out using the dough hook on an electric mixer at low speed for 2–3 minutes.
Timing If you wish to stagger your bread making, you can put the dough in the refrigerator to prove, where it will take about 12–24 hours, depending on the quantity.
Short-time bread doughs The short-time method of making bread cuts out the initial rising process and replaces it with a 5–10 minute resting period.

It involves using ascorbic acid (Vitamin C), which can be bought in 25, 50 or 100 mg. tablet form. It is crushed and added with the liquid. When using this method it is recommended that fresh yeast be used.

Genoese fruit ring (page 156), fairy cakes (page 154), coffee all-in-one Victoria sandwich with chocolate Stork icing (pages 152 and 169) piped in a lattice design using a ribbon tube, and Dundee cake (page 153)

Teas

Adding the eggs to the Stork margarine, sugar, flour and baking powder in a mixing bowl ready for beating in the all-in-one cake-making method.

The finished all-in-one Victoria sandwich cake filled and iced with Stork icing (see page 169) and decorated with chocolate triangles (see Chocolate boxes for method – page 156).

Creamed and all-in-one cakes

All-in-one Victoria sandwich

IMPERIAL/METRIC
4 oz./125 g. Stork margarine
4 oz./125 g. castor sugar
2 large eggs
4 oz./125 g. self-raising flour, sieved
    with 1 teaspoon baking powder
Filling
raspberry jam or Stork icing (see
    page 169)
Topping
icing sugar

Place all the ingredients for the cake in a mixing bowl and beat with a wooden spoon until well mixed – 2–3 minutes. Alternatively use an electric mixer and beat for 1–2 minutes. Place in either an 8-inch (20-cm.) or two 7-inch (18-cm.) greased sandwich tins lined on the bottom with greaseproof paper (see page 160).

Bake in the middle of a very moderate oven (325°F., 160°C., Gas Mark 3) for 35–40 minutes for an 8-inch (20-cm.) cake and 25–35 minutes for two 7-inch (18-cm.) cakes.

Turn out, remove the paper and cool on a wire tray. When cold sandwich the smaller cakes or split the larger cake and fill with jam. Dredge the top with icing sugar. Alternatively, fill and decorate with any flavour of Stork icing (page 169).

Freezing note Victoria sandwich cakes can be frozen with or without icing.

Variations
Traditional Victoria sandwich Use the ingredients as above but omit the baking powder. Cream the margarine and sugar together until light and fluffy. Beat in the eggs one at a time, adding a little of the sieved flour with the second egg. Fold in the remaining flour with a metal spoon. Continue as above.
Coffee cake Add 1 tablespoon coffee essence or 2 teaspoons instant coffee dissolved in 1 tablespoon hot water and cooled.
Illustrated on page 151

Honeynut ring cake ❄

IMPERIAL/METRIC
6 oz./175 g. Stork margarine
3 oz./75 g. castor sugar
3 tablespoons clear honey
3 large eggs, separated
8 oz./225 g. self-raising flour
1 teaspoon cinnamon
pinch nutmeg
2 oz./50 g. walnuts, chopped
2 tablespoons orange juice
grated rind of 1 orange
Decoration
icing sugar for dredging

Cream the margarine and sugar together in a mixing bowl until light and fluffy. Beat in the honey. Beat the egg yolks into the creamed mixture, mixing thoroughly. Sieve the flour, cinnamon and nutmeg and fold into the mixture with the walnuts, orange juice and orange rind.

Beat the egg whites stiffly and fold into the mixture. Pour into an 8-inch (20-cm.) greased and floured ring tin. Bake in the middle of a moderately hot oven (375°F., 190°C., Gas Mark 5) for 40–50 minutes.

Turn out carefully and cool on a wire tray. Dredge with icing sugar.
Freezing note Freeze before decorating.

Variation
Lemon rind and juice can be substituted for orange.

Mexican ring cake ❄

IMPERIAL/METRIC
4 oz./125 g. Stork margarine
4 oz./125 g. castor sugar
2 large eggs
2 tablespoons cocoa blended with 2 tablespoons hot water
4 oz./125 g. self-raising flour, sieved with 1 teaspoon baking powder
Decoration
coffee fudge icing (see page 170)
shredded or desiccated coconut, toasted

Place all the ingredients for the cake in a mixing bowl and beat with a wooden spoon until well mixed – 2–3 minutes. Place in a greased and floured 8-inch (20-cm.) ring tin. Bake in the middle of a very moder-ate oven (325°F., 160°C., Gas Mark 3) for 35–40 minutes. Turn out and cool on a wire tray.

Spread the icing over the ring cake, smoothing with a palette knife. Sprinkle with coconut.
Freezing note This can be frozen after it has been iced. Open freeze, then pack in a polythene bag. Unwrap before thawing.

Old English Madeira cake ❄

IMPERIAL/METRIC
6 oz./175 g. Stork margarine
6 oz./175 g. castor sugar
3 standard eggs
8 oz./225 g. plain flour, sieved with 1½ teaspoons baking powder
2 thin strips citron peel (optional)

Place all the ingredients except the citron peel in a mixing bowl and beat with a wooden spoon until well mixed – 2–3 minutes. Place in a greased and lined 7-inch (18-cm.) cake tin. Smooth the top and place the peel in the centre if used. Bake in the middle of a very moderate oven (325°F., 160°C., Gas Mark 3) for 1½–1¾ hours. Test with a clean skewer; if it comes out clean when inserted into the cake, it is cooked. Turn out, remove the paper and cool on a wire tray.
Note To line a cake tin, see line drawings on page 160.
Freezing note This cake can be frozen either whole or cut in slices and wrapped individually in cling wrap and foil.

Variations
Creamed cake This cake may be made by the creaming method.
Cherry cake Add 8 oz. (225 g.) glacé cherries, washed and halved. Bake for 1¾–2 hours.
Orange Madeira Add the grated rind of 1 orange and 1 tablespoon orange juice.

Valentine cake ❄

IMPERIAL/METRIC
basic all-in-one Victoria sandwich cake mixture (see page 152)
chocolate Stork icing (see page 169)
Decoration
chocolate vermicelli
mimosa balls

Make up the Victoria sandwich and place in a greased heart-shaped tin, approximately 8 inches (20 cm.) across the widest point and 7 inches (18 cm.) in length. Bake in the middle of a very moderate oven (325°F., 160°C., Gas Mark 3) for 40–45 minutes. Turn out and cool on a wire tray.

Make up the Stork icing. Cut the cake horizontally through the centre and sandwich the two halves together with a little of the Stork icing. Spread some of the icing around the sides and press the chocolate vermicelli on. Spread a little icing on top and pipe the remainder around the top edges. Decorate with mimosa balls.

Dundee cake

IMPERIAL/METRIC
6 oz./175 g. Stork margarine
6 oz./175 g. castor sugar
grated rind of 1 orange
4 standard eggs
7 oz./200 g. plain flour, sieved with ½ teaspoon baking powder
1 teaspoon mixed spice
6 oz./175 g. currants
6 oz./175 g. sultanas
6 oz./175 g. raisins
2 oz./50 g. glacé cherries, washed and halved
3 oz./75 g. mixed cut peel
Decoration
2 oz./50 g. whole blanched almonds

Place all the ingredients except the whole almonds in a mixing bowl and beat thoroughly with a wooden spoon until well mixed – 3–4 minutes. Place in a greased and lined 7-inch (18-cm.) round cake tin and smooth the surface with the back of a hot wet metal spoon. Arrange the whole almonds in circles round the top. (To line cake tin, see page 160.)

Bake in the middle of a slow oven (300°F., 150°C., Gas Mark 2) for 3–3½ hours. Test with a skewer before removing from the oven. Turn out, remove the paper and cool on a wire tray.
Note If wrapped and kept in an air-tight container this cake will keep well for several weeks.

Variation
Creamed cake This cake may be made by the creaming method but omit the baking powder.
Illustrated on page 151

Devil's food cake ❄

IMPERIAL/METRIC
6 oz./175 g. Stork margarine
6 oz./175 g. castor sugar
2 large eggs
6 oz./175 g. golden syrup
2 oz./50 g. ground almonds
6 oz./175 g. plain flour, sieved with
    2½ oz./65 g. cocoa
½ teaspoon bicarbonate of soda
    blended with 6 fluid oz./175 ml.
    milk
double quantities coffee fudge icing
    (see page 170)

Place all the ingredients except the icing in a mixing bowl and beat with a wooden spoon until smooth – 2–3 minutes. Pour into a greased and lined 8-inch (20-cm.) square cake tin. Bake in the middle of a slow oven (300°F., 150°C., Gas Mark 2) for 1¾–2 hours. Turn out, remove the paper and cool on a wire tray.

Spread the icing over the sides and top of the cake. Decorate as liked.

Freezing note Can be frozen plain or decorated.

Coffee walnut fudge cake ❄

IMPERIAL/METRIC
6 oz./175 g. Stork margarine
6 oz./175 g. castor sugar
3 large eggs
6 oz./175 g. self-raising flour, sieved
    with 1½ teaspoons baking powder
2 oz./50 g. chopped walnuts
1 tablespoon coffee essence
Filling and decoration
coffee Stork icing (see page 169)
3 oz./75 g. walnuts

Place all the ingredients for the cake in a mixing bowl and beat with a wooden spoon until well mixed – 2–3 minutes. Place in two 7-inch (18-cm.) greased and bottom-lined sandwich tins. Bake in the middle of a very moderate oven (325°F., 160°C., Gas Mark 3) for 35–40 minutes. Turn out, remove the paper and cool on a wire tray. (To line the sandwich tins, see page 160.)

To fill and ice, sandwich the two cakes together with a little of the icing. Spread most of the remainder on the sides and top of the cake. Chop all but eight of the walnuts and press around the sides. Pipe the remaining icing around the edge using a star nozzle and decorate with the reserved walnuts.
Freezing note Freeze plain or decorated but without the walnuts.

Fairy cakes ❄

IMPERIAL/METRIC
4 oz./125 g. Stork margarine
4 oz./125 g. castor sugar
2 large eggs
5 oz./150 g. self-raising flour, sieved
    with 1 teaspoon baking powder
Decoration
icing (see method)
miniature liquorice allsorts, fruit
    jellies, chocolate drops or other
    suitable sweets

Place all the ingredients for the cake in a mixing bowl and beat with a wooden spoon until well mixed – 2–3 minutes. Place in 18–24 greased bun tins or paper cases. Bake on the second shelf from the top of a moderately hot oven (375°F., 190°C., Gas Mark 5) for 15–20 minutes. Cool. Ice with Stork icing, fudge or glacé icing (see pages 169–170) and decorate with any of the suggested decorations.
Makes 18–24 fairy cakes
Freezing note Can be frozen plain or iced with Stork icing. Glacé icing is best put on cakes after thawing.

Variations
Butterfly cakes Remove a slice from the top of each cake and halve. Decorate the cakes with flavoured Stork icing (see page 169) and re-place the top halves to form butterfly wings. Dredge with icing sugar.
Chocolate cup cakes Add 1 tablespoon cocoa to the basic mixture and ice with chocolate glacé icing (see page 169).
Queen cakes Add 2 oz. (50 g.) sultanas and 1 oz. (25 g.) chopped glacé cherries to the basic mixture.
Fancy-shaped cakes Bake the mixture in a greased and lined 11- by 7-inch (28- by 18-cm.) swiss roll tin. Cut into fancy shapes, ice with Stork or glacé icing (see page 169) and decorate.
Illustrated on page 151

All-in-one lemon swiss roll ❄

IMPERIAL/METRIC
2 oz./50 g. Stork margarine
4 oz./125 g. castor sugar
2 large eggs
4 oz./125 g. self-raising flour, sieved
grated rind of 1 lemon
Filling and decoration
lemon curd
castor and icing sugar
crystallised lemon slices

Place all the ingredients for the cake in a mixing bowl and beat with a wooden spoon until well mixed – 2–3 minutes. Put the mixture in a greased and lined 11- by 7-inch (28- by 18-cm.) swiss roll tin. Bake in the middle of a fairly hot oven (400°F., 200°C., Gas Mark 6) for 10–12 minutes.

Place a sheet of greaseproof paper on top of a damp tea-towel. Dredge lightly with castor sugar. Turn the swiss roll out on to the sugared paper. Remove the paper and trim the edges of the cake. Spread quickly with lemon curd and roll up using the greaseproof paper as a guide. When cold unwrap and dredge with icing sugar. If liked mark the top with diagonal lines using a hot skewer. Decorate with lemon slices.
Freezing note Open freeze on a plate after decoration, then wrap in cling wrap and foil. Unwrap before thawing.

Variation
Use warmed jam instead of lemon curd for the filling.

'The Brighton Belle' ❄

IMPERIAL/METRIC

Cake
4 oz./125 g. Stork margarine
4 oz./125 g. castor sugar
2 large eggs
4 oz./125 g. self-raising flour, sieved
   with 1 teaspoon baking powder
2 tablespoons cocoa blended with
   3 tablespoons hot water, cooled

Filling and topping
castor sugar for sprinkling
3 tablespoons chocolate spread
1½ quantities chocolate Stork icing
   (see page 169)

Decoration
2 chocolate biscuits
3 liquorice whirls
1 packet liquorice allsorts
1 tube Smarties
desiccated coconut, some coloured
   with green food colouring

To make the cake, place all the ingredients in a mixing bowl and beat with a wooden spoon until well mixed – 2–3 minutes. Place three-quarters of the mixture in a greased and lined 11- by 7-inch (28- by 18-cm.) swiss roll tin and a quarter into a greased and bottom-lined 1-lb. (450-g.) loaf tin. Bake in the middle of a very moderate oven (325°F., 160°C., Gas Mark 3) for 15–20 minutes for the swiss roll and 10 minutes for the loaf tin. Turn the swiss roll out on to lightly sugared greaseproof paper placed on a damp tea-towel. Remove the paper, trim the edges of the cake and spread with chocolate spread. Roll up carefully and leave to cool on a wire tray. Turn out the cake from the loaf tin, remove the paper and cool.

To assemble the Brighton Belle, cut the loaf cake in half and hollow out the tops a little to make two trucks. Cover with chocolate icing. Cover the swiss roll with chocolate icing and place a chocolate biscuit at each end. Half unroll two liquorice whirls to make front wheels and mudguards. Use liquorice allsorts for the remaining wheels, buffers and funnels. Fill the trucks with Smarties and liquorice allsorts. Cover the silver board with desiccated coconut, unroll the remaining liquorice whirl and use as the railway track. Place the train on the track.
Freezing note Freeze before assembling.

'The Brighton Belle'

Whisked sponges

Swiss roll ❄

IMPERIAL/METRIC
2 large eggs
2 oz./50 g. castor sugar
2 oz./50 g. plain flour, sieved
Filling and decoration
castor or icing sugar
jam

Place the eggs and sugar in a bowl and stand it over a saucepan of hot water. Whisk, scraping down occasionally, until the mixture is pale and thickened and forms a trail – 10–15 minutes. Remove the bowl from the saucepan and continue to whisk until the mixture has cooled. Fold in the flour carefully, using a metal spoon, then pour into a greased and lined 11- by 7-inch (28- by 18-cm.) swiss roll tin. Bake in the middle of a fairly hot oven (400°F., 200°C., Gas Mark 6) for 5–8 minutes.

Meanwhile, place a damp tea-towel on the worktop and lay on top a sheet of greaseproof paper slightly larger than the cake. Dredge the paper with castor or icing sugar.

Turn the sponge out on to the paper and remove the paper. Trim the edges of the sponge. Spread jam over the surface and roll up using the greaseproof paper as a guide. Dredge again with sugar.
Freezing note Can be frozen, filled and wrapped in foil.

Variations
Lemon swiss roll Add the grated rind of 1 lemon with the flour and fill the cake with lemon curd.
Spiced cream roll Add 1 teaspoon cinnamon with the flour. Fill with ¼ pint (150 ml.) whipped cream.

Genoese fruit ring ❄ Chocolate boxes ❄

Scones and teabreads

Plain scones ❄

Genoese fruit ring

IMPERIAL/METRIC
3 large eggs
4 oz./100 g. castor sugar
1½ oz./40 g. Stork margarine
3 oz./75 g. plain flour, sieved
grated rind of 1 lemon
Filling and decoration
fresh fruit in season
¼ pint/150 ml. double cream,
 whipped

Place the eggs and sugar in a bowl over a saucepan of hot water and whisk until the mixture thickens and leaves a trail – 10-15 minutes. Melt the margarine in a saucepan. Cool slightly then fold the flour and melted margarine gently into the egg mixture using a metal spoon. Pour into a greased and floured fluted ring mould. Bake in the middle of a moderately hot oven (375°F., 190°C., Gas Mark 5) for 20 minutes or until firm to the touch. Turn out and cool on a wire tray.

Fill with fresh fruit in season and decorate with whipped cream.
Freezing note Freeze the baked ring in a polythene bag. To use, thaw then fill with fruit and cream.
Illustrated on page 151

Chocolate boxes

IMPERIAL/METRIC
3 large eggs
4 oz./100 g. castor sugar
3 oz./75 g. Stork margarine
3 oz./75 g. plain flour, sieved
Filling and decoration
8 oz./225 g. plain chocolate
3 oz./75 g. Stork margarine
6 oz./150 g. icing sugar, sieved
1 tablespoon orange juice
orange colouring (optional)

Place the eggs and sugar in a bowl over a saucepan of hot water and whisk, scraping down occasionally, until the mixture thickens and leaves a trail – 10–15 minutes. Remove. Melt the margarine in a saucepan and cool slightly. Fold the flour and melted margarine gently into the egg mixture using a metal spoon. Pour into a greased and lined 11- by 7-inch (28- by 18-cm.) swiss roll tin. Bake in the middle of a moderately hot oven (375°F., 190°C., Gas Mark 5) for 20 minutes or until the sponge is firm to the touch. Turn out, remove the paper and cool on a wire tray. Cut into 2-inch (5-cm.) squares.

To decorate the cakes, melt the chocolate in a basin over hot water – *do not overheat*. Pour over a sheet of waxed or greaseproof paper, spread quite thinly but *evenly* and allow to set. Cut into 2-inch (5-cm.) squares. Cream the margarine and icing sugar together, adding the orange juice gradually. Colour if liked. Spread a little icing on the four sides of each square and stick a chocolate square on each side. Use the remaining icing to pipe stars on the tops of the cakes, and decorate with leftover chocolate pieces.
Makes 15–20 boxes
Freezing note Open freeze and pack carefully in a rigid polythene container.

Variation
Add the grated rind of a lemon or orange to the eggs and sugar before whisking. Use the juice of the fruit for the icing.

Plain scones

IMPERIAL/METRIC
2 oz./50 g. Stork margarine
8 oz./225 g. plain flour
½ teaspoon salt
½ teaspoon bicarbonate of soda
1 teaspoon cream of tartar
1 egg, beaten
5 tablespoons milk

Rub the margarine into the sieved dry ingredients. Add the egg and milk and mix into a soft dough. Knead lightly on a floured worktop and roll out to a thickness of ½ inch (1 cm.). Cut out scones using a plain or fluted 2-inch (5-cm.) cutter and place on a greased baking sheet. Bake on the second shelf from the top of a hot oven (425°F., 220°C., Gas Mark 7) for 10–15 minutes. Cool on a wire tray.
Makes 10–12 scones
Freezing note Scones freeze well. Pack in rigid polythene boxes or polythene bags in rows.

Variations
All-in-one scones Substitute self-raising flour for plain flour. Omit the bicarbonate of soda and cream of tartar and add 1 teaspoon baking powder. Place all the ingredients in a bowl and mix to a soft dough.
Fruit scones Add 2 oz. (50 g.) currants or sultanas and 1 oz. (25 g.) castor sugar after rubbing in.
Wholemeal scones Substitute 4 oz. (125 g.) wholemeal flour and 4 oz. (100 g.) self-raising flour for the plain flour. Add 1 oz. (25 g.) castor sugar after rubbing in.
Illustrated on page 163
Cheese scones Add 1 teaspoon dry mustard and a pinch of cayenne pepper to the dry ingredients. Stir in 4 oz. (100 g.) grated Cheddar cheese after rubbing in.
Savoury Oxo scones Crumble 2 Red or Onion Oxo cubes into the dry ingredients. Serve with cheese or with soup.

Drop scones

IMPERIAL/METRIC
8 oz./225 g. plain flour
1 teaspoon cream of tartar
½ teaspoon bicarbonate of soda
1 oz./25 g. castor sugar
pinch salt
1 tablespoon golden syrup
1 standard egg
¼ pint plus 4 tablespoons/200 ml.
  milk

Sieve the flour and raising agents into a bowl. Add the remaining ingredients and beat together to form a thick batter.

Lightly grease a cast-iron frying pan or girdle with oil or cooking fat and place over a low heat. Allow it to become moderately hot. Drop tablespoons of the batter on the girdle or frying pan about 2 inches (5 cm.) apart. When bubbles appear on the surface, turn over and cook the other side. Continue until all the batter is used. Keep the scones warm in a clean tea-towel. Serve spread with margarine and jam or honey. Eat when freshly made or serve fried with bacon and egg for a delicious breakfast.
Makes approximately 25 scones

Orange and honey tealoaf

Cherry banana loaf

IMPERIAL/METRIC
2 oz./50 g. glacé cherries, washed
  and chopped
1 oz./25 g. walnuts, chopped
4 ripe bananas, mashed
4 oz./125 g. Stork margarine
6 oz./175 g. soft brown sugar
2 large eggs
8 oz./225 g. self-raising flour, sieved
4 oz./125 g. sultanas
Decoration
½ quantity glacé icing (see page 169)

Place all the ingredients for the loaf in a mixing bowl and beat well with a wooden spoon – 2–3 minutes. Place the mixture in a greased and bottom-lined 2-lb. (900-g.) loaf tin. Bake in the middle of a very moderate oven (325°F., 160°C., Gas Mark 3) for 1¼–1½ hours. Turn out, remove paper and cool on a wire tray.

Make up the glacé icing using half quantities and pour over the loaf, allowing it to trickle down the sides.

Tutti-frutti teabread

IMPERIAL/METRIC
4 oz./125 g. Stork margarine
4 oz./125 g. castor sugar
2 large eggs
10 oz./275 g. self-raising flour,
  sieved
8 oz./225 g. mixed fruit
1 tablespoon milk
few drops almond essence
8 sugar lumps, crushed

Cream together the margarine and sugar until light and fluffy. Add the eggs one at a time. Fold in the remaining ingredients, except the sugar lumps. Place in a greased and bottom-lined 2-lb. (900-g.) loaf tin. Sprinkle the top with the crushed sugar lumps. Bake in the middle of a moderate oven (350°F., 180°C., Gas Mark 4) for 1–1½ hours. Turn out and cool on a wire tray. Slice and spread with Stork.
Freezing note Freeze wrapped in foil or in a rigid polythene container; whole or in individual slices.

Orange and honey tealoaf

IMPERIAL/METRIC
4 oz./125 g. Stork margarine
3 tablespoons clear honey
2 oz./50 g. castor sugar
2 oz./50 g. walnuts, chopped
3 tablespoons orange juice
grated rind of 2 oranges
8 oz./225 g. self-raising flour, sieved
2 standard eggs
Decoration
clear honey

Place all the ingredients for the tealoaf in a mixing bowl and beat with a wooden spoon until well mixed – 2–3 minutes. Place in a greased and bottom-lined 2-lb. (900-g.) loaf tin. Bake in the middle of a moderate oven (350°F., 180°C., Gas Mark 4) for 1¼–1½ hours. Turn out, remove paper and brush with a little melted honey. Serve sliced and spread with Stork margarine.
Freezing note Freeze without decoration. Wrap in cling film and foil.

Cheese and walnut loaf ❄

IMPERIAL/METRIC
4 oz./125 g. Stork margarine
8 oz./225 g. self-raising flour, sieved
   with 1 teaspoon baking powder
1 teaspoon dry mustard
salt and pepper
½ teaspoon mixed herbs
2 oz./50 g. walnuts, chopped
1 egg
3 oz./75 g. Cheddar cheese, grated
¼ pint/150 ml. milk
Topping
tomato or cucumber slices

Place all the ingredients in a mixing bowl and beat until smooth – 2–3 minutes. Place the mixture in a greased and bottom-lined 1-lb. (450-g.) loaf tin. Bake in the middle of a moderately hot oven (375°F., 190°C., Gas Mark 5) for 40–45 minutes. Turn out, remove the paper and cool on a wire tray. Serve sliced, spread with Stork and topped with tomato or cucumber slices.
Freezing note Wrap the loaf in foil.

Rubbed-in method

Farmhouse fruit cake ❄

IMPERIAL/METRIC
4 oz./125 g. Stork margarine
8 oz./225 g. self-raising flour
4 oz./125 g. castor sugar
8 oz./225 g. mixed dried fruit
½ teaspoon mixed spice
2 large eggs
3 tablespoons milk
grated rind of ½ lemon

Rub the margarine into the flour until the mixture resembles fine breadcrumbs. Stir in the sugar, fruit and mixed spice. Beat the eggs and milk together and stir in with the lemon rind. Mix to a soft dough. Place in a greased and lined 6-inch (15-cm.) round tin, bake in the middle of a very moderate oven (325°F., 160°C., Gas Mark 3) for 1¼–1½ hours. Turn out and cool on a wire tray.

This cake will keep wrapped in an airtight tin for 1–2 weeks.

Variation
All-in-one cake This can be prepared by the all-in-one method, adding 1 teaspoon baking powder with the flour.

Shortbread ❄

IMPERIAL/METRIC
4 oz./100 g. Stork margarine
4 oz./100 g. plain flour
2 oz./50 g. icing sugar
2 oz./50 g. cornflour
castor sugar for dredging

Rub the margarine into the sieved flour, icing sugar and cornflour. Knead into a dough. Press the mixture into a 7-inch (18-cm.) tin or flan ring placed on a baking sheet. Smooth the mixture with the back of a metal spoon and prick with a fork. Bake in the middle of a very moderate oven (325°F., 160°C., Gas Mark 3) for 40 minutes, then reduce to 275°F., 140°C., Gas Mark 1 for a further 15–20 minutes. Cool slightly then cut into triangles ('petticoat tails'). Dredge with castor sugar.
Makes approximately 12 biscuits
Freezing note Freezes well.

Variations
Lemon shortbread Add the grated rind of 1 lemon.
Ginger shortbread Add 2 oz. (50 g.) chopped crystallised ginger.

Melting method

Florentines

IMPERIAL/METRIC
2 oz./50 g. demerara sugar
1 tablespoon golden syrup
2 oz./50 g. Stork margarine
1 oz./25 g. walnuts, chopped
1 oz./25 g. plain flour
1 oz./25 g. raisins
1 oz./25 g. mixed cut peel
2 oz./50 g. glacé cherries, washed
   and chopped
½ teaspoon cinnamon
3 oz./75 g. plain chocolate (optional)

Melt the sugar, syrup and margarine together in a saucepan over gentle heat. Remove from the heat and add all the remaining ingredients except the chocolate. Mix well. Place teaspoonfuls of the mixture about 3 inches (7 cm.) apart on greased baking sheets. Bake in the middle of a moderate oven (350°F., 180°C., Gas Mark 4) for approximately 10 minutes. Remove carefully and cool on a wire tray.

Melt the chocolate in a basin over hot water and spread a little on one side of each florentine if liked. These keep well in an airtight tin.
Makes approximately 16 biscuits

Brandy cornets

IMPERIAL/METRIC
2 oz./50 g. Stork margarine
1 tablespoon golden syrup
2 oz./50 g. soft brown sugar
1 teaspoon lemon juice
2 oz./50 g. plain flour, sieved
1 teaspoon ground ginger
½ teaspoon mixed spice
Filling
¼ pint/150 ml. double cream
1 egg white

Melt the margarine, syrup and sugar in a saucepan. Add the remaining ingredients and mix thoroughly. Place teaspoonfuls of the mixture about 3 inches (7 cm.) apart on greased baking sheets. Bake in the middle of a moderate oven (350°F., 180°C., Gas Mark 4) for 6–8 minutes. While the biscuits are still hot mould them around cream horn tins. Allow to cool before removing from the mould. If the biscuits harden before moulding return the baking sheet to the oven for a moment to soften them.

For the filling whip the cream and egg white until fairly stiff. Place in a piping bag fitted with a large star tube. Fill each cornet with cream. These keep well unfilled in an airtight tin.
Makes approximately 20 cornets
Note If you do not have cream horn tins you can mould the biscuits round a rolling pin, which will give you more open curls, or use a wooden spoon handle to make brandy snaps.

Variation
For special occasions, add 1 teaspoon sherry or brandy to the cream.

Brandy cornets

Chocolate and raisin flapjack ❄

IMPERIAL/METRIC
4 oz./125 g. Stork margarine
4 tablespoons golden syrup
2 oz./50 g. demerara sugar
2 oz./50 g. raisins, chopped
8 oz./225 g. rolled oats
$\frac{1}{2}$ oz./15 g. cocoa

Melt the margarine, syrup and sugar in a saucepan. Stir in the raisins, oats and cocoa and mix thoroughly. Place the mixture in a 7-inch (18-cm.) greased square tin and spread evenly. Bake in the middle of a moderate oven (350°F., 180°C., Gas Mark 4) for 25–30 minutes.

Whilst still warm cut into squares and allow to cool. These keep well in an airtight tin.
Makes 12–15 biscuits

Gingerbread ❄

IMPERIAL/METRIC
4 oz./125 g. Stork margarine
4 oz./125 g. soft brown sugar
7 tablespoons golden syrup (see note)
$\frac{1}{4}$ pint/150 ml. milk
8 oz./225 g. plain flour
3 teaspoons ground ginger
1 teaspoon bicarbonate of soda
1 large egg, beaten

Melt the margarine, sugar and syrup with the milk in a saucepan over a low heat, stirring continuously. Remove from the heat and cool. Pour into the sieved dry ingredients with the beaten egg. Mix together until smooth. Pour into a 7-inch (18-cm.) greased and lined square cake tin. Bake in the middle of a slow oven (300°F., 150°C., Gas Mark 2) for 2–2$\frac{1}{4}$ hours. Leave in the tin for 2–3 minutes before turning out on to a wire tray. Keep in an airtight tin for 1–2 weeks or freeze.
Note Black treacle may be substituted for half the syrup.
Freezing note Wrap in cling film and foil.

Variation
All-in-one gingerbread Place all the ingredients in a mixing bowl and beat together with a wooden spoon or electric beater until well mixed – 2–3 minutes. Proceed as above.

Lining a deep cake tin

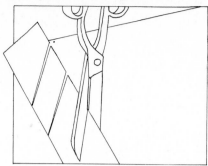

1.   *Cut a strip of greaseproof paper to fit the sides of the tin – about 2 inches (5 cm.) wider than the depth. Make a 1-inch (2$\frac{1}{2}$-cm.) fold along the length of the strip, cutting this fold at $\frac{1}{2}$ inch (1 cm.) intervals at an angle.**

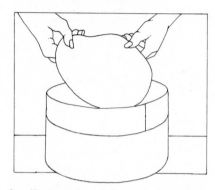

2.   *Having placed the strip of greaseproof round the inside of the greased tin, with the snipped fold lying flat against the base, cut a circle of greaseproof paper to fit the base of the tin.*

3.   *Brush all over with melted fat.*

Lining a sandwich tin

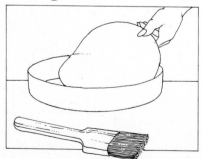

Lightly grease the inside of the tin. Line the base with a fitting circle of greaseproof paper and grease this.

*For rich cakes with long cooking times, double-line the tin and tie two strips of brown paper or newspaper around the outside of the tin and stand it on several thicknesses of paper on a baking sheet.

Biscuits and cookies

Boston brownies ❄

IMPERIAL/METRIC
4 oz./100 g. Stork margarine
8 oz./200 g. soft brown sugar
1 tablespoon coffee essence
2 large eggs
3 oz./75 g. plain flour, sieved with
   1 oz./25 g. cocoa and $\frac{1}{2}$ teaspoon baking powder
Coffee topping
3 oz./75 g. plain chocolate
3 tablespoons milk
1 oz./25 g. Stork margarine
1 teaspoon coffee essence
Decoration
walnut halves

Cream the margarine, sugar and coffee essence until light and fluffy. Add the eggs one at a time and beat well. Fold in the flour, cocoa and baking powder using a metal spoon. Place in a greased 11- by 7-inch (28- by 18-cm.) swiss roll tin and spread evenly. Bake in the middle of a moderate oven (350°F., 180°C., Gas Mark 4) for 25–30 minutes. Turn out and cool on a wire tray.

To make the topping melt the chocolate in a bowl over hot water. Add the milk and margarine and beat until smooth and glossy. Stir in the coffee essence. Spread over the brownies and cut into squares. Decorate with walnuts.
Makes 18–24 brownies
Freezing note Freeze iced, but without the walnuts. Open freeze, then wrap in foil or pack in a rigid polythene container.

Variation
All-in-one brownies Place all the ingredients for the cake in a mixing bowl and beat together with a wooden spoon or electric beater until well mixed – about 2–3 minutes. Bake as above.

Mocha pinwheels ❄

IMPERIAL METRIC
7 oz./200 g. Stork margarine
3$\frac{1}{2}$ oz./100 g. castor sugar
10 oz./275 g. plain flour, sieved
$\frac{1}{2}$–1 tablespoon coffee essence
1–2 tablespoons cocoa

Combine the margarine, sugar and flour and mix into a manageable dough. Divide the dough in half; knead the coffee essence into one half and the cocoa into the other. Roll out each half between two sheets of greaseproof paper to a 10- by 8-inch (30- by 20-cm.) rectangle, $\frac{1}{8}$ inch (3 mm.) thick. Place on top of each other and trim the edges. Roll up the dough tightly from one long side like a swiss roll. Chill until firm. Cut into slices and place on a greased baking sheet. Bake on the second shelf from the top of a moderately hot oven (375°F., 190°C., Gas Mark 5) for 10–12 minutes. Cool on a wire tray. This dough will keep uncooked, wrapped in foil or waxed paper, in a refrigerator for up to 2 weeks.

Makes 35–40 biscuits

Freezing note Can be frozen unbaked in the roll, packed tightly in foil; thaw then slice and bake; or freeze baked.

Viennese biscuits ❄

IMPERIAL/METRIC
8 oz./225 g. Stork margarine
3 oz./75 g. icing sugar
finely grated rind of 1 orange
7 oz./200 g. plain flour, sieved with
    2 oz./50 g. cornflour
orange Stork icing (see page 169)
Decoration
4 oz./125 g. plain chocolate
icing sugar

Cream the margarine and sugar together until light and fluffy. Add the grated orange rind, flour and cornflour and mix to a fairly stiff consistency. Place the mixture in a piping bag fitted with a large star tube and pipe into 3-inch (8-cm.) lengths or rosettes on a greased baking sheet. Bake on the second shelf from the top of a moderately hot oven (375°F., 190°C., Gas Mark 5) for 10–15 minutes. Cool on a wire tray.

Use the icing to sandwich the biscuits together in pairs.

Melt the chocolate in a basin over hot water. Dip in the ends of the biscuits and allow to set on a wire tray or waxed paper. Sprinkle with icing sugar.

Makes 14–16 pairs

Freezing note Freeze in a polythene bag when baked or in a polythene container after decoration.

Mocha pinwheels

Viennese biscuits

Ginger drop cookies ❄

IMPERIAL/METRIC
2 oz./50 g. Stork margarine
2 oz./50 g. soft brown sugar
4 oz./125 g. golden syrup
6 oz./175 g. self-raising flour, sieved
1 teaspoon ground ginger
Decoration
crystallised ginger

Melt the margarine, sugar and syrup. Cool, add the remaining ingredients and mix to a firm paste. Roll into balls the size of a walnut and place apart on greased baking sheets. Decorate with a thin slice of crystallised ginger on each. Bake in the middle of a moderate oven (350°F., 180°C., Gas Mark 4) for 10–15 minutes. Carefully remove from the baking sheets and cool.
Makes 15–20 cookies
Freezing note Freeze packed in a rigid polythene container or polythene bags.

Macaroons ❄

IMPERIAL METRIC
1 large egg white
4 oz./125 g. castor sugar
2 oz./50 g. ground almonds
1 tablespoon cornflour
few drops almond essence
rice paper, cut into rounds
few flaked almonds

Whisk the egg white until light and foamy. Beat in the sugar, ground almonds, cornflour and almond essence. Add a little extra ground almonds to stiffen the mixture if necessary (depending on the size of the egg). Place the rice paper rounds on a baking sheet and spoon small amounts on to them or pipe using a large plain tube. Place a flaked almond in the centre of each macaroon. Bake in the middle of a moderate oven (350°F., 180°C., Gas Mark 4) for 8–10 minutes. Cool on a wire tray.
Makes about 12 macaroons

Granny's cookie bars ❄

IMPERIAL/METRIC
3 oz./75 g. Stork margarine
2 tablespoons golden syrup
8 oz./225 g. muesli-type cereal
2 oz./50 g. dates, chopped
1 oz./25 g. glacé cherries, chopped
grated rind of ½ lemon
Topping
4 oz./125 g. plain chocolate

Melt the margarine and syrup and stir in the remaining ingredients. Place in a greased 7-inch (18-cm.) shallow square tin and smooth evenly.

Melt the chocolate and pour over the cookie mixture, smoothing evenly with a knife. Allow to set in a cool place and mark into bars.
Makes approximately 15 bars
Freezing note Pack in a polythene bag or rigid polythene container.

Almond curls ❄

IMPERIAL/METRIC
2½ oz./65 g. Stork margarine
2½ oz./65 g. castor sugar
1½ oz./40 g. plain flour
2 oz./50 g. flaked or shredded almonds

Combine the margarine, sugar and flour in a mixing bowl. Add the almonds and mix in well. Place teaspoons of the mixture on greased baking sheets (well apart as they tend to spread). Flatten with a wet fork.

Bake on the second shelf from the top of a fairly hot oven (400°F., 200°C., Gas Mark 6) for 6–8 minutes. Allow to stand for a few seconds then carefully remove with a palette knife. Curl around a rolling pin and allow to set.
Makes approximately 20 curls
Freezing note Can be frozen in polythene bags.

Baking with yeast

Basic white bread ❄ (traditional method)

IMPERIAL/METRIC
½ oz./15 g. fresh yeast or 2 teaspoons dried yeast
½ pint/275 ml. warm water
1 teaspoon castor sugar
1 lb./450 g. plain flour
1 teaspoon salt
½ oz./15 g. Stork margarine
beaten egg or milk for glazing

If using fresh yeast blend with ¼ pint (150 ml.) of the warm water and the sugar. If using dried yeast dissolve the sugar in ¼ pint (150 ml.) of the warm water and sprinkle the yeast on top. Leave until frothy – 10 minutes.

Sieve the flour and salt into a bowl and rub in the margarine. Pour in the yeast liquid and remaining warm water. Mix well until the dough begins to leave the sides of the bowl. Turn out on to a lightly floured worktop and knead thoroughly until the dough is elastic and smooth. Place in a greased polythene bag and leave in a warm place to rise – about 50–60 minutes.

Turn the dough out on to a floured worktop, knock out the air bubbles and knead. Shape the dough and fit into a 2-lb. (900-g.) greased loaf tin. Cover with greased polythene and return to a warm place to prove until the dough reaches the top of the tin. Brush with beaten egg or milk.

Bake in the middle of a very hot oven (450°F., 230°C., Gas Mark 8) for 30–40 minutes. If becoming too brown cover with foil. The loaf should sound hollow when tapped on the bottom. This proves that it is thoroughly baked.

This quantity will also make two 1-lb. (450-g.) loaves, but bake for only 25–30 minutes.

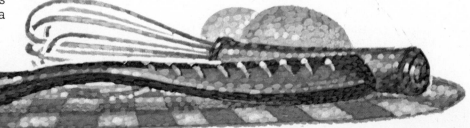

Freezing note Freeze bread tightly wrapped in foil or in a polythene bag, sliced or whole. The crust of crusty loaves tends to shell off when thawed but otherwise bread freezes very well.

Variations

Plait Use half the dough. When the dough has risen, knead and shape into an oval. Cut lengthways into three long strips to within 1 inch (2½ cm.) of the top. Plait and tuck the loose ends underneath. Place on a baking sheet, cover and prove in a warm place for 20–30 minutes. Brush with beaten egg or milk and sprinkle with poppy seeds. Bake near the top of a very hot oven (450°F., 230°C., Gas Mark 8) for 10

minutes. Reduce the oven temperature to 400°F., 200°C., Gas Mark 6, and bake for a further 10–15 minutes, covering with foil if necessary to prevent over-browning.

French loaf Use half the dough. When the dough has risen, knead and shape into a long oval roll. Place on a greased baking sheet and score diagonally across the top with a sharp knife. Cover and prove in a warm place for 20–30 minutes. Brush with beaten egg and bake near the top of a very hot oven (450°F., 230°C., Gas Mark 8) for 10 minutes, then reduce the temperature to 400°F., 200°C., Gas Mark 6 for a further 5–10 minutes. Cover with foil if necessary to prevent it becoming too brown.

White bread rolls sprinkled with poppy seeds (page 164), basic white bread loaf, wholemeal rolls (page 164), wholemeal scones (page 156), iced spicy bun round (page 165) and Chelsea buns (page 164)

Wholemeal bread ❄️ (traditional method)

IMPERIAL/METRIC
1 lb./450 g. plain flour, sieved with
   2 teaspoons salt
1 lb./450 g. wholemeal flour
1 oz./25 g. Stork margarine
1 oz./25 g. fresh yeast or 4 teaspoons
   dried yeast
4 teaspoons sugar
1 pint/575 ml. warm water

Place all the flour and salt in a mixing bowl and rub in the margarine (see step 1). If using fresh yeast mix the sugar with the flour. Blend the yeast with the water and pour into the flour (step 2). Mix to a soft dough which leaves the bowl clean. If using dried yeast mix half the sugar into the flour. Dissolve the remaining sugar in the warm water and sprinkle the dried yeast on top. Leave until frothy – about 10 minutes. Pour into the flour and mix to a soft dough.

Knead the dough on a lightly floured worktop until smooth (step 3). Divide the dough in half, knead each into a round and place in two greased 8-inch (20-cm.) round cake tins. Place the tins in greased polythene bags and leave in a warm place to prove until the dough reaches the tops of the tins.

Dust the tops with a little flour. Bake near the top of a very hot oven (450°F., 230°C., Gas Mark 8) for 20–30 minutes.

Freezing note See basic white bread (traditional method).

Variation
Use the dough to make 30 rolls. Bake for 10–15 minutes only.
Illustrated on page 163

Basic white bread ❄️ (short-time method)

IMPERIAL/METRIC
1 oz./25 g. Stork margarine
1½ lb./675 g. plain flour, sieved
   with 2 teaspoons salt and
   1 teaspoon sugar
1 oz./25 g. fresh yeast
14 fluid oz./400 ml. warm water
25 mg. ascorbic acid, crushed
   (see note)
beaten egg or milk for glazing

1. Rubbing the margarine into the flours and salt in a mixing bowl.

2. Pouring the yeast, sugar and water mixture into the flour, and mixing with a palette knife.

3. Kneading the dough on a lightly floured worktop until smooth and elastic.

Rub the margarine into the dry ingredients. Blend the yeast, warm water and ascorbic acid together and pour into the flour. Work into a dough using a palette knife. Turn out on to a well floured worktop and knead for 10 minutes. Place in a greased polythene bag and rest for 5 minutes.

Remove the dough from the bag and knead lightly. Place in a greased 2-lb. (900-g.) loaf tin. Return to the polythene bag and prove at room temperature for about 45–60 minutes.

Brush with beaten egg or milk. Bake in the middle of a hot oven (450°F., 230°C., Gas Mark 8) for 25–35 minutes. Remove from the tin and bake for a further 5 minutes. The loaf should sound hollow when tapped underneath.

Note Ascorbic acid can be bought in tablet form from leading chemists; the tablets come in 25-, 50- and 100-mg. sizes.

Freezing note This loaf freezes well.

Variations
This quantity will make two 1-lb. (450-g.) loaves, but bake for only 20–30 minutes. You can also make 20 rolls. Prove rolls for only 20 minutes, glaze, sprinkle with poppy seeds and bake for 10–15 minutes.
Illustrated on page 163

Chelsea buns ❄️

IMPERIAL/METRIC
half quantity basic white bread
   dough, traditional method
   (see page 162)
Filling
½ oz./15 g. Stork margarine, melted
1½ oz./40 g. castor sugar
1 teaspoon mixed spice
3 oz./75 g. currants
grated rind of 1 lemon
Glaze
2 tablespoons castor sugar
3 tablespoons hot water

Knead the risen dough and roll it out into a 12- by 9-inch (30- by 23-cm.) rectangle. Brush the melted margarine over the surface of the dough, then sprinkle over the sugar, spice, fruit and lemon rind. Roll up lengthways like a swiss roll and cut into eight equal slices. Lay the slices flat in a greased 8-inch (20-cm.) sandwich tin. Cover and leave in a warm place to prove for 15–20 minutes.

Bake in the middle of a very hot oven (425°F., 230°C., Gas Mark 8) for 20–25 minutes.

To make the glaze, mix the sugar and water together over a low heat until the sugar has dissolved. Brush over the buns as soon as they come out of the oven.

Makes 8 buns

Freezing note These freeze well unglazed. When thawed heat in the oven before glazing.
Illustrated on page 163

Danish pastries ❄

IMPERIAL/METRIC
5 oz./150 g. Stork margarine
half quantities basic white bread
   dough, traditional method
   (see page 162)
Filling 1
1½ oz./40 g. ground almonds
1½ oz./40 g. castor sugar
egg white to bind
Filling 2
1 oz./25 g. Stork margarine
1 oz./25 g. brown sugar
pinch nutmeg
1 oz./25 g. currants
Filling 3
little almond paste

Shape the margarine into a 5- by 10-inch (13- by 25-cm.) oblong. Roll out the dough into a 10-inch (25-cm.) square and place the margarine block in the centre. Fold the dough over and seal the edges. Carefully roll into a long strip and fold into three. Seal the edges. Rest the dough in a polythene bag for 10 minutes in a cool place.

Repeat the rolling, folding and resting twice more. Finally rest the dough for 10 minutes. The pastry is now ready to be rolled out and used.
Crescents Roll the dough out fairly thinly and cut into 5-inch (13-cm.) squares. Cut diagonally to form triangles. Place a small amount of any of the fillings (made by blending the ingredients) in the centre of each triangle. Roll up loosely from the base and bend into crescent shapes (see line drawing). Place on a greased baking sheet, cover and prove for 10–15 minutes.
Envelopes Roll out the dough fairly thinly and cut into 3-inch (8-cm.) squares. Place a little of the chosen filling in the centre. Damp all four corners, fold to the middle and seal. Place on a greased baking sheet, cover and prove as above.
Windmills Roll out the dough fairly thinly and cut into 4-inch (10-cm.) squares. Make diagonal cuts from each corner to within ¼ inch (1 cm.) of the centre. Place a small piece of almond paste in the centre, damp the corners and fold alternately to the centre. Press firmly to seal (see line drawing). Place on greased baking trays, cover and prove as above.

   Bake the Danish pastries near the top of a fairly hot oven (400°F., 200°C., Gas Mark 6) for 10–15 minutes. Cool on a wire tray. If liked, ice the pastries with a little glacé icing (see page 169).
Makes 12 pastries
Freezing note Freeze before icing.

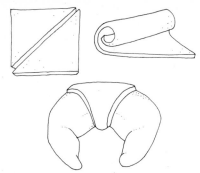

Crescents *Cutting 5-inch (13-cm.) squares of dough diagonally to form triangles. Placing a small amount of filling in the centre. Rolling up loosely and bending into a crescent.*

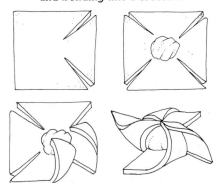

Windmills *Making diagonal cuts to within ½ inch (1 cm.) of the centre at each corner of 4-inch (10-cm.) squares of dough. Placing a little filling in the centre and pressing the four alternate points into the centre to form a windmill.*

Pizzas ❄

IMPERIAL/METRIC
one-third quantity basic white bread dough, traditional method (see page 162)
oil for brushing
8-oz./227-g. can tomatoes, drained and chopped
4 rashers bacon, chopped and fried
pinch basil
4 oz./100 g. Cheddar cheese, grated
2-oz./57-g. can anchovies
Garnish
parsley

Roll the dough out into a circle 8 inches (20 cm.) in diameter and place on a greased baking sheet. Brush the surface of the dough with oil, then cover with the to-matoes. Sprinkle over the bacon and herb and top with the cheese. Arrange the anchovies in a lattice design on top. Bake on the second shelf of a very hot oven (450°F., 230°C., Gas Mark 8) for 15–25 minutes. Garnish with parsley.
Freezing note Pizzas can be frozen baked or unbaked.
To freeze unbaked Wrap in polythene or heavy-duty foil. Remove the packaging and place frozen in a **cold** oven set to 450°F., 230°C., Gas Mark 8 and bake for 30–35 minutes.
To freeze baked Wrap the cooled pizza in heavy-duty foil or polythene. Remove the packaging and place frozen in a preheated fairly hot oven (400°F., 200°C., Gas Mark 6) for 20 minutes, or allow to thaw for 2 hours before heating as above for 10–15 minutes.

Iced spicy bun round ❄

IMPERIAL/METRIC
half quantity basic white bread
   dough, traditional method (see
   page 162)
1 teaspoon mixed spice
1 teaspoon lemon rind
2 oz./50 g. sultanas
1 oz./25 g. raisins
Icing and decoration
4 oz./125 g. icing sugar
2 tablespoons lemon juice
little water
angelica leaves

When the dough has risen, knock back and knead in the spice, lemon rind and fruit. Divide into eight portions and shape each into a bun. Place the buns in a circle almost touching each other in a greased sandwich tin. Cover and prove in a warm place for 20–30 minutes. Bake near the top of a hot oven (425°F., 220°C., Gas Mark 7) for 20–30 minutes. Remove from the tin.

   To make the icing, sieve the icing sugar into a bowl and stir in the lemon juice and sufficient water to make a smooth, fairly stiff icing. While the fruit bun is still warm, pour over the icing, allowing it to trickle down the sides. Decorate with angelica.
Makes 8 buns
Freezing note Freeze before icing.
Illustrated on page 163

Quantities for very rich fruit cakes

Ingredients	○ 5-inch/12-cm. □ 4-inch/10-cm.	○ 6-inch/15-cm. □ 5-inch/12-cm.	○ 7-inch/18-cm. □ 6-inch/15-cm.	○ 8-inch/20-cm. □ 7-inch/18-cm.	○ 9-inch/23-cm. □ 8-inch/20-cm.
Currants	5 oz./150 g.	6 oz./175 g.	8 oz./225 g.	10 oz./275 g.	13 oz./375 g.
Sultanas	3 oz./75 g.	4 oz./125 g.	5 oz./150 g.	7 oz./200 g.	9 oz./250 g.
Raisins	1 oz./25 g.	2 oz./50 g.	3 oz./75 g.	4 oz./125 g.	5 oz./150 g.
Glacé cherries	1 oz./25 g.	1½ oz./40 g.	2 oz./50 g.	2½ oz./65 g.	3½ oz./90 g.
Almonds, blanched and chopped	1 oz./25 g.	1½ oz./40 g.	2 oz./50 g.	2½ oz./65 g.	3½ oz./90 g.
Mixed cut peel	1 oz./25 g.	1½ oz./40 g.	2 oz./50 g.	2½ oz./65 g.	3½ oz./90 g.
Grated lemon rind	½	½	1	1	1
Brandy (optional)	1 tablespoon	1 tablespoon	1½ tablespoons	2 tablespoons	2½ tablespoons
Plain flour	3 oz./75 g.	4 oz./125 g.	6 oz./175 g.	7 oz./200 g.	9 oz./250 g.
Mixed spice	½ teaspoon	½ teaspoon	¾ teaspoon	1 teaspoon	1¼ teaspoons
Nutmeg	¼ teaspoon	¼ teaspoon	¼ teaspoon	½ teaspoon	½ teaspoon
Ground almonds	1 oz./25 g.	1 oz./25 g.	1½ oz./40 g.	2 oz./50 g.	2½ oz./65 g.
Stork margarine	2½ oz./65 g.	3 oz./75 g.	4 oz./125 g.	5 oz./150 g.	7 oz./200 g.
Soft brown sugar	3 oz./75 g.	3½ oz./90 g.	5 oz./150 g.	6 oz./175 g.	8 oz./225 g.
Black treacle	½ tablespoon	½ tablespoon	1 tablespoon	1 tablespoon	1 tablespoon
Eggs	2 standard	2 large	3 large	4 large	5 large
Grated orange rind	½	½	1	1	1

Quantities of almond paste to cover top and sides of very rich fruit cakes

Ingredients	○ 5-inch/12-cm. □ 4-inch/10-cm.	○ 6-inch/15-cm. □ 5-inch/12-cm.	○ 7-inch/18-cm. □ 6-inch/15-cm.	○ 8-inch/20-cm. □ 7-inch/18-cm.	○ 9-inch/23-cm. □ 8-inch/20-cm.
Ground almonds	4 oz./125 g.	6 oz./175 g.	8 oz./225 g.	12 oz./350 g.	1 lb./450 g.
Icing sugar	2 oz./50 g.	3 oz./75 g.	4 oz./125 g.	6 oz./175 g.	8 oz./225 g.
Castor sugar	2 oz./50 g.	3 oz./75 g.	4 oz./125 g.	6 oz./175 g.	8 oz./225 g.
Lemon juice	¾ teaspoon	¾ teaspoon	1 teaspoon	1½ teaspoons	2 teaspoons
Almond essence	1 drop	2 drops	2 drops	3 drops	4 drops
Eggs (approximate as size varies)	½ standard	½ large	1 standard	1 standard	1 large

Quantities of royal icing to cover top and sides of very rich fruit cakes

Ingredients	○ 5-inch/12-cm. □ 4-inch/10-cm.	○ 6-inch/15-cm. □ 5-inch/12-cm.	○ 7-inch/18-cm. □ 6-inch/15-cm.	○ 8-inch/20-cm. □ 7-inch/18-cm.	○ 9-inch/23-cm. □ 8-inch/20-cm.
Egg whites	1½	2	2	3	3
Icing sugar	12 oz./350 g.	1 lb./450 g.	1 lb./450 g.	1½ lb./675 g.	1½ lb./675 g.
Lemon juice	1 drop	1 drop	1 drop	2 drops	2 drops
Glycerine	¾ teaspoon	1 teaspoon	1 teaspoon	1½ teaspoons	1½ teaspoons

Note If only icing the top of the cake use half quantities. Additional icing will be required for decorating according to the elaborateness of the decorations required.

Quantities for very rich fruit cakes

○ 10-inch/25-cm. □ 9-inch/23-cm.	○ 11-inch/28-cm. □ 10-inch/25-cm.	○ 12-inch/30-cm. □ 11-inch/28-cm.	○ 13-inch/32-cm. □ 12-inch/30-cm.	○ 14-inch/35-cm. □ 13-inch/32-cm.	Ingredients
1 lb./450 g.	1 lb. 4 oz./575 g.	1½ lb./675 g.	1¾ lb./800 g.	2 lb./900 g.	Currants
11 oz./300 g.	13 oz./375 g.	1 lb./450 g.	1 lb. 3 oz./525 g.	1 lb. 6 oz./625 g.	Sultanas
6 oz./175 g.	7 oz./200 g.	8 oz./225 g.	9 oz./250 g.	10 oz./275 g.	Raisins
4 oz./125 g.	5 oz./150 g.	6 oz./175 g.	7 oz./200 g.	8 oz./225 g.	Glacé cherries
4 oz./125 g.	5 oz./150 g.	6 oz./175 g.	7 oz./200 g.	8 oz./225 g.	Almonds, blanched and chopped
4 oz./125 g.	5 oz./150 g.	6 oz./175 g.	7 oz./200 g.	8 oz./225 g.	Mixed cut peel
2	2	2	2	3	Grated lemon rind
3 tablespoons	3½ tablespoons	4 tablespoons	4 tablespoons	5 tablespoons	Brandy (optional)
11 oz./300 g.	14 oz./400 g.	1 lb./450 g.	1 lb. 3 oz./525 g.	1 lb. 6 oz./625 g.	Plain flour
1½ teaspoons	1½ teaspoons	2 teaspoons	2½ teaspoons	3 teaspoons	Mixed spice
¾ teaspoon	¾ teaspoon	1 teaspoon	1½ teaspoons	2 teaspoons	Nutmeg
3 oz./75 g.	3½ oz./90 g.	4 oz./125 g.	4½ oz./140 g.	5 oz./150 g.	Ground almonds
9 oz./250 g.	11 oz./300 g.	13 oz./375 g.	15 oz./425 g.	1 lb. 1 oz./475 g.	Stork margarine
10 oz./275 g.	12 oz./350 g.	14 oz./400 g.	1 lb./450 g.	1 lb. 2 oz./500 g.	Soft brown sugar
1½ tablespoons	2 tablespoons	2 tablespoons	2 tablespoons	3 tablespoons	Black treacle
6 large	7 large	8 large	8 large	10 large	Eggs
2	2	2	3	3	Grated orange rind

Quantities of almond paste to cover top and sides of very rich fruit cakes

○ 10-inch/25-cm. □ 9-inch/23-cm.	○ 11-inch/28-cm. □ 10-inch/25-cm.	○ 12-inch/30-cm. □ 11-inch/28-cm.	○ 13-inch/32-cm. □ 12-inch/30-cm.	○ 14-inch/35-cm. □ 13-inch/32-cm.	Ingredients
1¼ lb./575 g.	1½ lb./675 g.	1 lb. 14 oz./850 g.	2 lb./900 g.	2 lb. 2 oz./1 kg.	Ground almonds
10 oz./275 g.	12 oz./350 g.	15 oz./425 g.	1 lb./450 g.	1 lb. 3 oz./525 g.	Icing sugar
10 oz./275 g.	12 oz./350 g.	15 oz./425 g.	1 lb./450 g.	1 lb. 3 oz./525 g.	Castor sugar
2½ teaspoons	3 teaspoons	3½ teaspoons	4 teaspoons	4½ teaspoons	Lemon juice
½ teaspoon	½ teaspoon	¾ teaspoon	1 teaspoon	1¼ teaspoons	Almond essence
2 large	2½ large	3 large	3½ large	4 large	Eggs (approximate as size varies)

Quantities of royal icing to cover top and sides of very rich fruit cakes

○ 10-inch/25-cm. □ 9-inch/23-cm.	○ 11-inch/28-cm. □ 10-inch/25-cm.	○ 12-inch/30-cm. □ 11-inch/28-cm.	○ 13-inch/32-cm. □ 12-inch/30-cm.	○ 14-inch/35-cm. □ 13-inch/32-cm.	Ingredients
4	4	5	5	6	Egg whites
2 lb./900 g.	2 lb./900 g.	2½ lb./1¼ kg.	2½ lb./1¼ kg.	3 lb./1½ kg.	Icing sugar
3 drops	3 drops	4 drops	4 drops	5 drops	Lemon juice
2 teaspoons	2 teaspoons	2½ teaspoons	2½ teaspoons	3 teaspoons	Glycerine

Note ○ indicates a round cake □ indicates a square cake

Special occasion cakes

The table on pages 166–7 gives the quantities for different sizes of cake.
All-in-one method Prepare and protect the cake tin (see page 160). Place all the ingredients in a mixing bowl and beat together with a wooden spoon until well mixed – 3–6 minutes according to the size of cake. Place in the prepared tin and smooth the top with the back of a wet metal spoon.

Bake in the middle of a very slow oven (275°F., 140°C., Gas Mark 1). After the first 3 hours, test the cake at 30-minute intervals. Test by inserting a skewer into the cake, if it comes out clean the cake is cooked. Remove from the oven and leave in the tin for 15 minutes before removing. Remove the paper and allow to cool on a wire tray. Wrap in greaseproof paper and foil and store in an airtight tin.
Creaming method Cream the margarine and sugar together until light and fluffy. Beat in the treacle. Add the eggs one at a time, beating thoroughly and adding a little of the sieved flour with every egg. Fold in remaining flour and spices with fruit. Continue as above.

Celebration cake

IMPERIAL/METRIC
7-inch/18-cm. round rich fruit cake (see pages 166–7)
almond paste (see page 169)
fondant icing (see page 170)
few drops red food colouring
asparagus fern

Make up the rich fruit cake and bake as directed in the previous recipe.

Make up the almond paste and cover the cake.

Ice the cake with the fondant icing (see step-by-step photographs page 170). Reserve a little fondant icing to make roses. To make these, colour the fondant icing pink. Form a tiny piece of the icing into a cone to form the centre of the rose. Take another piece of icing and press flat to form a petal. Moisten the base of the cone and allow the first petal to curve round the centre. Continue to build up petals round the rose. Allow to dry and become hard before using.

Arrange the roses on top of the cake and decorate with small pieces of fern. Pipe a shell border around base of the cake with royal icing.

This cake can be used to celebrate weddings, anniversaries, birthdays, etc.

Celebration cake

Three-tier wedding cake

IMPERIAL/METRIC
6-inch/15-cm. square rich fruit cake (see pages 166–7)
8-inch/20-cm. square rich fruit cake (see pages 166–7)
11-inch/28-cm. square rich fruit cake (see pages 166–7)
Icing and decoration
almond paste (see page 169)
royal icing (see page 169)
colourings
silver cake decorations, asparagus fern, etc.
7-inch/18-cm. silver cake board
9-inch/23-cm. silver cake board
14-inch/35-cm. silver cake board
8 white or silver cake pillars

Make up the cakes as directed on this page. Wrap the cakes in greaseproof paper and foil. Keep in an airtight tin for 2–3 months to mature. Extra brandy can be poured over the cakes during this time. Prick the bases with a skewer and allow the brandy to penetrate before re-wrapping.

Cover the cakes with almond paste and ice them, allowing one week so that the layers of icing dry. Make up extra royal icing for decorating the cakes. Colour a small quantity of the royal icing pink to make the roses. Make sure the icing is fairly firm so it will hold its shape.

To make roses use a petal-shaped pipe in a greaseproof icing bag. Hold a wooden cocktail stick in one hand and hold the pipe flat against the stick, revolving it at the same time as piping to make the centre of the rose. Break off, then continue to build up the petals, turning the cocktail stick all the time. The flowers can then either be left on the sticks to harden or can be removed by pulling the stick through the coarse perforations of a grater, leaving the rose sitting on top of the grater. Allow to harden and store in a box. Roses can be highlighted with food colouring using a very fine paintbrush.

To assemble the cake use a star tube to pipe a shell border around the top and bottom edges of the cakes, and to make a design on the top. Arrange the pink roses on the sides of the cakes, securing with a little royal icing. If liked a simple lattice design can be made using a writing pipe. Arrange any silver decorations to be used and secure with a little icing. If using asparagus fern, assemble this actually on the day, as it will wilt. A small silver vase with fresh flowers makes an ideal centrepiece for the top of the cake. Position the pillars on the two largest cakes and assemble at the reception.

Icings

Glacé icing

IMPERIAL/METRIC
8 oz./225 g. icing sugar, sieved
2–3 tablespoons water or fruit juice

Place the ingredients in a mixing bowl and beat with a wooden spoon until smooth and glossy. Use immediately. This quantity will ice 18–24 small cakes, or half quantity will cover the top of an 8-inch (20-cm.) sandwich cake.

Variations
Chocolate Add 2 tablespoons cocoa or drinking chocolate with the icing sugar and use hot water to blend.
Coffee Use 1 tablespoon coffee essence and 1–2 tablespoons water.
Orange or lemon Substitute orange or lemon juice for 1 tablespoon of the water.

Stork icing ❄

IMPERIAL/METRIC
3 oz./75 g. Stork margarine
8 oz./225 g. icing sugar, sieved
2 tablespoons milk or fruit juice

Place all the ingredients in a mixing bowl and beat with a wooden spoon until smooth. This quantity will fill an 8-inch (20-cm.) sandwich cake and cover the top and sides.

Variations
Chocolate Substitute 1 tablespoon cocoa blended with 2 tablespoons hot water for 1 tablespoon of the icing sugar. Use only 1 tablespoon milk.
Coffee Substitute 1 tablespoon coffee essence for 1 tablespoon of the milk.
Lemon or orange Substitute 2 tablespoons orange or lemon juice for 2 tablespoons of the milk.

Frosting

IMPERIAL/METRIC
1 large egg white
6 oz./175 g. icing sugar, sieved
1 tablespoon golden syrup
3 tablespoons water
pinch salt
1 teaspoon lemon juice

Place all the ingredients in a bowl and whisk over a saucepan of boiling water with an electric mixer for 5 minutes, or hand-whisk for 10 minutes, until the mixture stands in peaks. Remove from the heat and continue to whisk until cool. Use immediately.

This quantity will cover the top and sides of a deep 8-inch (20-cm.) cake.

Royal icing

The table on pages 166–7 gives the quantities required for different sizes of cake. Sieve the icing sugar. Place the egg whites in a bowl and beat lightly with a fork until frothy. Add the icing sugar gradually, beating well until the icing is smooth, glossy and white. It should be thick enough to hold its shape when spread.

Beat in the glycerine and lemon juice, if used. (Colour if required at this stage.) Either cover with a damp cloth or place in a plastic container with a tight-fitting lid. Stand for 1 hour.

To ice a cake, secure the cake (covered with almond paste) to a board with a little Royal icing. Place a little icing on top; using a palette knife spread the icing smoothly and work out any bubbles that may appear. Draw a metal ruler firmly across the cake, remove the surplus icing and allow to dry for 24 hours. Repeat this process on the sides of the cake, holding a knife or plastic

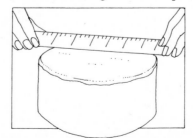

Having spread icing evenly over the surface of a cake, draw a metal ruler firmly across the top at an angle to remove surplus icing.

scraper vertically to remove the surplus. Allow to dry.

Repeat these layers. It is far better to have several thin layers of icing, as it will give you a smoother surface.

Make up a small quantity of Royal icing for decoration.

Almond paste

The table on pages 166–7 gives the quantities required for different sizes of cake. Put the ground almonds, icing sugar and castor sugar in a mixing bowl. Add the lemon juice, almond essence and enough beaten egg to mix to a dry paste. Knead together using the fingertips. Turn out on to a worktop dusted with icing sugar and knead until smooth.

To cover a cake with almond paste, brush the top and sides with boiled, sieved apricot jam. Roll out one-third of the almond paste to a round or square slightly larger than the top of the cake. Place the almond paste on top and trim off the surplus.

Roll out the remaining two-thirds of the almond paste into a long strip and cut to the exact length and depth of the sides of the cake. (If unmanageable cut the strip in half and cover in two pieces.) Place on the sides of the cake, joining the edges together.

Leave in a dry place for 1–3 days to dry out before icing.

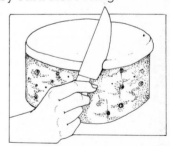

1. *Having placed a circle of almond paste on top of a cake, trim the edges with a sharp knife.*

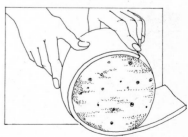

2. *Rolling the cake along the measured strip of almond paste. Seal the edges carefully at the side and top.*

Covering a cake with fondant icing

1. *Rolling out the icing on a board dusted with icing sugar into a circle 2 inches (5 cm.) larger than the cake to be covered.*

2. *Lifting the icing, over the back of the rolling pin, on to the cake covered with almond paste and brushed with egg white.*

3. *Moulding the icing over the cake with the fingers dipped in cornflour. Trim any excess icing from the base.*

Fondant icing

IMPERIAL/METRIC
12 oz./350 g. icing sugar, sieved
1 standard egg white
1 tablespoon liquid glucose, warmed
egg white for brushing
icing sugar and cornflour for rolling out and moulding

Place the icing sugar, egg white and liquid glucose in a mixing bowl and blend together, using the blade of a knife. Knead together, using the fingertips, to form a ball. Knead thoroughly on a worktop dredged with icing sugar until soft but manageable. Knead in more sieved icing sugar if necessary. (Colour if required at this stage.)

Roll out the icing until it is 2 inches (5 cm.) larger than the cake to be covered (see step 1). Brush the almond paste with the egg white. Carefully lift the icing on to the cake (step 2) and work quickly, with fingertips dipped in cornflour, to mould the icing over the cake (step 3). When completely covered trim the base of the cake and allow to harden. Decorate as liked. This quantity will cover the top and sides of a 7-inch (18-cm.) round cake or a 6-inch (15-cm.) square cake.
Note This icing will keep for 2 weeks if wrapped in polythene and sealed in a polythene container.

Liquid glucose may be purchased from any leading chemist.

Fudge icing

IMPERIAL/METRIC
2 oz./50 g. Stork margarine
3 tablespoons milk
8 oz./225 g. icing sugar, sieved

Place all the ingredients in a bowl over a saucepan of hot water. Stir with a wooden spoon until smooth and glossy. Remove from the heat and allow to cool. Beat well until thick.

This quantity will fill and ice the top of an 8-inch (20-cm.) sandwich cake.

Variations
As for Stork icing.
Coffee fudge icing For a stronger coffee flavour use 2 tablespoons coffee essence and 1 tablespoon milk.

Sandwiches

Stacked sandwiches

IMPERIAL/METRIC
brown or white bread
Stork margarine
Cream cheese and celery
4-oz./113-g. packet cream cheese
3 sticks celery, chopped
½ Onion Oxo cube, crumbled
Curried egg and cucumber
2 eggs, hard-boiled and chopped
2 tablespoons salad cream
1 Curry Oxo cube, crumbled
2-inch/5-cm. piece cucumber, chopped
Sardine and apple
4¾-oz./124-g. can sardines, drained
½ oz./15 g. Stork margarine
1 red apple, cored and chopped

To make each filling blend the ingredients together. Cut out 2- to 3-inch (5- to 8-cm.) circles of white or brown bread with a plain cutter. Spread each circle with a little Stork and sandwich together with the chosen filling. Use three circles of bread to each stacked sandwich. Decorate the top of each sandwich with a slice of hard-boiled egg, a cucumber twist, a radish rose, etc. Each filling makes six complete sandwiches, or you can mix and match them.
Freezing note Open-freeze sandwiches, then wrap in foil or pack in rigid polythene containers.

Pinwheel sandwiches

IMPERIAL/METRIC
1 sandwich loaf
Stork margarine
Cheese and chives
6 oz./175 g. Cheddar cheese, finely grated
few chopped chives
2–3 tablespoons salad cream
Tuna and gherkin
8-oz./198-g. can tuna fish
6 gherkins, chopped
½ oz./15 g. Stork margarine
Banana and honey
3 bananas, mashed
1 tablespoon honey
few drops lemon juice

Choose one of the given fillings. Slice a loaf thinly lengthways and remove the crusts. Spread with a little Stork and the chosen filling, made by blending the ingredients. Roll up carefully like a swiss roll. Wrap and chill until firm. Cut into slices and serve. Each filling makes enough to serve six people.
Freezing note Freeze sandwiches in the roll, wrapped in foil; thaw and slice.

Spread an equal number of slices of brown and white bread with Stork. Sandwich a white and a brown slice together with the chosen filling. Cut into four small square sandwiches. Arrange white and brown side uppermost alternately to give a chequerboard effect. Each filling serves six people.
Freezing note Freeze sandwiches uncut, with a sheet of greaseproof or film between each one.

Open sandwiches

IMPERIAL/METRIC
French bread, rye bread, baps, brown, wholemeal bread or toast
Stork margarine
Filling 1
sliced or rolled ham with a wedge or slice of orange and watercress
Filling 2
salami with gherkin fans
Filling 3
roast pork or beef with apple and cucumber
Filling 4
rollmops on a bed of lettuce
Filling 5
cottage cheese with tomato
Filling 6
chicken with mayonnaise and watercress
Filling 7
sliced liver sausage with cucumber and watercress

Spread the chosen base or bases with Stork and arrange the fillings on top. Arrange the sandwiches on trays and garnish with parsley.

Chequerboard sandwiches ❄

IMPERIAL/METRIC
brown and white bread
Stork margarine
Watercress and cottage cheese
½ bunch watercress, finely chopped
8 oz./225 g. cottage cheese
½ Onion Oxo cube, crumbled
Ham and horseradish
4 oz./125 g. ham, finely chopped
2 tablespoons horseradish sauce
3 tomatoes, skinned and chopped
Curried cucumber and cheese
4-inch/10-cm. piece cucumber, diced
4 oz./125 g. cream cheese
½ Curry Oxo cube, crumbled

Summertime loaf ❄

IMPERIAL/METRIC
1 uncut large white loaf
8 oz./225 g. Stork margarine
1 Onion Oxo cube, crumbled
Filling 1
1⅛-oz./32-g. jar fish paste
¼ teaspoon curry powder
Filling 2
2 oz./50 g. Red Leicester cheese, grated
1 tablespoon salad cream or mayonnaise
½ bunch watercress, finely chopped
Filling 3
4 oz./100 g. liver sausage
2 oz./50 g. finely chopped cucumber
Garnish
crushed cornflakes
mustard and cress
radishes

Remove all the outside crusts from the loaf and slice horizontally into six slices.

Mix the margarine and crumbled onion cube together and spread a little on each slice of bread. Reserve some and keep in a cool place.

Make up the fillings by combining all the ingredients for each one together. Sandwich the slices of bread together with the fillings, alternating to give a good colour combination. Reassemble the loaf and spread the outsides and top with the remaining margarine. Press crushed cornflakes on to all sides and sprinkle the cress over the top of the loaf. Garnish with radish roses.

To serve cut into slices and then fingers. This loaf makes a good alternative to ordinary sandwiches for a children's party.
Freezing note This loaf can be frozen filled but without the cornflakes and garnish, tightly wrapped in foil.

Entertaining

Planning a meal for friends or a family celebration is great fun but no one can pretend it does not involve extra work for the hostess. The casual 'come round and have something to eat tonight' invitation need not actually have much planning although even on this sort of occasion it helps. The more formal the occasion the more care and preparation must go into the planning of the meal so that the hostess appears at her own party cool and unruffled.

Cold wedding buffet (pages 174–5)

This is not easy when children have to be fed at regular times and the usual day-to-day chores done, so start with paper and pencil and make a list. It may sometimes be helpful to do this with the family although you may get some weird suggestions! A good idea is to enlist your children's help as they can be marvellous at counting knives, forks and spoons and arranging napkins and plates. This also keeps them involved and interested.

If you have a home freezer, party giving is easier as you can start days or even weeks in advance and have everything finished before the actual day, except setting the table, making salads and coffee. If you do not have a freezer and the party numbers are large, choose a simple menu which is within the scope of the cooking and storage space which you have available. Be careful not to select turkeys or ham joints which are too large for your oven.

Here are a few points to keep in mind whether you are planning a dinner, buffet party, coffee morning or even providing a tea at the cricket club:

1 Decide on the numbers for catering, write out the menu and then make a list of the dishes, cutlery and glasses you will need. If numbers are large, for example, a wedding buffet or birthday party, there are hire shops in most towns now and they can usually help you out.

2 Make a shopping list and timetable and plan advance preparation. Tick items off the list as they are bought or prepared.

3 Do not serve two egg, cheese, chicken or fish dishes on the same menu. Make sure the colours are as varied as possible too.

4 If you are doing everything yourself do plan an easy menu, for example a casserole which does not require last-minute adjustments. A large roast can lead to a hot, flustered hostess, who has been making gravy and serving vegetables between the first and second courses. A cold starter already set out on the table, such as a fruit cocktail, melon or pâté, allows you to relax and talk to your guests; as does a cold pudding or cheese board served after the main course.

5 Serve wines which you enjoy drinking. Remember sweet wines do not enhance the flavour of savoury dishes and are best served with the sweet course.

Cold wedding buffet

MENU FOR 20

Chilled cucumber soup
Garlic bread

Shooters' pie *(see page 76)*
Apricot-stuffed lamb
Cheese and asparagus quiche
Curried chicken pieces with spicy dips
Galaxy salad
Nutty coleslaw

Caramelised oranges
Black Forest gâteau

Cheese and coffee

Illustrated on pages 172–3

Apricot-stuffed lamb

IMPERIAL/METRIC
4½-lb./2-kg. shoulder of lamb,
    boned and rolled
salt and pepper
1 oz./25 g. Stork margarine
1 onion, chopped
4 oz./100 g. dried apricots, soaked
    overnight and chopped
3 oz./75 g. fresh breadcrumbs
2 tablespoons chopped parsley
1 Red Oxo cube, crumbled and
    dissolved in 3 tablespoons boiling
    water
1 large egg yolk
1 oz./25 g. cooking fat
Garnish
parsley sprigs

Unroll the lamb and season inside.
Melt the margarine and sauté the
onion for 5 minutes until soft. Mix
in the apricots, breadcrumbs, parsley, seasoning, beef stock and egg
yolk. Spread the stuffing over the
lamb, reroll and secure with string
and skewers to enclose the filling.
Weigh the joint and place in a roasting tin with the hot cooking fat.
Roast according to the chart on
page 45, basting several times
during cooking. Remove from the
tin, cool and chill. Serve in slices
arranged on a plate with parsley to
garnish.

Chilled cucumber soup ❄

IMPERIAL/METRIC
4 oz./100 g. Stork margarine
2 large onions, chopped
3 tablespoons flour
2½ pints/1¼ litres water
4 Onion Oxo cubes, crumbled
2 cucumbers, diced (approximately
    2 lb./900 g.)
salt and pepper
juice of 1 lemon
¾ pint/425 ml. single cream

Melt the margarine in a pan and
sauté the onion for 5 minutes until
soft but not coloured. Add the flour
and cook for 1 minute then add the
water, onion cubes and cucumber
and bring to the boil. Cover and
simmer gently for 30–40 minutes
until tender. Either liquidise or
sieve the soup, season to taste and
add the lemon juice. Cool then chill

thoroughly. Just before serving stir
in the cream and serve sprinkled
with chives or spring onion tops.
Freezing note This soup can be
frozen without the cream.

Garlic bread ❄

IMPERIAL/METRIC
4 oz./100 g. Stork margarine
3–4 cloves garlic, crushed
1 long French loaf or 2 Vienna
    loaves

Beat the margarine and garlic together until well blended. Slice the
loaf or loaves diagonally at ½-inch
(1-cm.) intervals leaving slices still
jointed to the bottom crust. Spread
both sides of each slice with garlic
spread and reassemble the loaf.
Wrap in foil and heat in a fairly hot
oven (400°F., 200°C., Gas Mark 6)
for 10–15 minutes. Unwrap and
serve hot or cold.

Cheese and asparagus quiche ❄

IMPERIAL/METRIC
8 oz./225 g. shortcrust pastry
    (see pages 12–13)
15-oz./425-g. can asparagus
    spears, drained
2 tablespoons finely grated onion
3 large eggs, beaten
½ pint/275 ml. milk
¼ pint/150 ml. single cream
salt and pepper
6 oz./175 g. Gruyère or Cheddar
    cheese, finely grated

Roll out the pastry on a lightly
floured worktop and use to line an
11-inch (28-cm.) fluted flan tin.
Reserve 12 even-sized asparagus
spears for decoration, chop the
remainder and put in the pastry
case. Whisk together the onion,
eggs, milk, cream and seasoning
and pour into the pastry case.
Sprinkle with grated cheese and

arrange remaining asparagus in a wheel design over the cheese. Bake on the second shelf from the top of a hot oven (425°F., 220°C., Gas Mark 7) for 20 minutes then reduce the heat to 375°F., 190°C., Gas Mark 5 and continue cooking for 25–30 minutes until golden brown and firm to the touch. Cool and serve cut into small wedges.
Freezing note Freeze wrapped in polythene.

Curried chicken pieces with spicy dips

IMPERIAL/METRIC
2 4½-lb./2-kg. oven-ready chickens
1 tablespoon curry powder
salt and pepper
2 oz./50 g. flour
2–3 standard eggs, beaten
2 packets golden breadcrumbs
  (or use fresh breadcrumbs)
fat for deep-frying
Garnish
mustard and cress
lemon slices

Skin and strip the flesh from the chickens and cut into thin pieces approximately 2 inches by 1 inch (5 by 2½ cm.). Combine the curry powder, salt, pepper and flour and coat the chicken pieces lightly in the mixture. Dip the pieces into beaten egg and then coat thoroughly in breadcrumbs. Fry in hot deep fat (360°F., 180°C.) a few pieces at a time, for 3–4 minutes until golden brown and cooked through. Drain thoroughly on absorbent paper and cool. Pile on to a large plate and garnish with mustard and cress and lemon slices. Serve with the dips in separate bowls.

Dips
Tartare dip Beat 2 teaspoons lemon juice, ½ crumbled Onion Oxo cube, salt and pepper, 1 tablespoon finely chopped onion, 1 tablespoon chopped capers, 4 finely chopped gherkins and 1 tablespoon chopped parsley into ¼ pint (150 ml.) mayonnaise.
Tangy cocktail dip Beat 1 tablespoon tomato purée, ½ teaspoon Worcestershire sauce, salt and pepper and ½ crumbled Onion Oxo cube into ¼ pint (150 ml.) mayonnaise.

Galaxy salad

IMPERIAL/METRIC
2 15-oz./425-g. cans artichokes,
  drained
1½ lb./675 g. French beans, cooked
1 lb./450 g. tomatoes, sliced
¼ pint/150 ml. French dressing (see
  page 131)
Garnish
watercress

Cut the artichokes into halves or quarters according to size and place in a bowl. Cut the beans into 2-inch (5-cm.) lengths and mix with the artichokes. Pile into the centre of one large or two smaller dishes and surround with sliced tomatoes. Spoon the French dressing over all the vegetables and garnish.

Nutty coleslaw

IMPERIAL/METRIC
2 lb./900 g. white cabbage,
  shredded
12 oz./350 g. carrots, peeled and
  coarsely grated
1 small onion, finely chopped
6–8 sticks celery, sliced
4 oz./100 g. walnut halves
¼ pint/150 ml. soured cream
¼ pint/150 ml. mayonnaise (see page
  132)
salt and pepper

Mix together the cabbage, carrots, onion, celery and walnuts in a large bowl. Combine the soured cream and mayonnaise and season well. Add to the cabbage mixture and toss thoroughly. Serve in two bowls.

Caramelised oranges

IMPERIAL/METRIC
20–24 oranges
2 lb./900 g. granulated sugar
1¼ pints/700 ml. water
few cloves

Thinly pare the rind from six oranges and cut into julienne strips. Cook in boiling water for 5 minutes and drain. Meanwhile, cut the rind and pith from all the oranges and cut into slices, removing any pips. Arrange in a bowl and reserve any orange juice.
  Dissolve the sugar in the water

and bring to the boil. Add 8–10 cloves and boil the syrup until it turns a pale golden brown. Remove from heat and immediately add 4 tablespoons cold water. When the bubbles subside and the mixture cools a little, add any juice from the oranges then pour carefully over the sliced oranges. Cool then chill. Serve sprinkled with the strips of orange rind. Cloves removed.

Black Forest gâteau ❄

IMPERIAL/METRIC
4 large/standard eggs
6 oz./150 g. castor sugar
4 oz./100 g. plain flour
¾ oz./20 g. cocoa
2 15-oz./425-g. cans black cherries
1 tablespoon arrowroot
orange liqueur or brandy
½ pint/275 ml. double cream
¼ pint/150 ml. single cream
3 flaked chocolate bars

Grease and line a 10-inch (25-cm.) round cake tin. Whisk the eggs and sugar together over a pan of hot water for 10–15 minutes, until the mixture is thick and leaves a trail. Remove from the heat and continue to whisk for 5 minutes until cool. Sieve the flour and cocoa together and fold evenly into the mixture. Turn into the tin. Bake on the middle shelf of a moderately hot oven (375°F., 190°C., Gas Mark 5) for about 40 minutes until firm to the touch. Turn on to a wire tray.
  Reserve six cherries for decoration and stone and roughly chop the remainder. Measure ½ pint (275 ml.) juice and bring most of it to the boil. Blend the arrowroot with the remainder and add to the pan. Bring back to the boil and simmer for 2 minutes. Add the chopped cherries and leave to cool. Cut the cake in half and sprinkle the base with 2–3 tablespoons liqueur or brandy. Spread the cherry mixture on top. Whip the creams together until stiff and spread a little on top of the cherries. Cover with the top of the cake then completely mask the cake in cream, leaving sufficient to make whirls around the top of the cake using a large star nozzle. Lightly crush the chocolate flakes and press all round the sides of the cake. Decorate the whirls with cherries and chocolate. Chill.

Hot buffet

MENU FOR 12

Melon and black grape cocktail
Salade niçoise

Cidered chicken
Succotash
Duchesse potatoes

Lemon soufflé
Fruit shortcakes

Cheese and coffee

Melon and black grape cocktail

IMPERIAL/METRIC
1 large ripe melon
8 oz./225 g. black grapes, halved and deseeded
few mint leaves, crushed
egg white (optional)
castor sugar (optional)
Garnish
6 sprigs mint

Halve the melon, remove the seeds and either make the flesh into balls with a scoop or cut into cubes. Place in a bowl with any juice from the melon, the grapes and a few crushed mint leaves. Chill.

If liked, dip the rims of six glasses first into lightly beaten egg white then castor sugar to give a frosted effect. Fill the glasses with melon and grapes. Garnish with mint.
Serves 6

Salade niçoise

IMPERIAL/METRIC
6 tomatoes, quartered
1 green pepper, deseeded and sliced
1 small onion, peeled and finely sliced
6 oz./175 g. cooked French beans
7-oz./198-g. can tuna fish, drained and flaked (optional)
salt and pepper
1 clove garlic, crushed
6 tablespoons French dressing (see page 131)
lettuce
3 hard-boiled eggs, quartered
few black olives and capers
1 can anchovy fillets, drained

Mix together the tomatoes, pepper, onion, beans cut into 2-inch (5-cm.) lengths and tuna fish. Season well, add the garlic and dressing and leave to stand for 15–30 minutes. Line a salad bowl with lettuce and spoon the tuna mixture on top with the quarters of egg, black olives, capers and anchovy fillets.
Serves 6

Cidered chicken

IMPERIAL/METRIC
2 5-lb./2¼-kg. oven-ready chickens or 12 chicken portions
2 onions, peeled and sliced
4 bay leaves
salt and pepper
juice of ½ lemon
3 Chicken Oxo cubes
6 oz./175 g. Stork margarine
6 oz./175 g. flour
¾ pint/425 ml. dry cider
½ teaspoon ground nutmeg
12 oz./350 g. streaky bacon rashers, derinded and chopped
24 button onions, peeled and blanched
8 oz./225 g. tiny button mushrooms
¼ pint/150 ml. double cream
Garnish
sprigs watercress

Place the chickens or portions in a large pan (or two smaller pans) with the onions, bay leaves, salt and pepper and lemon juice and just cover with water. Bring to the boil, cover and simmer for about 1 hour, until tender. Remove the chicken.

Strain the stock and reserve 2 pints (generous litre). Dissolve the chicken stock cubes in the stock. Melt the margarine in a large pan, stir in the flour and cook for 1 minute. Gradually add the cider and stock and bring to the boil, stirring continuously. Season to taste, add the nutmeg and simmer for 3 minutes.

Fry the bacon in its own fat then add the button onions and fry until golden brown. Drain and add to the sauce. Fry the mushrooms in the same fat for 2–3 minutes then add to the sauce, reserving a few for garnish. Strip the chicken from the carcasses, add to the sauce and simmer gently for 10 minutes. Adjust the seasoning, stir in the cream and serve. This dish can be prepared in advance and reheated in two casseroles in the oven for about 45 minutes. Serve garnished with the reserved mushrooms and watercress.

Freezing note This can be frozen before the cream is added. Add the cream when reheating.

176

Hot buffet

Succotash

IMPERIAL/METRIC
1½ lb./675 g. frozen peas
2 11½-oz./326-g. cans corn niblets
10-oz./283-g. can lima or butter beans
15-oz./425-g. can carrots
salt and pepper
1 oz./25 g. Stork margarine, melted

Cook the peas as directed on the packet then drain. Heat the corn niblets, beans and carrots in their own liquor then drain thoroughly. Combine the vegetables except the carrots, season lightly and toss in the margarine. Turn into a dish and surround with the carrots, tossed in margarine. Keep warm.

Duchesse potatoes

IMPERIAL/METRIC
3½–4 lb./1½–1¾ kg. potatoes, peeled
4 oz./100 g. Stork margarine
2 eggs, beaten
salt and pepper
little ground nutmeg

Cook the potatoes in boiling salted water until tender – 15–20 minutes. Drain thoroughly then mash or sieve. Beat in the margarine, eggs, seasoning and nutmeg and continue beating until very smooth. Place in a piping bag fitted with a large star vegetable nozzle and pipe into rosettes on well-greased baking sheets. Cook in a fairly hot oven (400°F., 200°C., Gas Mark 6) for 20–30 minutes until golden brown.
Note The potatoes can be cooked and piped on to trays in advance, then baked when required.
Freezing note Pipe the potato on to baking trays and open freeze. Remove and pack in rigid polythene containers. Thaw before cooking.

Variation
Substitute a pinch of garlic salt or ground cloves for the nutmeg.

Lemon soufflé

IMPERIAL/METRIC
3 large eggs, separated
8 oz./225 g. castor sugar
juice and grated rind of 2 large lemons
½ oz./15 g. gelatine
3 tablespoons water
½ pint/275 ml. double cream
½ oz./15 g. Stork margarine
1 oz./25 g. blanched almonds

Tie a band of greaseproof paper to come 1 inch (2½ cm.) above the rim round a 1½-pint (1-litre) soufflé dish. Place the egg yolks, sugar and lemon juice and rind in a bowl over a pan of hot water and whisk until the mixture is very thick and leaves a trail. Remove from the heat and whisk until cool. Dissolve the gelatine in the water in a basin over a pan of hot water, cool slightly and whisk into the mixture. Whip two-thirds of the cream until thick but not too stiff and fold into the mixture. Finally whisk the egg whites until stiff and fold evenly through the soufflé with a metal spoon. Pour into the prepared soufflé dish or a glass bowl and leave to set.

Melt the margarine in a pan and fry the almonds until browned.

Drain well and cool. Whip the remaining cream until stiff and use to decorate the top of the soufflé with the almonds.
Serves 6
Freezing note Freeze the soufflé without decoration. Thaw slowly in the refrigerator.

Variations
Coffee soufflé Instead of the lemons, stir 1 tablespoon coffee essence in 3 tablespoons water and whisk in with the gelatine.
Chocolate soufflé Omit the lemons and substitute 2 oz. (50 g.) plain chocolate melted in 3 tablespoons water, folded in with the gelatine.
Orange soufflé Substitute 2 oranges for the lemons.

Fruit shortcakes

IMPERIAL/METRIC
6 oz./175 g. plain flour, sieved
4 oz./100 g. Stork margarine
2 oz./50 g. castor sugar
½ pint/275 ml. double cream
2 tablespoons top of the milk
1 lb./450 g. strawberries

Place the flour in a bowl, add the margarine and sugar, rub in and then knead into a smooth dough. Roll out and cut into six fluted 3-inch (7-cm.) rounds and six fluted 2½-inch (6-cm.) rounds. Place on a baking sheet and prick well. Bake in the middle of a slow oven (300°F., 150°C., Gas Mark 2) for 15–20 minutes. Cool on a wire tray.

Whip the cream and milk together until stiff and spread or pipe a little on each of the larger rounds. Reserve six strawberries for decoration, halve the remainder and place on top of the cream. Cover with the smaller shortbread rounds and decorate the tops with the remaining cream and strawberries.
Serves 6
Freezing note Freeze the baked shortcakes only.

Celebration dinner

MENU FOR 8

Curried cheese ramekins or watercress soup
(see page 25)

Filet de bœuf en croûte
(illustrated overleaf)
Lemon carrots
Garlic French beans
New potatoes

Gingered pineapple and grape salad

Devils on horseback

Coffee

Curried cheese ramekins

IMPERIAL/METRIC
12 oz./350 g. cottage or cream
  cheese
2 10½-oz./298-g. cans condensed
  consommé
1 clove garlic, crushed
¼ teaspoon curry powder
Garnish
chopped chives

Place the cheese, one can of consommé, the garlic and curry powder in a liquidiser and blend until smooth. (This can also be done using a rotary whisk.) Pour into eight ramekins or glasses and allow to set in a cool place for a few hours.

Pour the remaining consommé on top and allow to set. Garnish.

Filet de bœuf en croûte ❄

IMPERIAL/METRIC
2 2-lb./900-g. fillets of beef
3 oz./75 g. Stork margarine
2 onions, chopped
6 oz./175 g. mushrooms, chopped
2 oz./50 g. bacon, chopped
2 tablespoons tomato purée
1 lb./450 g. flaky or rough puff
  pastry (see page 15)
beaten egg or milk for glazing
Garnish
watercress

Trim the meat, removing any excess fat. Tie the meat at intervals with string. Melt 2 oz. (50 g.) of the margarine in a large frying pan and fry the meat until browned all over – about 5–10 minutes – turning frequently (see step 1). Place the meat in a roasting tin, season and bake in a fairly hot oven (400°F., 200°C., Gas Mark 6) for 10 minutes. Remove from the oven and leave until cold.

Melt the remaining margarine and sauté the onions, mushrooms and bacon for 5–8 minutes until soft, then stir in the tomato purée. Spread this mixture over the partly cooked fillets (step 2).

Divide the pastry in half and roll out each half on a lightly floured worktop to a rectangle large enough to enclose the meat completely. Place a fillet in the centre of each piece of pastry and brush the edge with beaten egg or milk (step 3). Fold over the pastry (step 4), tucking in the ends to form a parcel (step 5). Decorate with pastry leaves made from the trimmings (step 6). Glaze with beaten egg or milk and bake in the middle of a hot oven (425°F., 220°C., Gas Mark 7) for 20–30 minutes. Garnish with watercress.
Freezing note Can be frozen unbaked. Open freeze then wrap.

1. *In a large frying pan, browning the tied fillet in melted margarine.*

2. *Spreading the sautéed onions, mushrooms and bacon mixture over the cooled, partly cooked fillet.*

3. *Brushing the edges of the pastry with beaten egg or milk. The fillet having been placed in the centre.*

Filet de boeuf en croûte

4. *Folding the flaky pastry dough over the prepared fillet.*

5. *Tucking in the ends of the pastry to form a neat parcel, sealed underneath.*

6. *Decorating with pastry leaves made from the pastry trimmings.*

Lemon carrots

IMPERIAL METRIC
2–3 lb./1–1½ kg. new carrots, scraped
2 oz./50 g. Stork margarine
1 teaspoon sugar
salt and pepper
grated rind of ½ lemon

Place the carrots in a saucepan with the margarine, sugar, seasoning and sufficient water just to cover the carrots. Bring to the boil, cover and simmer for 15–20 minutes. Drain and toss in a little melted margarine, with the lemon rind.

Garlic French beans

IMPERIAL/METRIC
2–2½ lb./1–1¼ kg. French beans
2 oz./50 g. Stork margarine
garlic salt to taste

Top and tail the French beans, leaving them whole. Cook in boiling salted water for 15–20 minutes.

Melt the margarine and toss the drained beans until well coated, sprinkle with a little garlic salt.

New potatoes

IMPERIAL/METRIC
3–3½ lb./1½–1¾ kg. new potatoes, scraped
salt
sprig mint
1–2 oz./25–50 g. Stork margarine, melted
chopped chives or parsley

Place the potatoes in boiling salted water, with a sprig of mint. Bring back to the boil and simmer for 15–20 minutes. Drain and toss in the melted margarine. Sprinkle with chives or parsley.

Gingered pineapple and grape salad

IMPERIAL/METRIC
1 oz./25 g. sugar
¼ pint/150 ml. ginger ale
2 medium-sized pineapples, or
    2 15-oz./425-g. cans pineapple chunks, drained
2 tablespoons Curaçao or Grand Marnier (optional)
4–6 oz./100–175 g. black grapes, halved and deseeded
4–6 oz./100–175 g. white grapes, halved and deseeded

Dissolve the sugar in the ginger ale. Cut the pineapples in half lengthways and remove the flesh, discarding the centre core. Cut the flesh into pieces and mix with the ginger ale and Curaçao. Skin the grapes if liked, mix with the pineapple and pile back into the pineapple shells. Serve with cream.
Note If using canned pineapple, serve in individual glasses.

Devils on horseback

IMPERIAL/METRIC
16 prunes, soaked overnight
8 rashers streaky bacon

Stone the prunes. Stretch the bacon with the back of a knife and cut each rasher into two strips. Roll a strip of bacon around each prune and secure with a cocktail stick. Grill under a moderate heat for 5–10 minutes, turning until the bacon is crisp, or bake in a fairly hot oven (400°F., 200°C., Gas Mark 6) for 10–15 minutes while the main course is being eaten.

Serve as a savoury after the meal or with drinks before.

181

Saturday evening meal

MENU FOR 6

Corn on the cob

Guard of honour
Braised celery
Spinach
Creamed potatoes

Coffee ice cream with
butterscotch sauce

Corn on the cob

IMPERIAL/METRIC
6 fresh corn on the cob (or
    frozen if fresh not available)
1 tablespoon sugar
Stork margarine for serving
freshly ground black pepper

Remove the outer husk and silky
threads of the sweetcorn. Add the
sugar to a large pan of fast boiling
water and immerse the sweetcorn.
Cook for 10–20 minutes until tender.
Drain. Press a cocktail stick firmly
in each end of the cobs to act as
'handles'. Serve with the melted
margarine and freshly ground black
pepper.

Guard of honour

IMPERIAL/METRIC
2 joints best end neck of lamb,
    chined (6–7 chops on each)
orange and celery stuffing (see
    page 90)
Garnish
parsley sprigs

Remove the fat from bones of meat
about 1 inch (2½ cm.) from the top.
Place the joints together, fat side
outside, allowing the bones to
cross over alternately, with the bases
together. Make the stuffing and use
to fill the cavity between the two
joints of meat. Cover the end of each
bone with a little foil to prevent

burning. Place the meat in a baking
tin. Roast in the middle of a moderately hot oven (375°F., 190°C., Gas
Mark 5) for 1¼–1½ hours.
    Remove the foil from the bones
and replace with cutlet frills if used.
Garnish with parsley.

Variation
Crown roast Instead of assembling
the joints with the fat side outside
and bones crossed, place the joints
with the fat sides inside forming a
circle. Secure with string. Stuff and
bake as for guard of honour.
Illustrated on page 91

Braised celery

IMPERIAL/METRIC
6 celery hearts
2 Chicken Oxo cubes, crumbled and
    dissolved in ⅔ pint/400 ml. hot
    water

Wash, scrub and remove any badly
discoloured outer stalks from the
celery. Blanch in boiling water for
5 minutes. Place in a casserole and
pour over sufficient chicken stock
to come a third of the way up the
dish. Cover and bake in the middle
of a moderate oven (350°F., 180°C.,
Gas Mark 4) for 1–1¼ hours or until
tender. Sprinkle with parsley.
Note Use a large can of celery
hearts if fresh are not available, and
braise for 30 minutes only.

Spinach

IMPERIAL/METRIC
2–3 lb./1–1½ kg. spinach
pinch salt
pinch nutmeg

Wash the spinach several times.
Discard any tough stalks and place
in a large saucepan with only the
water left on the leaves. Add a
pinch of salt, cover and simmer for
5–10 minutes. Drain very well,
pressing out as much water as
possible. Chop the spinach and
season with a little nutmeg to taste.

Creamed potatoes

IMPERIAL/METRIC
2½–3 lb./1¼–1½ kg. old potatoes
1 oz./25 g. Stork margarine
salt and pepper
pinch nutmeg
2–3 tablespoons milk

Peel and cover the potatoes with
cold salted water. Bring to the boil
and simmer for 20–30 minutes.
Drain well and mash with the margarine, seasoning, little nutmeg and
milk. Using a large star tube, pipe
the creamed potato into an ovenproof dish. Place under a hot grill to
brown the top lightly.

Coffee ice cream with butterscotch sauce ❄

IMPERIAL/METRIC
½ pint/275 ml. milk
2 large eggs, separated
3 oz./75 g. sugar
½ teaspoon vanilla essence
3 tablespoons coffee essence
½ pint/275 ml. double cream, lightly
    whipped
Sauce
1 tablespoon brown sugar
1 tablespoon golden syrup
½ oz./15 g. Stork margarine
2 teaspoons cornflour
¼ pint/150 ml. water
few drops lemon juice
2 oz./50 g. walnuts, chopped

Mix the milk, egg yolks, sugar, vanilla and coffee essence in a bowl over a pan of simmering water. Stir occasionally and cook until thickened – approximately 45 minutes. Allow to cool before stirring in the cream. Whisk the egg whites until stiff and fold into the mixture. Turn into a freezing tray or container and freeze. Just before it is completely frozen, remove and whisk again thoroughly. Return to the tray and freeze completely.

For the sauce, melt the sugar, syrup and margarine in a pan. Remove from the heat and add the cornflour blended with the water. Bring to the boil and add the lemon juice and walnuts. Serve the sauce hot or cold with the ice cream.

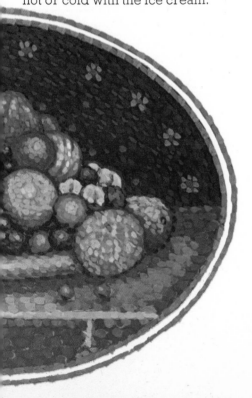

MENU FOR 12

Chilli con carne
Frankfurter and cheese hot dogs
Baked French bread

Fruity apples

Cider cup
Mulled burgundy

Chilli con carne ❄

IMPERIAL/METRIC
4 oz./100 g. Stork margarine
3 onions, chopped
1 green pepper, chopped
6 oz./175 g. celery, chopped
2 cloves garlic, crushed
12 oz./350 g. carrots, chopped
3 lb./1½ kg. raw minced beef
3 8-oz./227-g. cans tomatoes
20 prunes, soaked overnight and
    stoned
3 Red Oxo cubes, crumbled and
    dissolved in 1 pint/575 ml. hot
    water
1½ teaspoons Worcestershire sauce
2 tablespoons chilli powder
3 tablespoons tomato purée
salt and black pepper
2 14-oz./297-g. cans red kidney
    beans, drained and rinsed
Garnish
chopped parsley

Melt the margarine in a saucepan and sauté the onion, pepper, celery, garlic and carrot for 10 minutes. Add the meat and fry for a further 5 minutes before adding all the remaining ingredients except the kidney beans. Cover and cook over a gentle heat for 30–45 minutes, adding more water if necessary and stirring occasionally. When the meat and vegetables are tender, add the beans, return to the boil and simmer for a few minutes. Serve garnished with chopped parsley.
Freezing note If freezing, reduce the cooking time to 30 minutes. Add the canned kidney beans when reheating.

Frankfurter and cheese hot dogs

IMPERIAL/METRIC
24 frankfurters
8 oz./225 g. Cheddar cheese, cut
    into 24 slices
French mustard
24 long rolls
Stork margarine for spreading
Garnish
tomato wedges
parsley sprigs

Slit the frankfurters lengthways halfway through. Spread slices of cheese with French mustard and place in the slits. Place the frankfurters on a baking tray on the second shelf from the top of a moderate oven (350°F., 180°C., Gas Mark 4) and bake for about 10–15 minutes until sizzling.

Slit the long rolls and spread with margarine. Place a hot frankfurter inside each one. Return to the oven for 5–10 minutes to heat the rolls. Garnish each hot dog with a wedge of tomato stuck on a cocktail stick, and parsley sprigs.

Baked French bread ❄

IMPERIAL/METRIC
1 French loaf
4 oz./100 g. Stork margarine
½ Onion or Curry Oxo cube,
    crumbled

Slice the French loaf at an angle, taking care not to cut right through.

Mix the margarine with the crumbled curry or onion cube and spread in between each slice. Wrap the loaf in foil and bake on the second shelf from the top of a moderate oven (350°F., 180°C., Gas Mark 4) for 15 minutes. Serve hot.

Fruity apples

IMPERIAL/METRIC
12 cooking apples
12 tablespoons mincemeat
grated rind of 2 oranges
4 oz./100 g. demerara sugar
1 tablespoon grated lemon rind
¼ pint/150 ml. water
4 oz./100 g. Stork margarine, melted

Wash the apples and remove the cores carefully. Make a cut through the skins round the centre of the apples and place them in an oven-proof dish. Fill the cavities with the mincemeat mixed with the orange rind. Dissolve the sugar and lemon rind in the water, over a low heat. Pour over the apples. Brush each with melted margarine. Cover and bake in the middle of a moderate oven (350°F., 180°C., Gas Mark 4) for 1–1½ hours, depending on the size of the apples.

Cider cup

IMPERIAL/METRIC
juice and grated rind of 2 lemons
2 oz./50 g. castor sugar
2–3 tablespoons brandy
2 quarts/2¼ litres cider
2 pints/generous litre soda water or
   lemonade
2 red eating apples
few cloves

Mix the lemon juice and rind, sugar and brandy, and chill. Stir in the cider and soda water or lemonade, and strain the liquid. Cut the apples into slices and float these and a few cloves on top of the punch. Serve immediately.

Mulled burgundy

IMPERIAL/METRIC
1½ pints/850 ml. water
6 oz./175 g. castor sugar
6 sticks cinnamon
6 cloves
1 lemon, sliced
1 orange, sliced
1½ bottles burgundy or other
   full-bodied red wine

Bring the water, sugar and spices to the boil and simmer for 5 minutes. Add the lemon and orange slices and allow to stand for 10 minutes. Pour the wine into a large pan and strain in the water. Remove the lemon and orange slices from the strainer and return to the pan. Heat the wine until just below boiling point *but do not allow it to boil.* Serve very hot, in thick glasses with handles.

Informal meal

MENU FOR 6

Smoky kipper pâté

Carbonnade of beef
Braised leeks and carrots
Tossed green salad

Syllabub with brandy cornets
(see page 158)

Smoky kipper pâté

IMPERIAL/METRIC
4½ oz./125 g. Stork margarine
1 onion, finely chopped
1 clove garlic, crushed
12 oz./350 g. kipper fillets
6 oz./175 g. cottage cheese
1 Onion Oxo cube, crumbled
1½ tablespoons dry sherry
   (optional)
salt and pepper
Garnish
lemon twists
parsley

Melt 1½ oz. (40 g.) of the margarine and sauté the onion and garlic for 1–2 minutes. Add the roughly chopped kipper fillets and cook for a further 5 minutes. Remove from the heat and add the cottage cheese, onion cube, sherry if used, and seasoning. Mince or liquidise until smooth.

Place in six individual dishes. Melt the remaining margarine and pour a little over the surface of each dish. Chill in the refrigerator until set. Garnish each with a twist of lemon and parsley.

Freezing note This pâté can be frozen with or without the melted margarine on top, but without the garnish.

Carbonnade of beef ❄

IMPERIAL/METRIC
3 oz./75 g. Stork margarine
3 lb./1½ kg. stewing steak, cubed
2 medium-sized onions, sliced
2 cloves garlic, crushed
4 oz./100 g. bacon, chopped
2 oz./50 g. flour
¾ pint/425 ml. beer
2 Red Oxo cubes, crumbled and
    dissolved in ¾ pint/425 ml. hot
    water
salt and pepper
½ teaspoon ground nutmeg
1½ tablespoons vinegar
1 teaspoon sugar
1 bay leaf
Garnish
French bread, sliced and spread
    with French mustard
parsley

Melt the margarine and sauté the cubes of meat a few at a time until browned – about 5 minutes – then transfer to a casserole. Sauté the onion, garlic and bacon in the same fat until soft but not browned. Remove from the pan, stir in the flour and brown lightly. Gradually add the beer, beef stock and the remaining ingredients. Bring to the boil and pour over the meat and vegetables. Cover and bake in the middle of a very moderate oven (325°F., 160°C., Gas Mark 3) for 1½ hours.

Remove the lid and place slices of French bread, mustard side upper-most, on top of the meat so that half the slices are immersed in the gravy. Return to the oven for 30 minutes until crisp. Garnish with parsley.
Freezing note Can be frozen without the French bread on top.

Braised leeks and carrots

IMPERIAL/METRIC
2–2½ lb./1–1¼ kg. leeks
1½–2 lb./675 g.–1 kg. small new
    carrots, scraped
3–4 Chicken Oxo cubes, crumbled
    and dissolved in 1–1⅓ pints/
    575–750 ml. hot water
1 tablespoon chopped parsley

Remove the outside leaves and bases of the leeks. Trim the green tops and slice the leeks in half lengthways. Wash thoroughly. Place the vegetables in a shallow casserole and pour over sufficient chicken stock to come a third of the way up the casserole. Sprinkle with chopped parsley. Braise the dish in a moderate oven (350°F., 180°C., Gas Mark 4) for 40–50 minutes or until tender. Drain well and serve if liked with cheese sauce (see page 130).

Tossed green salad

IMPERIAL/METRIC
1 large lettuce
1 bunch watercress
2-inch/5-cm. piece cucumber
little chopped celery
½ green pepper, chopped
French dressing (see page 131)

Wash and dry the lettuce and watercress. Arrange in a salad bowl with the sliced cucumber, celery and green pepper. Just before serving toss in French dressing.

Syllabub with brandy cornets

IMPERIAL/METRIC
¾ pint/425 ml. double cream
2 egg whites
2–3 oz./50–75 g. castor sugar
¼ pint/150 ml. sherry or white wine
grated rind of 1 orange or lemon
brandy cornets (see page 158)

Whip the cream lightly. Whisk the egg whites until frothy and whisk into the cream with the sugar, until thick and frothy. Fold in the sherry or wine and grated orange or lemon rind. Serve with brandy cornets (unfilled) if liked (see page 158).

A guide to catering

Here is an approximate guide for portions and quantities to help with your catering. Amounts given apply to uncooked weight.
Soup 1 pint (575 ml.) gives 3 servings.
Fish 8 oz. (225 g.) on the bone per serving; 6 oz. (175 g.) filleted per serving.
Meat 4–6 oz. (100–175 g.) per serving for casseroling or grilling without the bone; 8 oz. (225 g.) per serving on the bone.
Vegetables Greens 1 lb. (450 g.) per 3 servings; peas, beans and root vegetables 1 lb. (450 g.) per 4 servings; potatoes 1 lb. (450 g.) per 3 servings.

Rice 2 oz. (50 g.) per serving.
Pasta 2–3 oz. (50–75 g.) per serving for a main course.
Pastry 2 oz. (50 g.) per serving for meat and fish pies.
Custard 1 pint (575 ml.) gives 6–8 servings.
Drinks 1 bottle wine serves 6 glasses, 1 bottle sherry serves 12–14 glasses, 1 bottle spirits serves about 20 tots.

Suggested quantities for 20

2 6-lb. (2¾-kg.) salmon or 4 3- to 4-lb. (1½- to 1¾-kg.) salmon trout.
2 12-lb. (5½-kg.) turkeys.
5 3½-lb. (1½-kg.) chickens.

2 lb. (900 g.) cooked rice with vegetables.
10 grapefruits and 10 oranges for a fruit cocktail.
8 oz. (225 g.) flaky pastry for 24 sausage rolls.
Sandwiches for 20 Allowing one round of sandwiches per person, you will need 40 slices of bread (1½ large loaves), 6–8 oz. (175–225 g.) Stork margarine for spreading. (1 large loaf yields 24–30 slices.) Sample fillings: 1¼ lb. (600 g.) grated cheese and about 10 tomatoes, sliced. *Or* 1 large and 1 small can tuna mixed with 2 tablespoons mayonnaise, and ½ cucumber, thinly sliced.

Home Freezing

Freezing is quickly becoming the most popular means of preserving food, replacing the more traditional methods of bottling, canning and drying. Unlike other forms of preserving, freezing does not destroy or alter anything in the food. As a result the natural cycle of food life is not destroyed but simply 'held in time'.

It is for this reason that food will come out of the freezer in the same condition as it went in – always provided that it is wrapped and sealed correctly. If it is not completely protected and airtight, food discolours and the outside is dried out. This condition is called 'freezer burn' and you should look out for it when you are selecting frozen chickens and turkeys.

The principles of freezing

Successful food freezing relies upon quickly reducing the temperature of the food to $-18°C$., so that all the water in the food is rapidly converted to ice in order to retard the development of the micro-organisms and enzymes. Food must be frozen quickly so that the ice particles that form are tiny. If you freeze slowly, the ice particles are large and will damage the cell structure of the food, causing valuable nutrients and flavours to leach out, sometimes altering its texture. It is for this reason that a freezer with a special low freezing temperature (with a fast freeze switch) should be chosen, this being used when fresh food is added to the freezer. Remember to add only small quantities of food, otherwise the temperature in the cabinet will be raised too far above $-18°C$. – 10 per cent of the total capacity of your freezer is usually recommended.

Water expands on freezing so remember to leave at least a 1-inch ($2\frac{1}{2}$-cm.) headspace when packaging foods with liquid, e.g. stews, to allow for this expansion.

Frozen fruits and vegetables can be as fresh as those from the green-grocer. Indeed they can be fresher and in better condition if the food has been frozen straight from the garden. Almost any food can be frozen, but whatever it is, it should be in tip-top condition. Fruit and vegetables should be just ripe, firm and if possible freshly picked. Meat and poultry must be of good quality, and any cooked foods should be cooled rapidly before packaging and going into the freezer. By doing this you can enjoy the advantages of producing from your freezer, at any time of the year, seasonal foods that look and taste as good and have the same food value as the day they were frozen.

Packaging for freezing

Packaging food for your freezer is all-important. The packaging material to use varies according to the type of food to be wrapped, but there are certain requirements to which all materials used for freezing must conform in order to achieve good results.

1 It must be moisture- and vapour-proof to prevent food drying out and·losing its flavour, or taking up the flavour of nearby foods.

2 It must be capable of being sealed or made airtight.

3 It must not react with the food.

The following are the most suitable and easily obtainable materials:

Polythene bags These must be of a suitable thickness, and are specially made with the freezer in mind. Twist ties are the most popular way of sealing the bags, but you can also buy a heat sealer to do the trick. This is a simple piece of equipment that fuses together the open ends of the bag so producing a perfect seal. Polythene bags are available in different colours for easy identification of food parcels in the freezer. They may be re-used providing they are thoroughly washed.

Boilable bags These are special polythene bags which withstand boiling and are relatively new on the market. They can be filled with food, sealed as an ordinary poly-thene bag and frozen. When required, the filled bag can be placed in boiling water which will thaw and reheat the contents. These

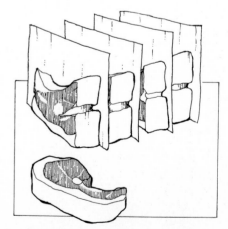

Freezing chops *Freezing chops individually by placing a sheet of grease-proof paper between each one to keep them separate. Wrap the chops in freezer foil or place in a polythene bag and seal.*

bags can also be re-used if not damaged.

Plastic containers There are many types available, but for freezing choose ones that can withstand very cold temperatures without warping and still give an airtight seal. They can be repeatedly re-used. Experiment too with used margarine tubs, cream and yogurt pots, etc., but remember they are not as durable and soon crack. Regular shaped containers are economical on freezer space as they stack easily.

Foil containers These include foil bags, dishes, plates, etc., some of which have lids provided. They can be used several times and are very convenient for packing soups, casseroles and pies according to the type.

Sheet foil For freezing purposes this needs to be of a special heavy thickness or alternatively a double thickness of ordinary foil can be used. Foil is self-sealing and is especially convenient for awkward shapes as it can be moulded easily. But remember it tears easily on jagged bones, so it is safer to over-wrap with polythene afterwards. Foil can be used to line casseroles and regular-shaped containers, and can then be filled, frozen and removed from the container, so leaving the container free for every-day use.

Sheet polythene This is also useful but it needs to be sealed by heat or with freezer tape. Ordinary tape peels off at freezer temperatures. Cling film wraps are not adequate on their own and really need over-wrapping but they are useful for

1. *Pouring a stew or similar mixture into a foil-lined casserole dish or container. Freeze.*

2. *Lifting the foiled-lined block from the dish. Overwrap the frozen block, label and refreeze.*

packing individual items within a large bag.

Greaseproof paper This is not suitable for an outer wrapping for food but is useful to separate a pile of chops or beefburgers for instance, or for dividing food into individual portions so that any number can easily be removed from the freezer when required, leaving the rest frozen.

As a final note remember to package food in the quantities you will want to use. It's no good freezing a pâté for 12 if you are only going to need four slices from it. So slice it before you freeze it, put a sheet of waxed paper or polythene between each slice and then wrap the whole thing in foil. If you make up a sauce, freeze it in $\frac{1}{2}$-pint (275-ml.) containers, not in one solid block. You can also freeze stocks and

sauces in ice trays; when frozen, turn the cubes out into a polythene bag and store. A little soda water squirted into the bag helps prevent the cubes sticking together. Eggs can be separated and returned to their cartons (if plastic) which should be opened flat and wrapped in polythene. The yolks can be removed for sauces, custards, etc., and the whites for meringues.

Finally, do label everything you put into the freezer. Colour coded labels are ideal for quick and easy recognition of foods. Make sure you put the date on as well as labelling the contents. A list of everything you freeze is handy inside the lid of the freezer, or alternatively compile your own freezer log book. All this adds up to successful, convenient and enjoyable freezing.

Open freezing raspberries and then packing carefully in a polythene bag. Seal with freezer tape or a twist tie.

Open freezing raspberries and then packing them in layers in a rigid polythene container with a lid.

Freezing washed, dried and trimmed chives in a polythene bag. Seal with freezer tape or a twist tie with an attached label.

Preparation and storage time for freezing foods

Preparation and freezing instructions	Food storage time	Preparation and freezing instructions	Food storage time
Fish Freeze white fish whole, in fillets or steaks. Steaks or fillets should be dipped in salt solution (1 oz. (25 g.) salt stirred into 1 pint (575 ml.) cold water) before freezing. If frozen whole it is best to glaze the fish after removing the fins, tail and guts. To do this place the prepared fish in the freezer unwrapped on a baking tray until it is solid. Then dip the fish into cold water and return it to the freezer for about 30 minutes. A film of ice will form over the surface. The process should be repeated two or three times before the fish is wrapped and ready to store.	**White fish** cod 6 months haddock 6 months plaice 6 months	Stone fruits should be packed in sugar syrup of concentration to suit the flavour of the fruit, e.g. a sour fruit requires a heavy syrup and sweeter fruit would be better with a thinner syrup. **Syrups** *thin* 4 oz. (100 g.) sugar to 1 pint (575 ml.) water (20 %) *medium thin* 7 oz. (200 g.) sugar to 1 pint (575 ml.) water (30 %) *medium heavy* 11 oz. (300 g.) sugar to 1 pint (575 ml.) water (40 %) *heavy* 1 lb. (450 g.) sugar to 1 pint (575 ml.) water (50 %) *very heavy* 1 lb. 9 oz. (700 g.) sugar to 1 pint (575 ml.) water (60 %)	
If oily fish are cut into steaks or filleted before freezing they should be dipped in ascorbic acid solution (1 teaspoon ascorbic acid to 1 pint (575 ml.) water) otherwise prepare as for white fish. Because fish has such a strong smell it is important to wrap it well. Foil or polythene are the easiest to use.	**Oily fish** mackerel 3–4 months herring 3–4 months salmon 3–4 months	Fruit which is liable to discolour, e.g. apples, peaches, apricots, must be coated with lemon juice or ascorbic acid solution (¼ teaspoon ascorbic acid to 1 pint (575 ml.) hot sugar syrup) before freezing. Currants, citrus fruits, melon, gooseberries, rhubarb and pineapple – for these fruits, wash and freeze spread out on a baking tray until solid. Then mix the fruit and sugar (4 oz. (100 g.) sugar per lb. (450 g.) fruit) together, if using sugar, and pack in polythene bags or containers allowing about ½ inch (1 cm.) headspace.	
Only shellfish which is really fresh should be frozen at home. Also, once it is defrosted it should be used straight away. Crab should be boiled in its shell for 15 minutes per lb. (450 g.), before freezing. The edible meat is removed and the shell washed and kept for serving the crab in.	**Shellfish** crab 3 months lobster 3 months	Open freeze berry fruits as described above but pack in containers without any sugar. No headspace need be allowed.	**Berry fruits** raspberries 6–8 months blackberries 6–8 months strawberries 6–8 months **Fruit purées** 6–8 months
Prawns and shrimps are best cooked in boiling water for 5 minutes and heads and tails removed before freezing. If very fresh they can be frozen raw.	prawns and shrimps raw 3 months cooked 2 months	Fruit can be frozen as a purée, either sweetened or unsweetened. Cook the fruit in very little water and when soft liquidise or sieve and pack into containers allowing ½ inch (1 cm.) headspace. Soft fruits can be puréed and frozen uncooked.	
Meat Bone where possible to economise on freezer space. Remove excess fat and protect protruding bones with pads of foil. Separate chops, steaks, hamburgers with greaseproof paper or foil. Wrap in foil or polythene bags. Can be frozen as casseroles etc.	beef 9–12 months veal 4–6 months lamb 9–12 months pork 4–6 months mince 2–3 months cooked 3–4 months sausages 1 month bacon 1 month	Orange, lime, grapefruit and lemon juices can be frozen in polythene containers or ice cube trays. (The rinds can also be grated and frozen and the fruit can be frozen whole.)	**Fruit juices** 4–6 months

Offal
Wash and dry. Remove blood vessels. Can be prepared as made-up dishes before freezing. Pack in polythene or foil.
	liver 2–3 months
	kidney 2–3 months
	sweetbreads and tripe
	  3–4 months
		Vegetables
		These should be washed and prepared as for cooking. To be sure of success the raw vegetables need blanching before freezing. This is especially necessary if they are to be kept for several months. The aim of blanching is to inactivate the enzymes which cause discoloration and off flavours. The raw vegetables should be put in a blanching or deep frying basket (about 1 lb. (450 g.) at a time) and the full basket immersed in a large pan of rapidly boiling water and returned to the boil. The blanching times should be timed from the point when the water returns to the boil. After the recommended time, remove the basket from the water and cool the vegetables quickly by immersing in very cold or iced water. Drain and dry well before packing and freezing. Polythene bags are the most suitable. Either pack in quantities which can be used at one time or open freeze the vegetables by laying them out on a baking tray. Pack into bags when solid so that they remain separate and free flowing.
			most vegetables
			  10–12 months
			vegetable purée
			  6–8 months
			mushrooms 6 months

Poultry Chicken and turkey can be frozen cooked or raw, whole or jointed. Joints may be coated with egg and crumbs before freezing. Giblets must be removed before freezing and the legs should be tied together and sharp edges protected with foil. Poultry should be closely wrapped and as much air as possible removed before sealing. *Always* defrost before use.	chicken 12 months turkey 12 months giblets 3 months stuffing 1 month		
Game Game should be hung, plucked and drawn. The shot removed and the inside wiped with a damp cloth before freezing. *Always* defrost before cooking.	duck 4–6 months goose 4–6 months rabbit 6 months hare 6 months		
Fruit Fruit should be prepared for the freezer in one of the following ways, according to type and personal needs.	most fruits 9–12 months pineapple 3–4 months		

Vegetable	Blanching time	Vegetable	Blanching time	Vegetable	Blanching time
Asparagus – thin stems	2 minutes	Carrots – sliced	4 minutes	Peas	1 minute
– thick stems	4 minutes	Cauliflower sprigs	3 minutes	Peppers – deseeded	3 minutes
Aubergines – cut in 1-inch (2½-cm.) slices	4 minutes	Celery – cut in 1-inch (2½-cm.) lengths	3 minutes	Potatoes – new	Cook until just tender
		Corn on the cob	4–8 minutes (depending on size)	– chipped	Part fry for 2 minutes
Beans – Broad	3 minutes			Spinach	2 minutes
– French	3 minutes	Courgettes – cut in ½-inch (1-cm.) slices	1 minute	Tomatoes	Cook for 15 minutes and purée.
– Runner	2 minutes	Marrow – cut in 1-inch (2½-cm.) slices	3 minutes		
Beetroot – whole	Boil for 40–50 minutes			Turnips – diced	3 minutes
Broccoli sprigs	3–5 minutes (depending on size)	Mushrooms	Sauté for 4 minutes in Stork	Herbs	They can be frozen in sprigs or in stalks.
Brussels sprouts	3–5 minutes	Onions – chopped	2 minutes		
Cabbage – wedges	4 minutes	Parsnips – sliced	2 minutes		
– shredded	1½ minutes				

Preparation and freezing instructions	Food storage time
Lettuce, cucumber, watercress, and mustard and cress lose texture on freezing and are not suitable for salads but freeze well when made into soups.	

Bread

Freeze whole loaves wrapped in foil or polythene, or slices separated by greaseproof paper and overwrapped. The crust tends to 'shell off' but the texture of the dough is well retained. Sandwiches can also be frozen.

Pack unrisen dough in sealed polythene bags with sufficient room for any rising while dough is freezing.

Knead after first rising then pack in polythene bag, removing air to prevent a skin forming.

Very convenient to keep a plastic bag of breadcrumbs in the freezer. They remain separate so can be used easily when required, for stuffings etc.

Croûtons can be frozen ready fried. Defrost in a hot oven on a baking tray.

Wrap yeast cakes etc. in foil or polythene with minimum airspace.

Pack yeast in ½–1-oz. (15–25-g.) quantities in foil or polythene. Defrost before use.

Food storage time:
- ready baked 4 weeks
- enriched bread 6 weeks
- sandwiches 4 weeks
- unrisen dough 2 months
- risen dough 2–3 weeks
- breadcrumbs 3 months
- croûtons 1 month
- yeast cakes, teabreads 3 months
- yeast pastries 2–3 weeks
- yeast 12 months

Cakes

Freeze in a polythene container. Allow to defrost before cooking.

Scones, iced and un-iced cakes can be successfully frozen. If elaborately decorated open freeze until solid so the decoration will not be damaged by wrapping. Glacé icing does not freeze well. Slices of cake can be frozen individually.

Food storage time:
- unbaked Victoria sandwich 2 months
- baked cakes and scones 3 months

Pastry

Freezes well whether unbaked or baked. Flan cases can be baked and frozen but are fragile so should be stored in a box. Pie crusts can be frozen with their filling or separately.

Food storage time:
- baked 6 months
- raw 3 months

Dairy produce

Do not freeze eggs in their shells or they will crack. Hard-boiled eggs do not freeze well. Break eggs, whisk lightly and add 1 teaspoon salt or 2 tablespoons sugar to each 1 pint (575 ml.) of egg. Pour into polythene containers, ice cube trays or empty plastic egg cartons. Note on label the quantity in each and whether sweet or savoury.

Food storage time:
- whole uncooked eggs 9 months

Mix yolks with salt or sugar as before to prevent the mixture solidifying, and freeze as before.

Freeze whites just as they are, in polythene containers. Defrost before use.

The best type of milk to freeze is homogenised pasteurised milk. It can be frozen in the carton but if bought in a bottle decant the milk into a polythene container. Allow ½–1 inch (1–2½ cm.) headspace.

Only double or clotted cream freezes without separating. It is best to lightly whip double cream with a little sugar before freezing. Alternatively, cream can be whipped and piped into rosettes on to foil, open frozen and packed when solid. Very useful for an instant decoration.

Some yogurts can be frozen in the cartons and are also available in freezer cabinets in shops. Do not freeze yogurt unless recommended on packet.

Hard cheeses freeze most successfully. The crumbly texture of some cheeses is emphasised on freezing but the flavour is retained well. Grated cheese can be used from a frozen state, simply crumbled to separate it. Cheese dishes also freeze well.

Overwrap packets of fat with foil or polythene. Flavoured butters such as parsley butter are useful to keep in the freezer – also butter curls for entertaining. The fats can be melted from frozen.

Ready-made or homemade ice cream makes a quick dessert. Allow to thaw slightly for about 15–30 minutes in the refrigerator before serving.

Food storage time:
- egg yolks 9 months
- egg whites 9 months
- milk 1 month
- cream
  - double 6 months
  - clotted 12 months
- yogurt 3 months
- cheese 6 months
- margarine, butter and cooking fat
  - salted 3 months
  - unsalted 6 months
- ice cream 3 months

Soups and sauces

Do not add cream to soups until after defrosting when ready for use. The seasoning usually needs adjusting after freezing.

Basic white and brown sauces, from which many variations can be made, are useful to keep in the freezer.

Cream sauces can only be frozen if made with double cream.

Mayonnaise separates so does not freeze successfully.

Food storage time:
- soups 3 months
- sauces 4–6 months

Pasta and rice

Cooked pasta and rice can be frozen on their own or as part of a made-up dish, when the storage times will vary.

Food storage time:
- pasta 2–4 months
- rice 4–6 months